THE PHARAOH'S FEAST

THE
PHARAOH'S FEAST

FROM PIT-BOILED ROOTS
TO PICKLED HERRING,
COOKING THROUGH THE AGES
WITH 110 SIMPLE RECIPES

OSWALD RIVERA

FOUR WALLS EIGHT WINDOWS
NEW YORK | LONDON

Published in the United States by

FOUR WALLS EIGHT WINDOWS

39 West 14th Street

New York, NY 10011

http://www.4w8w.com

First printing October 2003

Library of Congress Cataloging-in-Publication Data

Rivera, Oswald, 1944-
   The pharaoh's feast : from pit-boiled roots to pickled herring : cooking through the ages
with 110 simple recipes / by Oswald Rivera.
      p. cm.
   Includes bibliographical references and index.
   ISBN 1-56858-282-X (paperback)
      1. Cookery—History. 2. Cookery, International—History. I. Title.

TX645.R58 2003
641.5'09—dc22

2003060031

Printed in the United States
10 9 8 7 6 5 4 3 2 1

CONTENTS

Preface ıx

Introduction ı

ONE   In the Beginning 5

TWO   Land of the Pharaohs ı7

THREE   Classical Greece 28

FOUR   The Indus Valley 47

FIVE   Of Togas and Centurians 60

SIX   Medieval Europe 76

SEVEN   The Arab World 88

EIGHT   The Chinese Kingdom ı02

NINE   The New World Meets the Old ı33

TEN   The Americas ı55

ELEVEN   The Cooking World Expands ı74

TWELVE   The Industrial Era ı93

THIRTEEN   Modern Times 2ıı

Afterword 259

Bibliography 262

Index 269

We may live without poetry, music and art;
We may live without conscience and live without heart;
We may live without friends; we may live without books;
But civilized man cannot live without cooks.

Athenaeus

The Pharaoh's Feast is a cookbook with a simple premise: to show how cooking has evolved throughout recorded history. We've had thirty thousand years of war, famine, social upheaval, and yes, progress on many fronts, including the preparation of food. Usually, this has turned out to be a pleasurable pursuit. We've come a long way from the charcoal pits of our prehistoric ancestors. Just as primitive cave paintings evolved from rudimentary designs on stone walls into masterworks on canvas, so have pit-boiled roots and plants evolved into the steamed savories of today.

But how to present this progression? Fortunately, there are written records, some fragmentary, some extensive, from the middle of the fifth century B.C.E. onward. Before that time we can take pretty good guesses based on what the culture produced in terms of raw materials, crops, and tool technology.

With this information, I intend to extract the ingredients and methods used in common recipes of the day. Each section of the book will show what was produced and what was standard for the cooking of that era, giving suitable background and information on individual recipes that can be duplicated in one's kitchen. Thus the reader will get an idea what the common and not-so-common folk ate in classical Greece or imperial Rome. What was it like to have a meal in ancient Egypt, or the Byzantine Empire, or at the time of the Manchu Dynasty in China, or the caliphate in the Arab world, or India during the Middle Ages—all the way up to the present? Not only what they ate but what they drank, be it beer, wine, water, milk, or something in between.

The recipes given will be as accurate as possible but simplified. I am a believer that the easier the recipe, the better it is for everyone. Of course, some recipes unearthed, especially in the ancient texts, can be daunting. Today, who would want to prepare peacock's tongue in wild honey? Or even in modern times, something as esoteric as *tournedos rossini*—round slices of beef filler cooked with foie gras, truffles, and Madeira sauce? Still, I believe one can maintain the structure and the flavor of the dish without going to such extremes.

I shall keep it simple for simplicity's sake, yet, as much as possible, I'll be true to the original method of cooking and the ingredients used. There may be cases where special ingredients used in certain cuisines may not be readily obtainable. In those circumstances, I shall endeavor to substitute ingredients that are available and may render the same flavor. Some recipes may call for special cooking techniques. Again, I will adhere, as much as it is practical, to the standard described or utilize a similar method to get the same result. Some recipes and cooking styles, where the writing record is sketchy, may involve sheer speculation—and I'm sure academics will howl. Let me state for the record, this book is not an anthropological study nor do I claim to be an academic historian, though I have read and revere both disciplines. My goal is to inform and, to a certain extent, entertain. I hope the reader will have fun with the recipes and gain some insight as to how we got here from there, at least, where cooking is involved.

So, sit back, enjoy, and *bon appétit*!

When did it all begin? To which some would reply, "Who the hell cares?" Well, I, for one, care. And so do a lot others, I'd like to think. What we're discussing is that greatest of all adventures: how cooking evolved. We can all guess how it began: some prehistoric ape-man, possibly Peking man, a species of *Homo erectus*, made use of fire, probably half a million years ago. It doesn't take a brain surgeon to learn that, in addition to providing warmth, fire can be used for roasting food. Certainly the Neanderthals, the successor to *Homo erectus*, knew this. They, in turn, were supplanted by the current species known as *Homo sapiens*. Namely, us.

But, to get back to the initial query, Why should we care? Especially now when a run to the local supermarket can get you victuals and staples undreamed of by prehistoric man. Simply, because food mirrors society. There would be no civilization without it. It made us what we are today and, undoubtedly, will transform us in the future. What drove a simple apelike creature thirty million years ago to climb down from the trees and begin foraging on the ground? Wasn't he or she safer in the trees, instead of scampering about in vast savannas and grasslands? This protohuman was at the mercy of larger and far stronger beasts for now he was competing with lions and hyenas and saber-toothed tigers, not to mention huge mastodons, and every sort of peril in a perilous land. Could it be that the grassland supplied something more that he couldn't find in the trees—insects, lizards, grubs? Sure, not an appetizing menu but, for a hominid, something positively scrumptious, given that the fruit and nests in the trees had begun to disappear.

Soon, this four-legged creature began to roam about on two legs—which became more of a necessity, especially when he or she had to stand upright to get a sight on the next clearing or rock outcropping in order to hunt tomorrow's dinner.

We have all seen those *Discover* or *National Geographic* TV specials where prominent archeologists dig up bones and primitive tools and artifacts showing how humans lived and survived during the Paleolithic era. It wasn't Fred Flintstone or the denizens of Bedrock. We know that before primitive man roasted his food, he probably extracted the rich, juicy marrow within the bone of the animals he killed for food. Archeologists have found that bones littered the caves of these primitive ape-men. But when did he start cooking? He probably knew that bones could be heated and used as fuel; and it's easier to get to the marrow if the bone is still warm. But suppose you cook a whole side of meat over a fire? A primitive kind of charcoal cooking. This meant he could eat the meat of his former predators be they tigers, oxen, or rhinoceros. Which meant that his hunting techniques would have to change, and so would to a large extent, his diet.

Time passed, these prehistoric beings learned they had to adapt, not only to daily perils but to other changes as well. It was one thing to throw a rock at an animal to kill it, but now he had to contend with climatic changes. The Pleistocene era brought raging storms and frigid cold. This accelerated the development of these species. They were forced to socialize, communicate, develop the beginnings of some form of speech and some social structure. They had to perfect their tool-making capabilities. In terms of food, they ate to survive. Before long, they could improve on the cooking and the preparation, be it primitive roasting or cooking of meat and vegetables in a large pit.

The Neanderthals died out sometime around 30,000 B.C.E. With the advent of the *Homo sapiens*, the last ice age began to recede, sometime around 11,000 B.C.E. A milder climate change followed. This made it perfect for modern man to adapt more rapidly. This spawned the Neolithic revolution, where the hunter-gatherer became a grower. He began to cultivate plants and domesticate animals. Somewhere along the line he discovered the process of boiling. First, by heating stones, then by heating natural containers such as gourds or the shells of mollusks, and eventually, around 6,000 B.C.E., he utilized pottery, and then bronze. For this, it was convenient to have a source of fresh water. And, wherever such a source was found, be it rivers, lagoons, or lakes, irrigation soon followed, then ditches and canals. Villages began to arise in Africa, Europe, and western Asia. This growth led to farming, especially in the Near East. The villages became towns and the towns became walled compounds and the walled compounds became cities. All driven by one requisite: to make the land produce crops and the crops produce food that could be cooked and savored and bartered and stored. Civilization had come at last. An eminent anthropologist, Carleton Coon, may have put it best: "The introduction of cooking may well have been the decisive factor in leading man from a primarily animal existence into one that was more fully human."

With the coming of civilization, it gets interesting. Pardon the pun, but that's when humanity really gets cooking. Our evolution, our history, all of it is affected by this journey from hunter-gatherer to settled farmer to stock-breeder to builder. Once man discovers that there's more to eating than mere survival, well, his culinary horizon becomes limitless. Given the inclination, he can make the time and effort to *enjoy* food. After that, relatively speaking, it's a short hop from pit cooking to haute cuisine. Cooking adapts to changing conditions. New influences and new techniques bring new innovations. The revolution, with its fits and starts, is underway and it can't be stopped. And that's what this book intends to discuss: the unending influence of our culinary history. Civilizations rise and fall, but cooking remains. Some cultures elevate food preparation and consumption to an art form, ostentatious in its presentation, like with the Ancient Romans. Or during the height of Islamic culture, when an innovative cuisine, especially in Persia, reached its full flower while in Europe and the medieval world, cooking, by and large, regressed to its primitive origins. Throughout history, cooking has been used to influence, to cajole, to impress, to subdue, elevate, chasten, or glorify. The bigger the pot, the bigger the influence, the bigger the return. Or, the more subtle the cuisine, the higher the standing. There's a reason why, during the Crusades, the Arabic world considered the crusading Europeans who came to the holy land as mere barbarians. And who could blame them when confronted by a horde gorging themselves on rancid meat, bread, water or ale— no spices, no imported delicacies, no knowledge of the basics, either in cooking styles or nutrition.

There are meals that have literally changed history. Think of the Last Supper with Jesus Christ and his disciples. Or what was it that Cleopatra fed Mark Antony on that barge going up the Nile that got him into her clutches? Catherine de Medici takes her whole kitchen staff to France in 1533 and a national cuisine is transformed. Why is it that throughout history we have celebrated marriages, alliances, summits, and treaties with lavish meals and banquets? A special occasion will call for a special meal. The corn beef and cabbage for Saint Patrick's Day; that champagne dinner for your Valentine; the Jewish Passover meal; the *Id-al-Fitr* feast that signifies the end of Ramadan; the Thanksgiving Day turkey—all signify something special and culinarily appropriate. Even when we diet we pare down the food to what is "good" for us.

On the other side of the spectrum, if you fed somebody well, you could obviously get rid of them that way. The Romans perfected this. More than one Roman emperor met his end through a poisoned morsel. If you were to dine with the notorious Borgia family during the mid-Renaissance, you had better take along a food taster. Or, sometimes, food could do you in through bad preparation, bad ingredients, or lack of basic hygiene. The pestilence that hit Europe in the thirteenth century, the Black Death, owed as much to bad sanitation, where food was concerned, as to contagion. The open-air markets were situated in the midst of waste materials from slaughterhouses and refuse from the streets. There were black rats everywhere, feeding on that leg of mutton left in the gutter by a food vendor, and sewage flowed freely to provide a perfect breeding ground for disease. The diseased rat died, infected fleas jumped on the nearest human, and an epidemic ensued.

Fortunately, we learned through trial and error so that today we take our nourishment for granted. At least in the developed world. In what is commonly known as the Third World, and less developed countries, the strictures of the past still apply. But that's another story. The influence of cooking transcends all in human history. From its earliest inception to the present, you can't get away from it. You can tell a lot about a culture from its food and how it prepares it. The usual cliché is that hot tropic climates produce hot spicy foods, and cold moderate climates produce bland dishes. But is that so? How did our favorite foods evolve? How is it that some recipes have worldwide resonance? An Italian would recognize moussaka as a take-off on lasagna, and a Greek would say lasagna is just another form of moussaka. Why is it that almost every culture has a meatball soup, or a hearty stew where everything is thrown in, be it Spanish *asopao* , French *cassoulet*, Japanese *udom*, or Chinese *wo-min?* Or that rice dishes are common to almost every society, from *arroz con pollo* (chicken and rice) to *risotto*, to *rijst* (Dutch rice pudding). For that matter, where did Jell-o come from? Why is it that we Americans are so hung up on fast food? Where did pizza come from? Is that French pastry called a *napoleon* really named after the Corsican general? It's a journey that fascinates and enthralls. So let's give cooking the credit it is due. Let's bring it to the fore. And when you sit down to that snack, luncheon, or dinner, remember that nomadic being who first tried his hand at cooking—and enjoyed the results.

ONE

In the Beginning

Mess of Pottage, Lamb and Turnip Stew,
Tarru-bird Stew, Meat Stew,
Raised Turnips, Pigeon Stew

The first biblical account of a dish of food affecting human behavior occurs in Genesis 24:29-34, the first book of Moses, where Esau sells his birthright to his younger brother, Jacob, for a mess of pottage. Now, the Bible notes that Esau was a "cunning hunter; a man of the field; and Jacob was a plain man, dwelling in tents." Seems to me, Jacob was the cunning one, for he got his older brother to renounce his heritage for a plate of red lentils. This is a big deal by biblical accounts; Jacob was the grandson of Abraham, the patriarch of three of the world's greatest religions. It was Jacob who gave his people, the Israelites, a national conscience, and it could have been Esau—had it not been for those pesky lentils, and the fact that he was starving. So one shrewd brother flimflams the other, and history is changed.

Genesis 11:31 says that Abraham, originally Abram, migrated from "Ur of the Chaldeans" to the land of Canaan. Ur was an important city in Mesopotamia during the fourth and third millennia B.C.E. It was part of the Sumerian civilization; and we can surmise what kind of foods they enjoyed in Sumer at this time. They were among the first to produce and codify a sort of *Farmer's Almanac* (c. 2500 B.C.E.), which gave detailed instructions on farming methods and use of tools. We know that grain was the mainstay of the diet. This means they most likely ate barley, wheat, chickpeas, lentils, turnips, beans, onion, garlic, and leeks. Since Mesopotamia sits between the Tigris and Euphrates rivers, we can deduce that they also enjoyed plentiful fish. The Sumerians were also known as sheep herders, and mutton was common to their diet.

What did they wash it all down with? You'd never guess: beer. Yup, the lowly brew. Beer was the favored beverage for the ancient Sumerians and Egyptians, so now seems a good time to comment on this distinctive drink.

Most of us today think of beer as the poor man's staple. Still, for many it is probably the first taste of the forbidden fruit where imbibing liquor is concerned—who can forget his or her first beer bash? Also, to most of us, beer does not have the pedigree that wine or *fine spirits* do. Some ordinary working stiff with a beer can does not conjure up the same image as a boulevardier with a brandy snifter or wine glass.

The fact is that beer does have a pedigree. The oldest records on brewing beer are six thousand years old. Forty percent of Sumerian grain yield was used for beer production. In addition, eight types of barley beer, eight types of wheat beer, and three types from mixed grains seem to have been made. They even had a goddess, Ninkasi, who was in charge of beer production.

No less a work than the *Epic of Gilgamesh,* written in the third millennium B.C.E., attests to the importance of the lowly brew. In one of the first classical works of great literature, beer is credited, along with bread, for taking primitive man to a higher plain.

Enkidu, a shaggy unkept, almost bestial primitive man, who ate grass and could milk wild animals, wanted to test his strength against Gilgamesh, the demigod-like sovereign. Taking no chances, Gilgamesh sent a (prostitute) to Enkidu to learn of his strength and weaknesses. Enkidu enjoyed a week with her, during which she taught him of civilization. Enkidu knew not what bread was nor how one ate it. He also had not learned to drink beer. The (prostitute) opened her mouth and spoke to Enkidu: "Eat the bread now, O Enkidu, as it belongs to life. Drink also beer, as it is the custom of the land." Enkidu drank seven cups of beer and his heart soared. In this condition he washed himself and became a human being.

Though we may feel happy for Enkidu, beer, by and large, still gets a bum rap. According to Greek legend, Dionysus, the god of wine, fled Mesopotamia in disgust because its people had such an addiction to beer. Even later on, the Romans considered beer to be a barbarian drink.

Simply put, the lowly grain does not have the cachet of the noble grape. Wine is easier to mythologize. It's what I call the Og and Oggie syndrome. It goes something like this. Og and Oggie are two guys, part of a clan who live in a cave during prehistoric times. They don't cultivate crops as such but they pick berries and grapes, and they like to eat them. One day, Og, who's had his fill of grapes, throws the leftovers in the back of the cave. Let's say they land on a vessel of some kind, maybe a gourd or a big shell. The grapes are left there for some time, and they begin to ferment. A while later Oggie comes in and notices a sweet, redolent fragrance emanating from the back of the cave. He goes to the back and sees all these grapes stewing in the shell. He takes a whiff of this mash, and then he takes a sip. Then, another sip. The stuff is not bad. Oggie spends all afternoon swilling the juice.

And the transformation takes place. For the rest of the day, Oggie is running around, laughing, carrying-on, telling dirty jokes, having a high-ole-time.

His friend, Og, figures something is going on. He takes a trip back to the cave and discovers the fermenting grapes. Likewise, he takes a swig. Lo and behold, what is this thing? Man, does it make you feel good. He comes out of the cave feeling no pain—for the time being. The rest of the clan decides to sample this beverage. Next thing you know, the whole village is partying; and the rest is, as they say, history.

An oversimplification? Yes. But even this tale may have a grain of truth. With beer all we get is a mythical Greek god who hates the stuff. *The Epic of Gilgamesh* aside, nothing in beer conjures up the romance of other "more civilized drinks." For all we know, beer may have evolved through primitive bread making. During the Neolithic period raw grain may have been left to sprout. This sprouted grain may have been soaked in water, and the mixture allowed to ferment. The Egyptians took it one step further. They made a special dough from sprouted dried grains, partially baked the mixture, afterward soaked it in water and allowed the mixture to ferment. The liquid was then strained and you had beer. The Egyptians became quite adept at making these flavored beer breads; and the by-product was a range of spiced brews.

"This Bud's for . . . Ishtar," could have been a catchy P.R. phrase during the second millennium B.C.E. The Babylonians, the successors to the Sumerians, took their beer making very seriously. The Code of Hammurabi, the oldest collection of written laws, has one decree establishing a beer ration. This rationing was commensurate with one's social standing. A worker received the equivalent of two liters per day, a civil servant three liters, administrators and high priests (it figures) received five liters. Beer was used as barter, but it was also sold. Since it was closely allied with bread making, brewing was traditionally a female activity; and women usually sold the beer from their homes. Then as now, quality was the main concern. The Code of Hammurabi even has a stricture condemning ale houses that sold under-strength, overpriced beer.

The Roman author, Diodorus Siculus, described Egyptian beer as being "Nearly equal to wine in strength and flavour." The fact is that in ancient times beer was cloudy and unfiltered. Additions of fruit, spices, and flavorings could have produced a fairly mild, sweet, and aromatic product. The type of beer most commonly drunk was called *haq,* and it was made from a red barley grown in the Nile. Beer was so important to Egyptian society that the scribes created an extra hieroglyph for *brewer.* Some beers achieved an alcohol content of about 12 percent and were so good that Athenaeus, a classical scholar, stated that "Those who drank this beer were so pleased with it that they sang and danced, and did everything like men drunk with wine." Shades of Og and Oggie.

Another piece of extraneous information: the word beer comes from the Latin word *bibere*, meaning "to drink." Think about that the next time you hoist one at a ball game, picnic, or barbeque.

So, if you desire, you can have beer with our very first recipe, given below, to exemplify the beginning. And which may explain why poor Esau gave it all away for a mess of pottage.

MESS OF POTTAGE

1 cup dried lentils
4 cups water
3 tablespoons olive oil
2 medium onions, peeled and sliced from the stem down into ½-inch-thick
  half-moons
2 cloves garlic, peeled and minced
Salt and ground black pepper to taste
2 fresh, ripe tomatoes, sliced into half-moons

1. Wash the lentils under cold running water.
2. In a large pot or casserole (a Dutch oven is good for this), cover the lentils with water. Cover, bring to a boil, and cook over medium heat for 10 minutes.
3. Meanwhile, heat the oil in a medium skillet and add the onions and garlic. Sauté for about 3 minutes or until the onions brown at the edges.
4. Add the onions and garlic to the lentils, plus the salt and pepper. Simmer over low heat, stirring occasionally, for 30 to 45 minutes until the lentils are tender, adding more water if the mixture becomes too thick.
5. Serve garnished with tomatoes

YIELD: 4 TO 6 SERVINGS

Lamb and Turnip Stew

The Sumerians *really* liked mutton. From what we gather from their vocabulary, they had quite a few words to describe all variety of sheep. That being the case, I've included a recipe for lamb. They also ate goat. The record shows they ate beef, though not in as great quantity as sheep. Cattle may not have been all that appetizing since they were slaughtered when they were old and no longer suitable for grazing, rendering tough and stringy meat when it was finally cooked. Who wants to eat shoe leather when you can have the meat of a fattened and tender lamb? Today, this meal would be served with boiled potatoes. In the time of the city of Ur, the accompaniment would have been wheat, millet, or barley bread.

 3 to 3 ½ pounds sliced lamb shoulder, or lamb stew meat
 1½ teaspoons whole black peppercorns
 6 or 7 turnips, peeled and cut into large chunks*
 Salt to taste
 2 cups boiling water
 ⅓ cup flour
 ¼ cup cold water

1. Wash the lamb under cold running water and pat dry with paper towels.
2. Place the peppercorns in a mortar and pound until crushed. If you don't have a mortar or similar receptacle, place peppercorns between two sheets of waxed paper and crush with the bottom of 14 ½-ounce can.
3. In a heavy pot or Dutch oven, layer the meat and turnips, sprinkling each layer with salt and crushed peppercorns.
4. Add the boiling water. Bring to a boil and simmer until the meat is tender, about 1½ hours.
5. Taste the stock and season with more salt and pepper, if necessary. It should be quite peppery.
6. Mix the flour with the cold water and stir into the pot to thicken the gravy.

Yield: 6 servings

*If turnips are not to your liking, cabbage, cut in large wedges, can be substituted.

TARRU-BIRD STEW

This recipe for Tarru-Bird Stew comes from three Akkadian tablets from the Yale Babylonian Collection. The tablets contain a collection of recipes from the old Babylonian period, approximately 1700 B.C.E. They are not a cookbook. Rather, they are more of a culinary record written for administrative purposes so that the recipes could be codified for the benefit of those who would enjoy them—the big wigs in the hierarchy. They do show that Mesopotamia had a vibrant and sophisticated cuisine for its time. As for tarru, the translator notes that it can mean fowl. This recipe may have been made with wild pigeons, quail, or partridge—any small bird. Naturally, the recipe is arcane, but using common sense, one can come up with something worthwhile. It's your basic stew. The translation from the tablet makes that clear: "Meat from fresh [?] leg of mutton is needed. You set in water. You throw fat in it. You dress the *tarru* [in order to place in a pot]. Coarse salt, as needed. Hulled cake of malt. Onions, *samīdu*, leek, garlic, milk: you squeeze [them together in order to extract the juice which is to be added in the cooking pot]. Then, after cutting up the tarrus, you plunge them in the stock [taken out] from the crock [and previously prepared with the above-mentioned ingredients], you place them back in the crock [in order to finish the cooking]. To be brought out for carving."

Some words inscribed on the tablets have yet to be translated (such as *samīdu*). Also, one of the ingredients given in the recipe is "hulled cake of malt." I've substituted malted milk powder—and it works. For the fresh leg of mutton, set in water, with fat in it, I've taken that to mean a rich mutton broth. In its place I recommend any rich meat or beef broth. For the fowl, Cornish game hens or poussin (young chickens) can be used. The dish goes well with boiled potatoes or steamed rice.

2 Cornish game hens or poussin
1 small onion, peeled and finely chopped
1 whole leek, rinsed and finely chopped (green part only)
2 cloves garlic
4 tablespoons milk
4 cups beef broth or bouillon

1 tablespoon shortening or 2 tablespoons vegetable oil
Salt to taste
2 teaspoons malted milk powder

1. Rinse the Cornish hens under cold running water and pat dry with paper towels. Split the hens in half.
2. Put the onion, leek, and garlic into a mortar and pound until everything is crushed together. If you don't have a mortar and pestle, you can place the ingredients in a heavy bowl or saucepan and crush with a potato masher or the back of a spatula or large spoon. Add the milk, and mix. Do not cheat by emulsifying in a food processor—it will come out too watery.
3. Place the Cornish hens in a large pot, casserole, or Dutch oven. Add the beef broth, shortening, salt, and malted milk powder. Bring to a boil, stirring constantly. Lower the heat and simmer, covered, for ten minutes.
4. Add the onion mixture. Cover and continue simmering until the hens are tender (10 to 15 minutes).
5. Place the hens on a serving platter as is. Or you can carve them into smaller pieces, if desired, with the broth served over them.

Yield: 4 servings

MEAT STEW

The Yale Babylonian Collection Tablet 4644 has instructions for meat stew. It states: "Take some meat. Prepare water. Throw fat in it. Then add [the word is lost], leeks, garlic, all crushed together, and some plain *šuḫutinnū*." The lost ingredient I figure is onion. The ancient Mesopotamians seemed to have loved every member of the onion family. They also had an affinity for foods soaked in fats and oils. Yet, oddly, they weren't as partial to salt as we are.

> 2 pounds boneless stewing lamb or beef round steak, well trimmed and cut
>   into 1-inch chunks
> 1 medium onion, peeled and finely chopped
> 1 whole leek, rinsed and coarsely chopped (green part only)
> 2 cloves garlic
> 4 cups water
> 1 tablespoon shortening or 2 tablespoons vegetable oil

1. Wash the meat under cold running water and pat dry with paper towels.
2. Put the onion, leek, and garlic into a mortar and crush everything together. If you don't have a mortar and pestle, you can put the ingredients in a heavy bowl or saucepan and crush with a potato masher or the back of a spatula or large spoon.
3. Place the meat in a Dutch oven or heavy kettle, add water, shortening, plus the onion mixture. Bring to a rapid boil, while stirring. Cover and simmer over low heat for 1 hour.

YIELD: 4 SERVINGS

RAISED TURNIPS

This is one of the few vegetable recipes found on the tablets. Babylonian cuisine corresponded closely to the Mediterranean diet of today. For most people, it was a vegetarian diet supplemented by milk, cheese, and fish. Only the upper classes ate meat and game with all of the intricate seasonings.

1 whole leek, rinsed and finely chopped (green part only)
1 clove garlic
5 large white turnips, peeled and cut into cubes (about 5 cups)
1 tablespoon shortening or 2 tablespoons vegetable oil
1 small onion, peeled and finely chopped
½ teaspoon ground coriander
½ teaspoon ground cumin
2 tablespoons fresh chopped mint

1. Put the leeks and garlic in a mortar and pound until crushed
2. Place the turnips in a saucepan with water to cover. Add the shortening, onion, coriander, and cumin. Bring to a boil, and stir in the leek mixture. Cover and simmer on low heat until just tender (10 to 12 minutes).
3. Add the mint and cook 2 minutes more.
4. Remove the turnips to a platter and serve with some of the stewed liquid poured over them.

YIELD: 4 SERVINGS

PIGEON STEW

This entree is from the Yale Babylonian Collection Tablet 4644: "Pigeon Stew: Split pigeon in two. There must also be meat. Prepare water. Throw in the fat. Salt, hulled malt, onions, *samīdu*, leeks and garlic: all herbs should be softened in some milk (before adding them to the pot). To be presented for carving." For the pigeons I use partridge. Quail or squab can also be used in the recipe.

> 4 partridges
> 1 medium onion, peeled and finely chopped
> 1 whole leek, rinsed and coarsely chopped (green part only)
> 2 cloves garlic, peeled and crushed
> 4 tablespoons milk
> 5 cups beef broth or bouillon
> 1 tablespoon shortening or 2 tablespoons vegetable oil
> Salt to taste
> 2 teaspoons malted milk powder

1. Rinse the partridges under cold running water and pat dry with paper towels. Split the partridges in half.
2. In a medium bowl, combine the onion, leek, and garlic. Add the milk and mix well.
3. Place the partridges in a large pot, Dutch oven, or kettle. Add the broth, shortening, salt, and malt. Bring to a boil over high heat. Stir in the onion mixture. Lower heat and simmer, covered, until the partridges are tender (about 20 minutes).
4. Place the partridges on a platter as is. Or carve into smaller pieces and serve with the broth poured over them.

YIELD: 4 SERVINGS

TWO

LAND OF THE PHARAOHS

MELOKIYAH, BOILED AND ROASTED DUCK,
GREEN SALAD, FUL MEDAMES, KOFTA,
BAMYA, SWEETENED DATES

B ack when I was a boy during the Peloponnesian Wars, one of my favorite pastimes was to catch the double feature at the Eagle Theater on 103rd Street and Third Avenue in New York City. Alas, this movie house, along with the Third Avenue El, no longer exists. Yet great memories arise from there. Apart from a double feature, you also had two or three cartoons and a news feature. All for the magical price of a buck. This was long before the modern day cineplex, D.V.D.s, and videos. Most kids today wouldn't know what a double feature is.

It was here, in the darkened confines of the Eagle Theater, that I first learned about the outside world. Not only that, I got a glimpse into history as it reeled along, with dubious authenticity, on the movie screen. This was the late 1950s and the movie spectacular was still in its flower. Those of us of a certain age can recall it: a great sprawling costume drama with a cast of thousands. The type of flic made legendary by Cecil B. De Mille. It was here that I first got a glimpse of ancient Rome in all its decadent wonder. This was the era of the biblical epics like *The Robe, Memetrius and the Gladiators, King of Kings, Sign of the Pagan, The Ten Commandments,* etc. As a kid from East Harlem, it always fascinated me that these oversized morality plays featured scantily clad, nubile young things prancing about. And each had the tamed-down mandatory orgy scene. Judah Ben-Hur may have been a good hero, but he'd still mess around with the pagan temptress when the script called for it.

My first exposure to ancient Egyptian civilization came from one of these features—as depicted in the back lots of M.G.M. and Paramount. It's a forgettable gem of a picture called *Land of the Pharaohs;* and it featured the great British actor, Jack Hawkins, as the pharaoh, and a young Joan Collins as the courtesan with designs on the pharaoh's empire.

What I found interesting in these Hollywood-versed renditions of history was that the protagonists, when they weren't fighting and conquering, would be drinking and feasting. So, I would think to myself, That's how the other half lives. Or, at least, lived back in the bad old days. It wasn't till years later that I discovered that most of the information given in these celluloid masterpieces was either false or misleading, even down to the costumes and food depicted. Most ordinary folk in ancient Egypt did not eat like that or drink wine out of oversized goblets. The great civilizations that arose out of the Tigris-Euphrates Valley and the Nile depended on grain and, by extension, their granaries. It was the Egyptians who first discovered the art of making bread. But what date? Historians cannot say. Wheat was prolific in Egypt, even more so than in Mesopotamia. Someone, somewhere, may have discovered that dough made from water and the flour of raw grain could produce an early type of flat bread. By the beginning of the dynastic period in Egypt, a form of leavened bread was in use.

We do know, or can speculate, that there was a difference between the diet of a peasant and a royal in pharaoic Egypt. On the lowest rung of the ladder, if you ate anything at all, it was probably bread, beer, and onions. Those who were above the hoi polloi, they had it better. An excavated tomb of a rich Egyptian from the third millennium B.C.E. showed that this matron had packed along not only barley and porridge, but cooked quail, fish, beef, bread, pastries, figs, berries, cheese, wine, and beer. When she reached the next world, she sure as hell was going to be well fed.

The Egyptians were fortunate that the Nile supplied marshlands abundant with fowl, fish, and vegetables such as wild celery, lotus root, cucumbers, and leeks. They also ate peas and beans. With regard to meat, such as sheep, goat, or pig, this was reserved mainly for special occasions since there was little grazing land. Simply put, meat was expensive. The Egyptians were among the first to store salted fish, and even export it to such areas as Palestine and far off Syria. In terms of delicacies, the historian Herodotus notes that small birds were very popular among the well-to-do. The one thing they did not have was sugar. Royals and aristocrats used honey as the main sweetener. Poor folk, which was the vast majority, used dates and fruit juices.

MELOKIYAH

As can be deduced, if you were atop the food chain, you ate very well. But even peasants could get by, as shown in the recipe below. It is for Melokiyah, a gelatinous soup that traces its lineage to dynastic Egypt. Melokiyah is a plant with dark green leaves and small, yellow flowers. Even in the land of the pharaohs most peasants had a small plot of land for their own use and in summer this was exclusively for the cultivation of melokiyah. Even today, Melokiyah is popular among Egyptians. I'm told the best Melokiyah can be found in Aswan and Luxor, in Upper Egypt.

Admittedly, finding fresh melokiyah may be difficult. You can get dried or frozen from any Middle Eastern store or specialty market, or even in the frozen section of a large supermarket. If you can't find it, a good substitute is spinach. But, let me say up front, it's not as tasty.

Compared to other recipes, Melokiyah may take a little bit more time and effort, but, believe me, it's worth it. If you are fortunate enough to find an Egyptian restaurant that serves fresh Melokiyah, forget about everything else on the menu and go for it.

Melokiyah can be prepared with fish, beef, or chicken. For this recipe, I have chosen chicken as a compliment to the stock.

1 fryer chicken, 2½ to 3 pounds, cut into serving pieces
1 medium onion, peeled and cut in half
Salt to taste
1 bay leaf
3 to 4 cardamom seeds*
Olive oil
1 pound frozen or dried melokiyah
4 cloves garlic, crushed
1 teaspoon ground coriander
1 teaspoon lemon juice
Cooked rice (enough for four people)

1. Rinse the chicken pieces under cold running water and pat dry with paper towels.
2. In a large pot, Dutch oven, or heavy iron casserole, add the chicken and water to cover. Add the onion, salt, bay leaf, and cardamon seeds. Bring to a boil, cover and simmer until the chicken is tender.
3. Remove the chicken from the pot, place in a medium skillet and fry quickly in 3 tablespoons of olive oil. Set aside and keep warm.
4. Remove the bay leaf and onion from the stock pot. Mash the onion and return it to the pot. Boil the soup stock and add the melokiyah. Adjust the seasoning and simmer on low heat for 3 to 5 minutes. Do not overcook or melokiyah will fall to the bottom of the pot. You want it suspended in the water.
5. Mix the garlic and coriander. Heat 2 tablespoons of olive oil in a skillet and fry the mixture until golden. Toss the mixture into the boiling melokiyah and simmer for about 2 minutes. Add the lemon juice.
6. To serve, place cooked rice in a serving bowl, add chicken, and cover with the soup. Or you can serve individually on plates with rice, a piece of chicken on top, and soup to cover.

YIELD: 4 SERVINGS

NOTE: You can double the recipe ingredients for six servings or more.

Available in Asian or Middle Eastern stores.

BOILED AND ROASTED DUCK

Duck was a very popular fowl in ancient Egypt. It was served either roasted or stuffed. The stuffing was either crushed wheat or millet. Stuffed duck is time consuming so I suggest roasting. You're probably wondering, how did the ancients bake or roast? We know they baked bread and roasted various foods, but how was it done? The Egyptians were innovative. Not only did they use the spit-roasting method, but they also stewed, braised, and even baked using fired clay vessels.

I find the best duck for roasting is Muscovy duck. It isn't as fatty as its Long Island brethren. Also, wild or Bavarizan duck tends to be less fatty.

Today, a good accompaniment to this dish would be boiled potatoes. In contemporary Egypt this dish is served with potatoes stuffed with fried minced meat.

1 4 - to 5-pound duck
1 tablespoon ground cumin
1 large onion, quartered
Salt and ground black pepper to taste
1 lemon
3 tablespoons tomato paste

1. Rinse the duck under cold running water and pat dry with paper towels.
2. Place it in a large pot or Dutch oven with water to cover. Bring the water to a boil. Stir in the cumin, onion, salt, and pepper. Cover and simmer until the duck is tender (45 minutes to one hour).
3. Preheat the oven to 375 degrees.
4. Remove the duck to a roasting pan or ovenproof platter. Cut the lemon in half and squeeze the juice over the duck. Cover evenly with tomato paste.
5. Place the duck in the oven and roast until brownish red (about 15 to 20 minutes).

YIELD: 4 TO 6 SERVINGS

Green Salad

Egyptians of the dynastic era enjoyed figs, dates, and pomegranates, not only as desserts but throughout the meal. They liked strong tasting vegetables such as garlic and onions. And vegetables were often served with an oil and vinegar dressing. Here is a green salad using vegetables the Egyptians may have enjoyed.

1 small bunch celery (about ¾ pound)*
3 large ripe tomatoes, sliced into half-moons
2 medium-sized cucumbers, washed, scrubbed, and sliced
1 medium red onion, peeled and thinly sliced
2 tablespoons red wine vinegar
2 tablespoons olive oil (extravirgin is best)
Juice of half a lemon
Salt and ground black pepper to taste
½ teaspoon ground cumin

1. Wash the celery under cold running water. Remove the root ends and leafy tops and cut the ribs into ½-inch pieces. Place in a bowl or on a platter.
2. Add the tomatoes, cucumbers, and onion. Toss to mix.
3. In a cup, combine the vinegar and olive oil. Add the lemon juice, salt, and pepper. Stir and pour on the salad. Sprinkle with cumin, and serve.
   YIELD: 4 TO 5 SERVINGS

*Green beans can be substituted for the celery. In this case, take ½ pound of green beans, trimmed and broken into bite-sized pieces, and cook or steam until crisp-tender. Drain and rinse in cold water, mix with other ingredients, and add the dressing.

FUL MEDAMES

Ful Medames or Fuul Medammis is one of those rare dishes that harks back to ancient times but is still popular today. The ancient Egyptians ate it for breakfast. Today Egyptians not only cook it at home, but it can be purchased from street vendors and in bazaars. In olden times it was made from ancient beans—which would be hard to find at present. These days the most popular legumes used are fava beans. This dish can be made from any other bean—just avoid the canned variety.

2 cups dried, small fava beans
3 cloves garlic, peeled and crushed
⅓ cup olive oil
Juice of 1 lemon
Salt and ground pepper to taste
½ teaspoon ground cumin
½ teaspoon ground coriander
Fresh flat parsley, chopped

1. Rinse the beans thoroughly. Place them in a large pot or bowl, cover with cold water, and let them soak at room temperature overnight or for at least 8 hours.
2. Drain the soaked beans, place them in a medium saucepan or cast-iron pot, and cover with water. Bring the water to a boil, reduce the heat, cover, and simmer the beans for an hour or more until they are very tender (but not pasty or soupy), adding more water as they cook if necessary.
3. Drain the beans and transfer to a bowl. Stir in the garlic, two tablespoons of the olive oil, lemon juice, salt, pepper, cumin, and coriander. Mix well.
4. Serve the beans in individual wooden bowls. Sprinkle each with parsley and drizzle with the remaining olive oil.

YIELD: 6 TO 8 SERVINGS

Kofta

Kofta are Egyptian meatballs. A dish as old as time itself, it has spread to other parts of the Middle East and beyond so that it's even popular in such areas as Afghanistan, where they have their own version, naturally termed, *Afghani kofta*. It can be made with beef, but the traditional choice is ground lamb. Let me state that the Egyptians had ovens, however primitive. As noted, they knew how to broil and roast. It can be assumed that this dish was grilled in a manner similar to the way we would do it today. And today, this dish would be served with pita bread.

6 whole black peppercorns
Salt to taste
1 pound ground lamb
1 whole leek, washed and finely chopped
Fresh flat parsley, chopped

1. In a mortar, crush the peppercorns along with the salt.
2. In a bowl, combine the lamb with the leek, peppercorn, and salt. Shape the mixture into ovals the size of walnuts.
3. Thread the meatballs on skewers and grill for about 5 minutes, until brown. Turn and grill on the other side. Serve sprinkled with the parsley.

YIELD: 4 SERVINGS

Bamya

The mucilaginous green pods we know as okra were enjoyed in pharoaic Egypt. This fruit of a tall tropical and semitropical plant (*Abelmoschus esculentus*) found favor in a dish called Bamya. This stew, which is still popular in the Middle East, can be prepared with lamb or beef and is normally served with rice. Plain Bamya is nothing more than sautéed okra sprinkled with lemon juice and served with whatever spices are available.

The problem with okra is that it's kind of slimy. For this dish to work, the okra must be cooked, as in step 1 below, so that it is no longer so.

1½ pounds okra
2 tablespoons olive oil
Salt and ground black pepper to taste
Juice of 1 lemon

1. Trim the tips of the okra pods, and dump the okra into rapidly boiling water for 2 minutes. Drain, rinse in cold water, and pat dry with paper towels.
2. Heat the olive oil in a skillet or frying pan. Add the okra and lightly fry over medium heat, stirring gently (about 3 minutes).
3. Season with salt and pepper. Sprinkle with lemon juice and serve.

Yield: 3 to 4 servings

Sweetened Dates

Pomegranates, figs, and dates were among the fruits enjoyed in Ancient Egypt. Figs, with their high sugar content, were relished by the rich and poor alike. Baskets of figs were among the provisions given to the dead when they took their journeys to the other side. Figs were good for the living too. They served as laxatives. Something that would appeal to a people who had a habit of fasting and purging themselves.

Dates, like figs, were eaten fresh, and their juice was often used as a sweetener.

This recipe was, and is, one of the most popular ways to prepare dates. It makes a good dessert.

2 cups fresh dates
½ cup water (approximately)
1 teaspoon ground cinnamon
½ teaspoon ground decorticated cardamom*
1 cup chopped walnuts
⅔ cup honey (more or less, as needed)
1 cup ground almonds

1. Place the dates in a medium bowl. Add a little water at a time while mashing the dates with a large wooden fork or potato masher to form a paste. The amount of water used is a judgment call. You need enough to form a paste but not a liquid.
2. Fold in the cinnamon, cardamom, and walnuts. Mix well and shape into little balls the size of gumdrops or just bigger than regular marbles.
3. Pour the honey into a dish. Pour the almonds into another dish.
4. Roll the balls in the honey until they are coated. Then roll in the almonds until coated. Serve at room temperature.

Yield: about 6 servings

*Ground decorticated cardamom can be found in health food stores or specialty markets.

THREE

CLASSICAL GREECE

BARLEY BREAD, MNESITHIUS CABBAGE,
FISH A LA MITHAIKOS, ROAST LEG OF LAMB,
CIRCE'S KYKEON, BAKED WHOLE FISH,
RABBIT ATHENAEUS,
PHILOXENUS' CHEESECAKE

It was at P.S. 25, in East Harlem, where dear old Miss Robinette first introduced us to the heroes of classical Greece. We were forced to read portions of Homer's *Iliad*—a long, turgid poem for adults let alone unctuous sixth-graders. Thank God in those days we had Classic comic books. Remember those? If a kid was assigned a book report on some notable work of fiction, all he had to do was get a Classic comic book, which gave you the gist of the story. I may be wrong, but I don't think those comic books are around anymore. They've all been replaced by Monarch Notes, which is a shame. I learned a lot about the classics from these dubious renditions.

Later on, I slogged through the *Iliad* and the *Odyssey* out of sheer curiosity. The *Iliad* centers on Achilles, a Greek warrior who (when he's not sulking in his tent or doing battle) in Book IX of the epic hosts Odysseus with a banquet outside the walls of Troy. He begins by telling his friend Patroclus: "Bring out a bigger bowl, my lord Patroclus, put less water in the wine, and give every man a cup. Here are my dearest friends under my own roof." After the toasting is over, they start preparing the meal. It continues, "Patroclus carried out his comrade's orders. He put down a big bench in the firelight, and laid on it the backs of a sheep and a fat goat and the chime of a great hog rich in lard. Automedon held these for him, while Achilles jointed them, and then carved up the joints and spitted the slices. Meanwhile, Patroclus, the royal son of Menotius, made the fire blaze up. When it had burnt down again and the flames had disappeared, he scattered the embers and laid the spits above them, resting them on dogs, after he had sprinkled the meat with holy salt. When he had roasted it and heaped it up on platters, Patroclus fetched some bread and set it on the tables in handsome baskets; and Achilles divided the meat into portions. . . . Patroclus threw the ritual pieces on the fire, and they all helped themselves to the good things spread before them."

It's not a regal meal by any standard. What we get from this tableux is that the Homeric heroes gorged themselves on burnt meat. Luckily, this was to change. Two thousand years after the Trojan War, Greeks were dining on such delicacies as fatted geese and sea urchins. Of course, not all Greeks had access to such exotic fare. Basic Greek food before and during the golden age was rather plain. Greeks of all strata had an affinity for what can only be referred to as "grain pastes." These could be made of barley or wheat. Pliny the elder has Greek and Italian recipes for pastes made out of barley. They were known by the Greek word *maza*, which can also translate to cake or porridge. But this barley paste was not a cake or porridge as we know it. It was more like a seasoned paste. In one of Pliny's recipes he states the Greeks soak the barley in water for a few days, then leave it to dry for a night. The next day they dry it by a fire and grind in some sort of mill, mix in three pounds of flax seed, half a pound of coriander, and an eighth of a pint of salt. What this would taste like, I hazard to guess. Wheat was processed more or less in the same fashion. It was soaked in water for about ten days, boiled, then the peelings were discarded and the rest was sundried. This was also the starter for making breads and desserts. Flour was also made from barley; and barley bread, olives, figs, and goat's milk cheese rounded out the basic diet. Sometimes they washed it down with wine, but more often the poor man's drink was goat's milk or water. The rich had access to more meat, such as goat, mutton, or pork, and game such as deer or wild boar. The poorer classes usually ate meat during public religious celebrations, which involved animal sacrifice, normally a goat or a cow. The ancient Greeks ate plenty of seafood; but again there was that disparity between rich and poor, which became more pronounced after the fifth century B.C.E. The peasant usually got by with the occasional salted fish *(tarichi)* while the well-to-do ate sardines, sea urchins, cuttlefish, prawns, and mullet.

The Greeks were fans of two other dietary staples—the olive and the grape. During the Bronze Age, Crete became an island state of note due to its cultivation of the olive. Excavation of the palace of Nestor at Knossos yielded jars that at one time contained olive oil mixed with aromatic herbs. Greece was to become so dependent on the olive that in the sixth century B.C.E. the Athenians forbade the export of olive oil. Olive oil became the preferred cooking medium, not only because of the flavor it imparted but also because through long-term use it made the cooking pots nonstick. And this, long before Teflon.

Greeks were the first to dabble in fine wines. Wine, of course, had been around long before the Greeks. It had been cultivated in Mesopotamia by 3000 B.C.E., but it was the Greeks who first placed a personal stamp on it. In the Mediterranean world during the classical age, Greek wines were renowned. Greeks not only cultivated *vin ordinaries*, or table wines, but they also produced distinct vintages. The common man, however, had to make do with less refined fare—such as Retsina wine. And, believe me, Retsina is an acquired taste. Ever wonder where it comes from? It may have to do with the fact that in ancient times wine was fermented in vats smeared inside and out with resin to make them watertight. It's the resin that, even today, gives the wine its distinctive taste. This may be one of the reasons why Greeks, like

the Romans, who came after them, drank their wine mixed with water—
normally two parts water to one part wine. They did not have the modern
methods of pasteurization and fermentation of today's vigneron. So, to
improve taste and longevity, special herbs and mixtures were added, including in some cases even condensed seawater and chalk. Of course, if you
wanted to get a buzz, you could always forget about the taste and the water
and have it straight. Those who could afford it could indulge in exquisite vintages such as the famed Pramnian mentioned by Homer. And they liked their
wine sweet, almost honeylike. These were the great growths enjoyed by the
rich and well-to-do. And everyone of note had his favorite. Archestratus,
about whom we shall speak more at length, praises the qualities of the wine
produced on the Isle of Lesbos with full poetic measure:

> *Then when you take up a full measure of Zeus the Savior*
> *it ought to be an old, quite grey-headed*
> *wine, its moist hair covered with a white flower,*
> *that you drink, a wine from wave-girt Lesbos by birth.*
> *I also praise the Bibline wine from Holy Phoenicia,*
> *although I do not rank it equal to Lesbian. For you are previously unacquainted with*
>   *it and taste it*
> *For the first time,*
> *you will think it more fragrant than Lesbian,*
> *but when it is drunk, it is much inferior, whereas*
> *Lesbian wine*
> *will seem to you to share the rank of ambrosia rather than of wine.*

A vibrant, expanding culture will produce a vibrant, expanding cuisine.
Just as they improved their vinification techniques, so did Greek cookery
improve. This became more pronounced in the diet of the rich. The upper
classes now indulged in sumptuous feasts and elegant presentations. It was
all to reach its height and glory during the Athenian golden age during which
the city-state of Athens enjoyed a period of greatness. This is the Athens of
Pericles and Socrates and the great philosophical schools. The first recipe
books of antiquity begin to appear at this time. Extracts have remained from
works on gastronomy and cooking by such authors as Herakleides of Syracuse, Mithaikos and Glaucus of Locris. But the most famous is the work of
Archestratus, who is credited with compiling what could be regarded as the

world's first cookbook. This work is known as *The Hedupatheia*, a poetical treatise on fine food and dining written in hexemeter. Archestratus was an Epicurean of the highest order. His work would have vanished completely were it not for another gourmet, Athenaeus of Naukratis, whose *The Deipnosophists* contains some sixty fragments of the poem. This book, also known as *The Sophists at Dinner*, is a dialogue of wise men who, at a Greek banquet, hold forth on many topics, including food and cooking. According to Athenaeus, "This Archestratus out of love of pleasure made a careful circuit of the entire earth because, I think, he wished to inquire painstakingly into everything associated with the belly. . . ."

Archestratus was among the first of the recorded gastronomes, if that term can be used for a fourth century Greek pedant. Across the centuries I would love to have hung out with this guy. Wading through his musings, he comes across both as an expert and a pompous dilettante. Check this out:

> And to you as you are drinking your fill let someone bring a dainty such as
> a sausage, and a stewed son's womb that has embarked
> in cumin and in pungent vinegar and silphium,
> and the tender race of whatever roasted birds are in
> season. Pay no attention to those Syracusians,
> who act like frogs and merely drink without eating anything.
> Pay no heed, but to at the foods
> I mentioned. All those other dainties are
> evidence of wretched beggary-boiled chickpeas
> and fava beans and apples and dried figs. But I praise
> the flat-cake of born in Athens. And if you do not have it there,
> go off elsewhere and look for Attic honey,
> since that is what makes it saucy.
> That is how a free man ought to live, or else go down
> unto destruction beneath the earth and beneath the pit and Tarturos
> and be buried countless stades deep.

Archestratus shows us a lot with his writings. We're all familiar with the type: the one who will pontificate on all the vagaries of *haute cuisine*, who will vouch for the most obscure ingredients, and who will take tea with his pinky finger extended. The kind of person whom my father would call a *pendejo* , a Puerto Rican word for someone who, among other things, is full of himself. Still, for all his airs, Archestratus keeps his cooking simple. His preparation falls into two categories: dry cooking—that is, frying, roasting, and baking; and wet cooking—stewing, poaching, and braising. His guiding principal is that food should be prepared as simply as possible to retain its inherent flavor. It should not be overwhelmed with strong sauces. One of his recommendations for roasted hare is to have it "hot and seasoned with salt alone," and not inundated with "sauces made of sticky things and over rich in oil and cheese, as if they were preparing the dish for a weasel." Instead, good food should have "the excellence of pleasure in themselves." The seasonings he recommends are salt, olive oil, cumin, vinegar, some unspecified herbs, cheese, and silphium. Okay, what is silphium? It is a spice also known as *asafoetida*, which is the resin of the plant *ferula asafoetida*, which is related to fennel. For cooking purposes, the closest and most convenient substitute today would be *hing*, a powdered mixture consisting of asafoetida, flour, and tumeric. This is used in Indian cooking and can be found in most Indian food stores. When using the *hing*, it should be used sparingly. It does have a strong taste and smell.

As you will note in the section on imperial Rome, the Romans used silphium extensively in their cooking. It was also reputed to have strong medicinal properties.

For the ancient Greeks, the main meal of the day was dinner. Or what they called the *deipnon*. Meals were often eaten outdoors, or al fresco, as one would term it today. And here we come to the other great Greek activity related to dining: the symposium. This was an institution that flourished in the Greek city-states from approximately the early to the late fifth century B.C.E. It was an exclusive male gathering of aristocratic friends that followed a prescribed ritual. First a procession of the guests who would attend a banquet, then the banquet or dinner itself, and finally the drinking party, which included not only philosophical and literary discourse but also singing and dancing. This might include dancing girls and musicians and other performers such as acrobats and actors. Whatever you might say about the philosophical nuances of the symposium, it seems to me that by the end of the evening, you probably had a bunch of drunkards with garlands around their heads, chasing female dancers and slave boys with wine jugs.

What food was served at these functions? Like most Greek meals, it began with bread, either wheat or barley, then some appetizers, or savories. This could range from fresh fruit, to fish or fowl, or even goose or peacock eggs; then on to the meat such as stewed goose or spit-roasted lamb. The final dessert course might consist of cheese, sweetmeats, and dried fruit, such as figs and raisins, and nuts, such as almonds and chestnuts.

One thing that those movies of my youth did get right when portraying classical Greek and Roman culture: they did dine reclining on couches. This became a common practice from the fifth century on. Men at dinner parties reclined on their left side and ate with their right hands off individual tables. According to Athenaeus, he quotes one Alcman demanding that etiquette required: "Couches seven, and as many tables laden with poppy-bread, and bread with flax and sesame seed, and in cups . . . golden sweets."

Naturally, not all Greek citizens of the classical era enjoyed such sumptuous dinners. Despite its claim to being the birthplace of democracy, ancient Greece, like most of the ancient world, had its share of disparities. Slaves and peasants predominated. During the classical era, cooking as a profession was the province of free male citizens. But as time progressed and especially after the Hellenistic era, many of the cooks were slaves who specialized solely in this province. If you couldn't afford a good slave cook, I guess you had to do it on your own. Which leads to the question, what utensils did they use? What was the ancient Greek kitchen like? We know there was no refrigeration; and obviously they ate a lot of boiled meat, which lasted longer. A lot of the surviving recipes call for roasting, braising, and grilling. This called for spit-roasting equipment probably suspended over a hearth made of brick or tile. The hearth most likely had a charcoal pit with a gridiron standing over the coals. Here you could place the clay pots and earthenware vessels, which were more common since metal pots and pans, mainly copper and lead, were more expensive. Meats and vegetables were usually cooked in a large pot known as a *gastra*, which could also be a cauldron, suspended by chains over the fire.

So you're probably thinking: What about ventilation? How could anyone survive in such a kitchen? Pastoral Greeks would cook outdoors. Indoors, hopefully there were windows, and if not, then there was probably a hole in the roof just above the hearth.

BARLEY BREAD

Athenaeus informs us that Herakleides of Syracuse defined a bread called *kyboi*, which literally means *dice*, as "square loafs of bread, seasoned with anise, cheese, and olive oil." This recipe sparked my interest. We know that barley bread was popular among the ancient Greeks, so why not try it with the ingredients given here, namely the anise, cheese, and olive oil? For the anise, I decided on aniseed, the licorice-flavored seed from the anise plant that has been around since time immemorial. Deciding which cheese to use was another judgment call. The ancient Greeks made many varieties of cheese; but there's not much information on them. My guess is that it was mainly goat's milk cheese. So I've settled on feta, that popular cheese in Greece and elsewhere that has been around since the Middle Ages.

I've tried this recipe with barley flour; and also with a combination of barley and whole wheat flour. When barley flour is used, the bread comes out somewhat heavy with a darker, course texture and richer flavor. Some people might prefer this. Could be that in poor households this was the norm. Those better off would probably have mixed the barley flour with some other flour to produce a less course bread with a softer crust. That's the recipe I've decided to go with. The recipe also calls for honey. Honey was one of the prime flavors used in Greek cuisine. They used it in sauces and even mixed it with wine to make it more palatable. In this recipe the honey is used to counteract the saltiness provided by the feta cheese. I prefer pure, raw unprocessed honey, which you can find in health food stores.

Those who are purist bread bakers will note that I don't leaven the bread for a prolonged period of time. The leaven, also called the starter, is just a piece of the raw dough that is left to ferment overnight. The ancient Greeks kept this starter *(prozymi)* in a clay jar and used it as needed when baking bread. For the sake of convenience, I dispense with this fermentation process. If you are a purist and prefer the extended leavening process then, before baking the bread, dissolve yeast in water, add 2 cups of barley flour, blend to form a dough, and store the dough overnight in a glass dish. The next day, combine with the cheese and honey mixture given below, add the remaining dough, and bake as per the instructions.

¾ cups milk
½ cup honey
½ cup feta cheese, crumbled
3 tablespoons olive oil
1 cup warm water
2 envelopes active dry yeast
3 cups barley flour
3 cups whole wheat flour
1½ tablespoons whole anise seed

1. In a small pan or skillet, heat the milk until boiling. Stir in the honey and cheese. Cook over medium heat, stirring constantly, until the cheese melts. Add 2 tablespoons of the olive oil, and mix. Let the mixture cool until lukewarm.

2. Meanwhile, place the water in a large bowl. Sprinkle in the yeast, and stir to dissolve. Add 1½ cups barley flour and 1½ cups whole wheat flour, and blend well with a wooden spoon. Add the cheese mixture, the anise seed, and the remaining flour. Knead well with your hands to form a stiff dough. The dough will be somewhat viscous. Sprinkle a little additional whole wheat flour until you get the desired consistency. Roll the dough into a ball. Cover with a cloth or towel and let it rest for 20 minutes.

3. Liberally grease a 9 x 5 x 3 loaf pan with olive oil. If you can locate a clay loaf pan, so much the better. Lightly moisten your hands and press the dough into the pan. Cover with a cloth or towel and let rise for 2 ½ hours. Note that the dough will not double in volume when it rises, but it will expand somewhat in the oven.

4. Preheat the oven to 375 degrees. Brush the top of the dough with olive oil, place it in the oven and bake for about 45 minutes.

YIELD: 1 LOAF

THE PHARAOH'S FEAST

MNESITHEUS CABBAGE

Cauliflower, leeks, lettuce, cucumbers, radishes, onions, artichokes, celery, and carrots were among the vegetables consumed by the Greeks. They also had onions and garlic, and cabbage, which was very popular because of its reputed medicinal properties. Oribasius, a physician who lived in the fourth century of the Common era recommended cabbage as a cure for those troubled by gout and dysentary. He quotes one Mnesitheus of Cyzicus advising "You should cut up cabbages with a very sharp knife, then wash them and allow the water to draw off; cut up together with the cabbage a sufficient quantity of coriander and rue; then sprinkle with honeyed vinegar, and grate on top a small quantity of asafoetida. "

The recipe seems simple, but for two factors. Mnesitheus mentions rue. This is a culinary herb, *Ruta graveolens*, which is now seldom used. It can be found in its dried form in any good health food or gourmet store. It is an evergreen and if you can find it fresh, more power to you. The other factor is honeyed vinegar. According to Oribasius, this honey vinegar mixture was called *oxymel;* and it involved simmering the honey, adding vinegar, boiling it down, and mixing it with water. You can try this method, if you desire. I take the easy way out by simply mixing the honey and red wine vinegar and sprinkling it over the vegetable.

The recipe does not mention cooking the cabbage at all. I prefer blanching the cabbage in water over eating it raw. Though I'm sure if you finely slice the cabbage, cooking may not be needed.

1 medium-sized cabbage, washed, leaves separated, and ribs trimmed
Salt to taste
2 teaspoons ground coriander
2 teaspoons dried rue
¼ cup honey
2 tablespoons red wine vinegar
A pinch hing*

1. Blanch the cabbage for 5 to 8 minutes in boiling salted water. Rinse in cold water, drain, and finely slice.
2. Place the cabbage in a bowl or a round dish. Add the coriander and rue.
3. Combine the honey and red wine vinegar and sprinkle over the cabbage. Toss.
4. Sprinkle the *hing* over the cabbage, toss, and serve.

YIELD: 4 TO 6 SERVINGS

NOTE: If you want a more authentic preparation, purchase whole Moroccan coriander and crush 1 tablespoon of the stuff in a mortar. This can be used in place of the store-bought ground coriander and will impart a richer flavor.

Hing can be found in most Indian food stores.

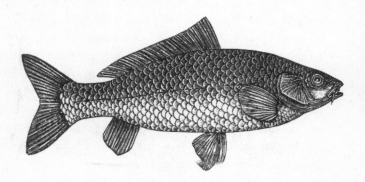

THE PHARAOH'S FEAST

FISH A LA MITHAIKOS

According to reliable Athenaeus, a fellow gourmand, Mithaikos, in the only preserved fragment from his cookbook, has given us a succinct and simple recipe for preparing fish. In this case, ribbonfish: "As for the ribbonfish, after you gut it, cut its head off, rinse it, and cut it into slices, pour cheese and olive oil over it."

The recipe seems simple enough. But what fish to use? In the Mediterranean world of Archestratus and Athenaeus, there was plenty of fish available. Ancient recipes include porgy, mackerel, and even shark. For this recipe any kind of whole fish can be used—hake, red snapper, blue fish, sea bass, striped bass, etc. The other factor is what kind of cheese to use. As noted, sheep or goat's milk cheese would be the obvious choice. I tried this recipe with feta cheese, and it didn't work. I've settled on Pecorino Romano, a sheep's milk cheese, which has a bold, sharp flavor. Another would be French chevre, also a goat's milk cheese.

1 whole fish, 2½ to 3 pounds, cleaned and scaled, head and tail removed
Salt to taste
¾ cup grated Pecorino Romano cheese, or Chevre cheese, crumbled
3 tablespoons olive oil

1. Preheat the oven to 400 degrees.
2. Wash the fish, inside and out, under cold running water and pat dry with paper towels. Rub the fish with salt.
3. Cut the fish into 1-inch slices.
4. In a small bowl, combine the cheese and olive oil. Mix well.
5. Place the fish slices in a roasting pan or baking dish large enough to hold them comfortably.
6. Spread the cheese mixture over the fish.
7. Bake, uncovered, for approximately 30 minutes or until the fish flakes easily when tested with a fork.

YIELD: 4 SERVINGS

ROAST LEG OF LAMB

Okay, how do we tackle that roasted sheep and goat meat that Achilles served his friends during the siege of Troy? This is rather interesting. Apicius, in his tome on cookery, *De Re Coquinaria*, includes recipes for steamed and marinated lamb. But Apicius was a Roman, and this is the Greek section. So I've inquired how Greeks would roast a leg of lamb today, thinking it might give me a clue concerning its preparation in ancient times. We know among the ingredients used by the ancients were olive oil, garlic, wine, honey, and such herbs as marjoram and cumin. So, why not keep it simple? Just like Achilles did when hosting Odysseus?

> 1 4-pound whole leg of lamb
> ¼ cup olive oil
> ½ teaspoon dried marjoram*
> ½ teaspoon salt
> ½ teaspoon ground cumin*
> 3 cloves garlic, peeled and cut into slivers

1. Preheat the oven to 400 degrees.
2. Rinse the meat and wipe with damp paper towels.
3. In a small bowl, mix a marinade by combining the olive oil, marjoram, salt, and cumin.
4. With the tip of a sharp knife, cut inch-deep slits all over the lamb and insert a sliver of garlic in each.
5. Rub the marinade over the leg of lamb and let it rest for at least half an hour.
6. Place the lamb in a roasting pan and roast for 20 minutes or until the meat is brown and crusty. Reduce the heat to 325 degrees and roast 2 to 2 ½ hours more, until done.

YIELD: 6 SERVINGS

THE PHARAOH'S FEAST

NOTE: For a variation on this dish—which would make use of that ancient Greek affection for wine and honey—mix 3 tablespoons of honey with ½ cup of dry red wine. Baste the lamb frequently with this mixture until done.

*You can substitute fresh marjoram and cumin seeds for the dried ingredients. If you do, use 1 teaspoon of fresh, chopped marjoram and combine it with 1 tablespoon of cumin seeds. Combine with the salt and pound in a mortar. Blend in the olive oil and rub the mixture over the lamb.

CIRCE'S KYKEON

When I was an impressionable lad back on the block, the movie, *Ulysses*, came out starring Kirk Douglas. Ostensibly, it's based on Homer's *Odyssey*. Now, I must be honest about this. One of the reasons I went to see this movie was because it also featured an Italian actress, Silvana Mangano. Ms. Mangano was a very healthy woman possessing (what would be termed in more sedate times) a magnificent carriage. Every guy on the block went to see the movie.

For me, there were other positive aspects to the flick. It got me interested in this fellow, Ulysses. After wading through the *Odyssey*, I discovered that this guy, also called Odysseus, was something else. In the *Iliad* he is always referred to as the "wily Odysseus." It's an apt description. He may not have had the brawn of an Achilles or the fighting skill of a Hector, but he did have brains. He was the one who came up with the idea of the big wooden horse that tricked the Trojans into defeat and ended the ten-year war.

Odysseus did have two flaws—he was proud and obstinate. He defied the gods and they made his life into a toilet. For a decade he tried to get back home to his faithful Penelope but the gods, pissers that they were, thwarted him at every turn.

One of these episodes involved Circe, a sorceress, who turned the men who sailed with Odysseus into hogs. She did it by feeding them a kind of porridge, which Homer describes as a mix of "cheese, barley meal and yellow honey with wine from Pramnos." She also added drugs for the desired effect. The porridge Circe most likely gave the men was *kykeon*.

Kykeon was popular throughout the ancient Greco-Roman world. The Romans had their version of it and so did the Carthaginians. I've decided to follow Circe's recipe—without the bonus ingredients. Since it is something like a porridge, Kykeon has to be thick. The thickening agent is barley. But what cheese to use? I settled on that old Greek standby, feta. Although I'm sure any other good goat cheese can be used. Circe's recipe calls for Pramnian wine. Any sweet wine will do (I used Tokay).

1 cup hulled barley
2 cups water
1 cup grated feta cheese
3 tablespoons honey
½ cup sweet red wine

1. Place the barley in a medium saucepan, add the water, and bring to a boil. Cover and simmer on low heat until thickened (30 to 40 minutes).
2. Stir in the cheese, honey, and wine. You can add more honey or wine depending on the consistency desired.
3. Allow to sit for a couple of minutes, and serve.

YIELD: 4 SERVINGS

Baked Whole Fish

In the Fish a la Mithaikos recipe (see page 39), Athenaeus recommends that the fish be cooked with its head cut off. But in other sections of his writings he recommends that a fish be served whole, as in this version where he quotes from a book called *The Banquet* by Philoxenus of Leucas:

The sea-perch, the turbot, the fish with even teeth and with jagged teeth must be sliced, else the vengeance of the gods may breathe upon you. Rather, bake them and serve them whole for it is much better so.

I am perplexed about the "even teeth" and "jagged teeth." But I take old Philoxenus at his word in terms of cooking the fish whole. We know that in general, his chronicler, Athenaeus, recommended seasonings such as salt, olive oil, marjoram, cumin, and cheese (along with silphium and some unspecified herbs). This would be a very easy way to cook a fish. As Athenaeus recommends, it could be turbot, perch, or any other white-fleshed fish such as sea bass, stripe bass, pike, fluke, etc.

1 whole fish, 2½ to 3 pounds, cleaned and scaled but with head and tail attached
1 teaspoon salt
2 teaspoons dried marjoram
1 teaspoon ground cumin
2 teaspoons red wine vinegar

1. Preheat the oven to 400 degrees.
2. Wash the fish, inside and out, under cold running water and pat dry with paper towels.
3. Place the fish in a roasting pan or baking dish large enough to hold it comfortably.
4. In a small bowl, combine the salt, marjoram, cumin, and vinegar.
5. With a sharp knife, make 3 to 4 vertical slits on both sides of fish. Rub the seasonings thoroughly into the skin.
6. Bake, uncovered, for approximately 30 minutes or until the fish flakes easily when tested with a fork.

Yield: 4 servings

RABBIT ATHENAEUS

. . . hot and seasoned with salt alone, pulling it off the spit while it is still a bit on the rare side. Do not let it trouble you when you see the juice dripping from the meat, but eat it greedily. The other ways of preparing it are, in my opinion, much too much too elaborate—sauces made of sticky things and over-rich in oil and cheese; as if they were preparing the dish for a weasel.

Here Athenaeus takes to task those who would overcook a hare—or, for our purpose, a rabbit. Again, I take it as the gourmand advises—hare or rabbit simply roasted with salt alone. I'll prepare the recipe as given; but, if preferred, other seasonings such as black pepper and oregano can be added. If you have a rotisserie grill, the rabbit can be cooked as stated. Otherwise, cut it into serving-sized pieces and bake at 400 degrees for about 45 minutes. Sage though he may be, I do not concur with Athenaeus about eating hare on the rare side with the juice (actually, blood) dripping from the meat.

If you can't find a rabbit in your local supermarket, you may have to order it from your butcher or buy it at a poultry market. The rabbit will come skinned, either whole or cut into serving-sized pieces.

1 2-pound rabbit, ready to cook
Salt to taste
2 to 3 tablespoons olive oil

1. Wash the rabbit under cold running water and pat dry with paper towels.
2. Season the rabbit inside and out with the salt.
3. Brush inside and out with the olive oil.
4. Place the rabbit on the spit rods of a rotisserie, inserting the rods from head to tail. Be sure to get the weight evenly distributed on the rods.
5. Roast until the rabbit is tender (about 45 minutes). When a fork or knife slips into the thigh easily, the rabbit is done. A meat thermometer should read 175 degrees Fahrenheit.

YIELD: 4 SERVINGS

PHILOXENUS' CHEESECAKE

In the quotations attributed to *The Banquet* by Philoxenus, there is a reference to a "Cheesecake, made with milk and honey, a sweet that was baked like a pie." This was news to me. They had cheesecake in classical Greece, and all this time I thought cheesecake was something modern. The next question is, how was it made back in the old days? (And we are talking about the *old days* here.) The sources are sketchy on this. The Romans had *libum*, a honeyed cake made with cheese to which they added an egg. Whether this was similar to the cheesecake referred to by Philoxenus, I do not know. I can only guess that Greek cheesecake also contained egg. We do know that Roman cooking, especially at the time of the Roman Empire, was influenced very much by Greek cuisine. So it's possible that the two honeyed cakes shared some ingredients. The final hurdle is what cheese to use? This being a Greek cheesecake, I went with feta. Admittedly, feta is quite salty. However, a good measure of honey counteracts that. Let me add that this is not the rich and creamy creation that we know today. Juniors and Baby Watson had not yet been invented.

1 cup whole wheat flour
1 pound feta cheese, grated
½ cup milk
1 egg
1 cup clear unprocessed honey

1. Preheat the oven to 425 degrees.
2. Place the flour in a bowl. Add the cheese and milk and stir until a soft consistency.
3. Add the egg and mix well. Form into a soft dough and shape it onto a greased 9-inch pie plate.
4. Warm the honey in a small saucepan and pour over the cake.
5. Bake until golden brown (about 40 minutes). Serve warm. If you prefer a sweeter cake, you can pour more warm honey over the cake and allow it to soak for 30 minutes before serving.

YIELD: 4 SERVINGS

FOUR

THE INDUS VALLEY

KING SRENIKA'S BASH

When Alexander the Great and his army invaded India in 327 B.C.E., India, to most Greeks, was a mysterious and exotic land. It was the farthest of their eastern conquests, a land both alluring and enigmatic. What was probably unknown to the invaders was that a thriving civilization, as old as that of Mesopotamia and Egypt, had arisen along the flood plains of the Indus and Saraswati rivers in what is now Pakistan and Northwest India. Two great cities, Harappa and Mohenjo-Daro, thrived in the Indus Valley. At its height, around 2200 B.C.E., Harappa, the larger of the two, covered about 370 acres and may have been populated by 80,000 people, making it as populace as the ancient city of Ur in Mesopotamia. Among their claims to fame, the enterprising residents of Harappa are credited with domesticating the Indian jungle fowl—what is known today as a *chicken*.

Sadly, no ringing archeological record remains of this civilization. They didn't leave behind any towering monuments or pyramids or burial mounds. But almost two thousand elaborately carved stone seals have been found. These miniature pictorial images were stamped on clay tablets and were most likely used to keep inventory of goods. Most of the symbols represent animals. But the inscriptions are yet to be deciphered.

Sometime between 1900 and 1700 B.C.E., the cities and their vast trading networks collapsed. Why? Nobody can say for sure. At one time it was believed that Indo-Aryan invaders from the north came in and conquered Harappa and the neighboring territory. Yet none of the archeological remains show evidence of destruction or warfare. Perhaps the Indus River shifted and flooded the plains. Or maybe some other ecological disaster occurred. We don't know.

We do know that the Aryans descended upon India in the second millennium B.C.E. Who were these Aryans? They were not, as Nazi ideology attests, of pure Caucasian strain. They were one of the prehistoric peoples who are believed to have migrated into Europe and India from central Asia.

What is interesting about the Aryans is that they may have been the first to ban the slaughtering of cows in India. It is possible the Aryans brought their own cattle with them when they invaded India. Their breed of cattle was soon superseded by the breed more native to the region and better equipped to handle the tropical climate. Could it be that the tropical breed gave less milk than the Aryan type? Another theory suggests that the cattle population was decreasing. Couple that with a populace who thrives on dairy products, and what have you got? A scarcity of said dairy products. A live cow can give more milk than a dead one. The *Rig-veda*, a sacred text that coincides with the first encounter of the Aryans in India, mentions that the flesh of horses, rams, sheep, and buffaloes could be cooked. In terms of cattle, it only mentions barren cows, as in the barren cows that were slaughtered at the celebration of a marriage and used for food. Later on, in another text, the *Atharva-veda*, even eating of hoofed animals, including cattle was now forbidden. Though they could still be used for ritual slaughter by the Brahmins, the high Aryan priests. In this regard, a barren cow could be sacrificed to the deities Vishnu and Varuna. But even this gave way when Buddha and Mahavira came on the scene.

Mahavira and his disciples, the Jians, were opposed to ritual animal sacrifice. The Buddha himself declared that all meats were uneatable for any reason. This had to do with a very sophisticated idea: the transmigration of souls. This doctrine holds that a living thing goes through a number of incarnations, culminating with the spiritual union embodied by the release from the cycle of rebirth. This applies to all things, be it a man, an insect, or a cow.

This idea was so pervasive that, in time, even the Brahmin priests, succumbed to its allure. By 465 C.E. the *Vayu Purana*, one of the ancient compilations of religious instruction, had declared the slaughter of animals as improper for sacrifices and that one should perform sacrifices with cereals. Animal sacrifice had given way to vegetarianism, which now had religious sanction. If there were any doubt as to the sacredness of the cow, by 300 C.E. the *Vishnu Dharma Sutra* stated that a person should not eat when, among other things, a Brahmin, a king, or a cow meets with an accident.

Buddhism and Jainism first flourished in northern India. By the end of the first millennium, these ideas had spread to southern India. Despite outside influences and invasions some of the basic concepts of these religions lived on in Hinduism, among them the sacred cow. This meant that dairy products became ever more vital. In the *Puranas*, or scared writings, there are seven magical oceans, or ingredients, representing the basic needs of mankind. Three of them are dairy products: milk, curds, and ghee (boiled and clarified butter). Because all the milk solids have been removed, ghee could be stored for a long time (it's the milk solids that turn rancid in butter). In a land where dairy products were king and where there was no refrigeration, ghee became indispensable for cooking.

Although beef is strictly forbidden with accordance to Hindu strictures, not all Brahmins became vegetarian. Kashmiri Brahmins continued eating mutton and chicken dishes; and the Brahmins of Bengal, with their access to major waterways, never gave up their fish dishes. Despite inroads of vegetarianism, in northwestern India foreign influence was extensive, ranging from Aryan, Persian, and Greek to nomadic Central Asian, and meat was, and still is, more commonly consumed in this area.

When one talks of Indian food today, one talks of a diversity of regional cuisines. The same could be said of India in the first millennia. Peas, beans, and lentils could be found in almost every part of the country. Same for sugarcane, plantains, and fruits such as mango. Wheat and barley grew year round in the north, and during the winter in the south. In the plains, rice was a predominant crop. Along the coasts, foreign influence was also prevalent; and Arab traders along the Malabar and Coromandel coasts introduced nutmeg, mace, coriander, cumin, and cloves to Indian cooking. This complimented and enhanced the array of spices such as pepper, cardamom, and ginger already in use in southern India.

So, what was a typical meal like during the first millennium? As always, those higher up, had it better. According to written accounts during the period, a rich person ate "shining white rice, broths of golden colour, butter, curries, well cooked savoury dishes, thick curds, milk, milk rice, sweets and water perfumed with camphor." While the poor ate "boiled rice grown stale, half cooked gourds, and certain badly cooked vegetables as well as some gruel mixed with plenty of mustard." Some peasants may have subsisted solely on rice and whey.

Curry is as ubiquitous to Indian cuisine as hamburgers are to American cooking. At its basic, curry, derived from the original term, *kari*, is a sauce that goes over rice or wheaten pancakes known as *chapatis*. This is how Europeans described it when they first encountered this dish. Another term, *karil*, was adopted by the Portugese and is still in use in Goa today. The dish was basically onions cooked in ghee, flavored with, among other things, coriander, cumin, tumeric, pepper, and diluted with coconut milk or *dahi*, a soured milk product. Today's western curries with their so-called curry powders bear no resemblance to the Indian original. In addition, one should not confuse curry with curry leaves, or kadhi leaves, which come from a plant that grows wild in most forest regions of India and which is used as a seasoning in food.

What were the common drinks? For lesser mortals, apart from water and milk, drinks were made from a combination of water, sugarcane juice, honey, molasses, and the juice of the rose-apple. The rich could indulge in drinks made from mango syrup and lime juice, and even rice beers. If you were well-to-do, then you could afford grape wine imported from Rome and northern Kabul.

What were the kitchen and its cooking utensils like? The art of cooking was so important it was considered one of the sixty-four fine arts. Kitchens were generally located in a well-lighted, clean, quiet, and secluded place where "strangers had no access." Proficiency in cooking was considered an essential qualification for a wife-to-be. The food was cooked over a fire of burning chaff (straw or hay cut fine). Utensils included an earthenware pot, a frying pan, and an oven on charcoals. The rich and upper caste had utensils made of gold or silver. Middle-class people had vessels made of other metals. For the poor, they had to make do with coconut or palm leaves sewn together as plates and, if they were lucky, maybe some bits of earthenware. Those who could afford them, used saucepans and stewpans and drank from cups made of conch shells or gourds that were engraved with designs. Everyone was generally expected to eat facing the east, sitting on a seat and not on a cot. Priests sat on separate small chairs with trays of food placed before them. Two principal meals were eaten during the day, and it was considered improper to take a third. Here we get into the Ayurvedic doctrine of proper nutrition.

The Ayurvedic tradition, a system of health and well-being that also incorporates the diet, spans at least five thousand years in India. This system states that cooking is a spiritual as well as a meditative experience. The kitchen is situated in the southeast corner of the house. This is the "fire corner" where the good energy of the sun prevails. In this respect the kitchen is as important as a temple in the Indian home. A balanced diet is crucial to the Ayuverdic tradition. This even applies to proper digestion. Only fresh ingredients should be used when cooking, and slow cooked foods are easier to digest because they retain more of the basic nutrients.

Indians of the first millennium were advised to chew their food well. Each meal consisted of thirty-two mouthfuls, and as a general rule each person was encouraged to visualize the stomach as consisting of four parts. The first two parts were to be filled with solid food, one fourth with liquid, and the final fourth part should be left empty for the movement of wind.

There is a surviving written account of a royal feast given toward the end of the first millennium by one King Srenika. The menu was quite extensive. The first course consisted of fruits such as pomegranates, grapes, and jujubes, "which can be chewed with teeth." The second course had fruits that could be sliced such as sugarcane, dates, oranges, and mangoes. The third course consisted of such well-cooked preparations "as could be taken by licking." In the fourth course sweets were served. The fifth course was fragrant boiled rice. The sixth, "broths prepared by mixing many food stuffs." The seventh consisted of preparations of curds. The eighth and last course was half boiled milk with sugar, honey, and saffron. The cups and dishes were removed and the hands washed with fragrant water between the sixth and seventh courses, and also at the end of the meal.

Trying to emulate such a menu could take some doing. To get the feel of such a repast I've decided to create a dish from each course and see where it takes us. The recipes here are designed for four to six servings.

KING SRENIKA'S BASH

FIRST COURSE

This is fairly simple and straight forward: a mélange of fruits. The deal about fruits that "could be chewed with teeth"—we can only guess. Perhaps, for whatever reason, this course excluded fibrous fruits like mangoes, which are mentioned in the second course with "fruits which could be sliced." Still, it's strange that pomegranates would be included in this course. Pomegranates have a red pulp with many seeds. As my father would say, it's messy eats, chewed or otherwise. And jujubes. I've never eaten jujubes. I'm told it's an edible fruit from the lotus tree. Okay. If you can find them, enjoy. Otherwise, arrange plump red grapes on a platter, the sweeter the better, and sprinkle them with pomegranate seeds.

SECOND COURSE

2 sticks sugarcane, about one foot long*
3 naval oranges, peeled and sectioned into quarters.
3 ripe, medium-sized mangoes, peeled and sliced

1. Peel the sugarcane by removing the outer stalk. Cut the sugarcane pieces lengthwise, and then into finger-length pieces.
2. On a serving platter, arrange the sugarcane pieces, orange sections, and mango slices in a pleasing circular pattern.

*If your area has any Caribbean or Asian markets, then, most likely, you can obtain sugarcane. It will come cut into various lengths, usually about one foot. My friends from the islands inform me that there are two types of sugarcane: regular sugarcane and pineapple sugarcane. The latter is thicker in diameter and sweeter. I would suggest pineapple sugarcane for this recipe. If not, then regular sugarcane will do. Try to obtain young, tender stalks.

Here it gets interesting. Well-cooked preparations "as could be taken by lick-ing." We have no idea what this means and can only guess. There is a fruit course, a sweet course, a rice course, etc. So I'm guessing that this could be a main course, probably vegetables since King Srenika seems to have ruled in the south. This is a mixed vegetable dish of South Indian origin. The recipe calls for ghee, which is fairly simple to make. Take one stick of sweet butter and melt it over a low flame in a heavy-bottomed saucepan. Bring to a low boil and simmer until the white milk particles separate from the fat and begin to turn a golden brown. It is important that the butter not burn. It should only bubble until the milk solids appear as a froth floating on the top. What you have left is a yellow liquid, which should be strained through a triple layer of cheesecloth and stored in an airtight jar or container. At room temperature ghee can be stored for at least a week. When refrigerated, it turns into a solid that can be turned again into a liquid by heating over low heat. If you want to save time and effort, prepared ghee can be found in most Indian stores.

4 tablespoons ghee
½ teaspoon black mustard seeds
½ teaspoon cumin seeds
1 small onion, chopped
1 medium red pimento (sweet red pepper), seeded and sliced lengthwise into
   ¼-inch-thick pieces
2 cloves garlic, peeled and finely minced
1 medium cauliflower, divided into florets
½ teaspoon ground turmeric
Salt to taste
1 pound, fresh green beans, cut into 1-inch length
¼ teaspoon ground coriander
¼ teaspoon cayenne pepper
½ cup water
1 medium ripe tomato, chopped
Juice of half a lime

THE PHARAOH'S FEAST

1. In a large pot, skillet, or wok, heat the ghee over low heat. Add the mustard seeds, cumin seeds, onion, pimento, and garlic. Sauté with a wooden spoon until the onion becomes soft but not too brown. Add the cauliflower, turmeric, and salt. Add 3 tablespoons of water, reduce the heat to low, cover the pot, and simmer for about 5 minutes.
2. Add the green beans and remaining spices and sauté about 2 minutes until well mixed. Add water and cook, covered, over low heat until the beans are tender.
3. Add the chopped tomato and squeeze the lime juice over the vegetables.

FOURTH COURSE

This is relatively simple, sweets are served. But what kind of sweets? This was not a dessert course. That came after. I gather it was probably something to cleanse the palate between courses. Indian sweets can run the gamut from a rice pudding (*firni*) to *gula jamon*, sweet balls in a flavored syrup. I've settled on Halva, one of the easiest Indian sweets to make. Simple Halva, also known as *sheera*, would be made for special guests, or at religious occasions such as a wedding.

6 cardamom pods*
2 cups water
¾ cup honey
¾ cup ghee (see page 54)
1 cup cream of wheat, farina, or semolina (uncooked)
1 tablespoon chopped almonds
1 tablespoon pistachio nuts, chopped
¼ cup raisins

1. Pinch the cardamom pods open and scrape out the black seeds inside. Discard the shells, place the seeds in a mortar, and finely crush. Set aside.
2. In a saucepan, mix the water and honey, and cook over low heat until it's syrupy (about 5 minutes). Do not boil. Remove from the heat and let cool.

3. In a skillet or frying pan, cook ½ cup of the ghee over low heat for 2 minutes. Gradually add the cream of wheat, stirring with a wooden spoon for about 5 minutes over medium heat. Add the almonds and pistachios and continue to cook for another 5 to 7 minutes until the cream of wheat turns a slightly reddish color.
4. Add honey syrup. This will spatter. So stand back and be careful not to get burned. Add the raisins and continue stirring for about 5 minutes. The halva will thicken into a soft, lumpy consistency. As soon as this happens, pour it into a shallow serving dish. Add the ground cardamom seeds and remaining ¼ cup of ghee. Spread out over the serving dish, and refrigerate for ½ hour.
5. Remove from the refrigerator, cut into slices or squares, and serve.

NOTE: In the days before refrigeration, Halva use to be served as is. A handful of the warm or cooled sweet would be dished out into a coconut or palm leaf, or onto the hand of the guest.

Available in Asian markets.

FIFTH COURSE

Fragrant boiled rice to me would mean spicy boiled rice. Rice with sesame seeds is a popular dish in southern India. So, here goes.

2 cups long grain rice, preferably basmati
4 cups water
Salt to taste
1 cup fresh, shelled peas
2 tablespoons ghee (see page 54)
1 teaspoon mustard seeds
12 curry leaves
½ cup sesame seeds
1 tablespoon lemon juice

1. Wash the rice at least three times in cold water and drain to rid it of starch.
2. In a heavy saucepan, kettle, or pot, bring the water and salt to a boil. Add the rice, stir and bring to a second boil. Add the peas and continue

cooking, stirring for 1 minute. Cover and simmer on low heat until the water is absorbed (20 to 30 minutes).

3. While the rice is cooking, heat the ghee in a saucepan or skillet. Add the mustard seeds and curry leaves and stir-fry until the curry leaves are brown and the mustard seeds begin to pop.

4. Add the sesame seeds and continue cooking over medium heat until the sesame seeds are golden brown.

5. Add the sesame seasoning to the rice and stir to mix.

6. Sprinkle the lemon juice over the rice and serve.

Sixth Course

Now we get to the broths. These are prepared by "mixing many food stuffs." Are we talking about hearty broths, light soups, what? Today, in southern India, the second course of a meal is usually *rasam*, a spicy soup that is served with rice. Traditionally it is a tamarind concoction. And tamarind pulp is hard to get in most areas. That leaves us with the other prominent souplike dish in Indian cooking, *dal*. Which literally means split lentil. Yet here it gets complicated. In Indian cuisine not all *dals* are lentils, as we would define them in the West. The thick soup known as *chana dal* is made from the garbanzo bean. *Mung dal* is made with mung beans. *Toor dal* uses what we know as pigeon peas that have been split in half. In Indian cooking they are known as split lentils. This is the recipe I've decided to go with.

Toor dal, also called *tur dal* or *toovar* can be found in any Indian market or store. You may find, upon purchasing, that it comes covered with a layer of oil. If that is the case, don't get shook up. The oil acts as a preservative to insure freshness without using chemical additives. Just wash the *dal* under running water until it's clear of the oil coating.

6 cups water
Salt to taste
1 cup toor dal *
¼ teaspoon ground turmeric
¼ teaspoon ground cumin
¼ teaspoon ground coriander
fresh ginger, 1-inch piece, peeled and grated
3 teaspoons ghee (see page 54)
¼ teaspoon black mustard seeds

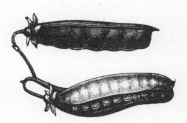

1 red chili pepper, seeded and halved
1 medium ripe tomato, chopped
Juice of ½ lemon

1. In a heavy saucepan, pot, or kettle, bring the water and salt to a boil.
2. Add *toor dal.* Bring to a second boil. Cover and simmer on medium heat for 40 minutes. Uncover and add the turmeric, cumin, coriander, and ginger. Stir well with a wooden spoon. Cover and cook for another 10 minutes. Remove the cover and let the *dal* simmer until the next step is complete.
3. Heat the ghee in a small saucepan or skillet over low heat. Add the mustard seeds and chili pepper. When the mustard seeds pop, add this mixture to the *dal.* Cover the pot for 2 minutes. Uncover and stir with a wooden spoon. Immediately add the tomato and squeeze the lemon juice over the *dal.* Stir to mix and serve.

SEVENTH COURSE

To my mind, preparation of curds in Indian cooking would mean yogurt, and this in turn would mean *raitas*, or yogurt-based dishes that refresh and cool the palate in between hot and spicy courses. Most *raitas* are made with yogurt mixed with fruit or vegetables. Fruits have already been served so I would tend to think vegetable *raitas* would grace King Srenika's table at this point. Such a dish, with cucumber, follows.

½ teaspoon cumin seeds
2 cups plain yogurt
1 large cucumber, peeled, seeded, and cut into thin strips
1 small onion, finely chopped
Pinch of cayenne pepper
3 to 4 sprigs fresh mint for garnish

1. Roast the cumin seeds in a small skillet or saucepan, shaking constantly until brown. Remove from the pan, place in a mortar and finely crush.

2. In a medium bowl, combine the yogurt with the cucumber and onion. Add the cumin seeds and mix well.
3. Sprinkle the cayenne over the yogurt and garnish with mint. If desired, the *raita* can be served chilled.

EIGHTH COURSE

The plates have been removed, the royal hands have been washed in perfumed water. Now comes the denouement (I love them twenty-dollar words). The final course is half-boiled milk sweetened with sugar, honey, and saffron. What could be simpler? One can assume this was not a cold beverage. It had to be thickened by boiling and sweetened with the ingredients given. The saffron was used to give the beverage a golden hue. Indians today enjoy a similar drink, *kesar doodh* or simply, saffron milk. Below is a variation that King Srenika's guests would have enjoyed.

10 to 12 strands of saffron
9 tablespoons warm milk
6 cups milk
*6 cardamom pods**
2 whole cloves
2 sticks cinnamon
3 tablespoons pure cane sugar
3 tablespoons honey

1. Soak the saffron in the warm milk for 10 minutes.
2. In a small saucepan, heat 2 cups of the milk. When it is very hot, add the cardamom pods, cloves, cinnamon, and the soaked saffron with its milk. Stir while cooking on a low flame until slightly thickened and the milk has turned a yellowish color.
3. Remove or strain out the cardamom, cloves, and cinnamon. Stir in the sugar and honey. Serve hot or cool.
   NOTE: The honey and sugar can be increased or decreased according to taste.

   * *Available in Asian markets.*

FIVE

Of Togas and Centurians

ROMAN BREAD, MULSUM,
ARTICHOKES, OIL AND MINCED EGGS,
ROMAN SAUCE FOR BOILED MEAT,
ROASTED RABBIT, ROAST FISH, TIROPATINAM

The scholar-statesman Abba Eban noted that the Roman Empire had two unifying elements—Roman law and Roman power. Indeed it did. They believed in power, and they believed in peace. But, peace at a price.

The Romans are a contradiction. In one respect they gave the world a unique system of laws, an excellence in literature, art, and architecture. On the other hand theirs was an empire built on the sweat of slave labor and the subjugation of other cultures. The same society that gave us the works of Tacitus, Cicero, and Virgil also gave us spectacles of mass slaughter in the Coliseum and cycles of repression toward its own people and others. How to explain this? The same can be said of their food. And here contradictions abound.

This monumental empire, which stretched from the sands of the Sahara to the moors of Scotland, first began as a small Iron Age settlement on the banks of the Tiber River in peninsular Italy. During its first centuries, Roman food was quite plain. The basic diet consisted of wheat, olives, pork, and fish. This began changing toward the end of the third century when Roman conquests introduced new tastes and foodstuffs. You had exotic spices from Indonesia, pickles imported from Spain, ham from Gaul, wine from the provinces, oysters from Britain, and pomegranates from Libya. New seasonings, ingredients, and flavors were imported from all over the Mediterranean, from North Africa, Egypt, the Middle East, and, most notably, Greece.

Greeks and Romans had a funny relationship. The Greeks considered the Romans to be no more than mere barbarians. The Romans considered the Greeks to be esthetes and inferior. Nevertheless, the Romans took to this new cuisine with martial fervor, modifying it, enhancing it, and sometimes taking it to new extremes. Whereas the Greeks may have limited their seasonings to a few essential ingredients, the Romans went whole hog, employing everything from dill, anise, honey, dry and sweet wine, cumin, poppy seeds, coriander, hyssop, thyme, vinegar, oregano, and anything else they could get their hands on. Honey also came into wide use. This led to a combination of sweet flavors mixed with whatever array of spices were available. The former spare cuisine of the republic became the rapacious banquets of the Empire.

This leads to the other rap against the Romans: ostentation in their presentation, which equals decadence. No more is this described, or lampooned, than in *The Satyricon* of Pretronius in which Trimalchio, a nouveau riche former slave treats his guests to such dainties as dormice seasoned with honey, a wild sow with its belly full of live thrushes, quinces stuck with thorns to look like sea urchins, and a hare tucked out with wings so that it resembled Pegasus, the flying horse of Greek mythology.

Supposedly, Gaius Petronius, who lived in the first century of the Common era, was emperor Nero's official advisor on matters relating to luxury and extravagance. His title was *arbiter elegantiae*. That should say it all.

Yet while the rich may have dined on exotic fare, the basic diet for the common man remained the same. The poor subsisted, just like their Greek counterparts, on grain pastes, which the Romans called *puls* or *pulmentum*. They also ate coarse bread and a polentalike porridge made from millet. The well-to-do drank wine. The poor drank water.

Cooking was a problem for the poor. Rome itself was filled with overcrowded and unventilated tenements called *insulae* where cooking went hand in hand with fire, which in these tall narrow confines was a real problem. As a result, cooking was to be avoided. The less privileged Romans might purchase some salt fish or sausage from street vendors or what the epigrammatist Martial decried as "thrusting shopkeepers" with their stalls "encroaching everywhere."

The ruins of Pompeii give us an idea about Roman town house kitchens. Other excavations afford us glimpses of what Roman cookery was like in the first century. Karanis, a farming town in Roman Egypt, was excavated by a team from the University of Michigan from 1923 to 1935. From both sites we know that kitchen implements included a mortar and pestle for crushing and grinding spices, earthenware cooking pots and serving vessels, household jugs for pouring wine and water, and even bronze kitchen knives.

It is interesting to note that the Romans did have glassware. The modern conception is that Romans drank their wine out of cups and goblets made out of pottery. The fact is that from the earliest Roman times, glass was available, although its prohibitive cost made it a luxury item. Glassblowing came into play in the second half of the first century, and the site at Karanis included glass objects such as flasks, drinking glasses, and jugs. Glass was continually used until the fourth century when it declined in popularity and production became more limited.

From the site in Pompeii we know that the dominant cooking conveyance, as in Greece, was the hearth, with its charcoal pit and raised tile edge. Wealthy households had kitchen slaves, usually a male, who did the cooking. In common homes and in the countryside most likely the women did the cooking. Normally, a Roman ate four meals a day. There was lunch (*ientaculum*), midday meal (*praendium*), a snack in the afternoon (*merenda*), and the evening meal (*cena*). On special occasions, a man of means might host a banquet. This was an opportunity to show off and impress his peers. The vulgarities of Trimalchio notwithstanding, there was a protocol to be observed. This can be deduced from a quotation painted on the wall of a dining room in Pompeii: "Kindly restrain your quarrelsome words, if possible. If not, get up and go home. Keep your sweet eyes and lewd looks from straying to other men's wives and let chastity shine in your face."

The banquets were held in a special dining room, the *triclinium*, where guests reclined on divans, propping themselves on their left sides, and drinking and eating with their right hands from a pedestal table that held platters of food. They did use fingerbowls and napkins, which came in handy since mostly they ate with their fingers. Forks hadn't made their appearance yet. Knives and spoons were used but only occasionally. The meal began with a sweet aperitif, *mulsum*, a wine and honey mix. Then the successive courses were served; and here, early in the dinner, the guests ate without drinking. Afterwards, they drank without eating. Wisely, like the Greeks, the Romans normally drank their wine mixed with water. During the *comissatio*, as this cocktail hour was called, guests were expected to exchange learned views on all topics. If the guests included a resident philosopher or tutor, then he would expound or philosophize. The goal was for the *triclinium* to become a literary salon, something similar to the Greek symposium.

As to the food served, here, we have to go to the sources. The closest thing we have to a cookbook from that time is the work of Apicius, *On Cookery*, or *De Re Coquinaria*. Apicius could be considered the Roman counterpart to Archestratus (remember him in the Greek chapter?). Apicius, who was accustomed to a high standard of living, was said to have poisoned himself when he discovered he had a mere ten million sesterces left in the bank. He reckoned this paltry sum was not enough for a man of his infinite tastes. Figure that ten million sesterces is equivalent to just under three-quarters of a ton of gold bullion. This dude knew how to live. As for his recipes, some, admittedly, are off the wall by today's standards. I don't think you would get many takers for such delicacies as sterile sow's womb, parrots, jellyfish, porpoises, and larks' tongues. But some of the recipes could hold their own even today. The emperor Vitellius might delight himself with peacock brains, nightingale tongues, and lamprey roe, while Juvenal, a poet and a strict moralist, might dine more modestly on a "plump kid, tenderest of the flock" and some wild asparagus.

For all its majesty, this vast empire would not have been possible without the vaunted Roman war machine. What did they eat? The prominent view is that, like the Roman poor, they didn't eat that much meat. Their rations were mainly grains and cereals. Food supplies came from civilian sources, either purchased from merchants at a fixed price, or by requisitioning under a tax system on the local economy. The army stationed in Britain needed, annually, some 530,000 bushels of corn. Yet an analysis of animal bones found in Roman forts in Britain and Germany shows that the legions ate considerable amounts of ox, sheep, pork, and goat, not just the expected grains, cheeses, and vegetables. It could be that when the grain supply was low, the army had to make do with what was available.

What did Roman food taste like? We can only guess. Cooking over a hearth is not the same as cooking on a modern computerized range, be it gas or electric. Also, what was the quality of the food like in Ancient Rome? How fresh was it? What was the quality of the raw ingredients be it animal or vegetable? Remember, there was no refrigeration, transportation was slow, food had to be stored and warehoused. Perhaps the affinity Romans had for strong-flavored sauces had to do with masking the taste and texture of the food. A citizen in the countryside might have access to a garden. But even here one is at the mercy of the elements. How would it be for the common Roman living in the streets of a giant metropolis? Even a patrician with access to the latest foreign spices had to contend with a rancid meal now and then. Not only that, among the Roman aristocracy, lead poisoning was a major problem. This could be due to the fact that in wealthy households, lead cooking pots and vessels were the norm.

Today, from our vantage point, fresh vegetables, meats, fish, and poultry are not a problem—normally. Especially, if you have access to a good health food store or produce market. We can only try to emulate the recipes from a bygone empire and hope for the best, which brings us to some of the unfamiliar ingredients and seasonings used in Roman cooking:

Garum or *liquamen*: This fish sauce was an essential element of ancient Greek and Roman cooking. The production of *garum* would not sound appetizing today. Part of the process involved letting salted fish ferment in the hot sun for up to seven days. In modern-day cooking a good substitute would be Vietnamese bottled fish sauce, *nouc mam,* or Thai *nam pla.*

Silphium: This herb was discussed in the Greek section (see page 33), where I recommend the Indian spice, *hing.* Again, use sparingly since it has a very pungent flavor.

Rue: the herb also know as *Ruta graveolens.* The dried version can be found in any good health food store or herbal shop. If you known someone who grows it (it's a hardy evergreen), then just chop up as many leaves as needed.

Other unfamiliar ingredients used by the Romans include *caroenum* (boiled grape must used as a sweetener in sauces), *passum* (raisin wine), *defrutum* (either fig syrup or grape must). Based on the methods and ingredients used, one can deduce that ancient Roman cooking was something unparalleled up to that time. Roman society had gone through tremendous changes and transformations, and this was reflected in its cuisine. We are all familiar with the picture of the gluttonous Roman patrician scarfing down grapes and wine. But that is only half the tale. Romans were adventurous in their cooking. And that is the highest compliment one can pay to the cuisine of any society.

ROMAN BREAD

The ancient city of Pompeii, which was destroyed by the volcanic eruption of Mount Vesuvius in 79 of the Common era, has yielded plaster casts of round loafs of bread. These loafs were baked in round ceramic bowls, which were very popular among the peoples of the Mediterranean. The method of cooking remains essentially the same as it is today. The ancient physician Galen, in one of his medical treatises, writes: "Baked bread in large ovens, however excels in all good qualities, for it is well flavoured, good for the stomach, easily digested, and readily assimilated." The process entailed sifting ground and dried flour, mixing it with yeast, salt, and water, kneading, shaping, and baking it in an oven.

The Romans produced many types of bread. There was honey and oil bread, a salty raised loaf called *cappadocian*, bread with poppy seeds, wafer bread, cheese bread, and a variety of other flavored breads that would be eaten as a snack, *prandium*, or as a meal in themselves. Wheat flour was widely used since barley flour was regularly eaten by slaves, and considered "beneath" most people. As Greek cuisine made its mark on the empire, the Romans began using a variety of different flours, sometimes in one loaf. In the recipe that follows, the result will be a chewy, hardy peasant bread that the plebeians may have enjoyed in the streets of Rome.

> ¼ cup warm water
> 1 package active dry yeast
> 2 teaspoons salt
> 1¼ cups lukewarm water
> 2 cups unbleached white flour
> 1 cup whole wheat flour
> ½ cup rye flour
> Olive oil

1. Place ¼ cup of the warm water in a large bowl. Sprinkle in the yeast and stir to dissolve.
2. Dissolve the salt in the lukewarm water and add to the yeast. Slowly stir in ¾ cup of the white flour, the whole wheat flour, and rye flour. Blend well.

3. Stir in the remaining flour to make a stiff dough. Turn out on a floured board, cover, and let rest for 10 to 15 minutes. Knead until smooth and elastic, about 10 minutes.

4. Place in a greased bowl, preferably ceramic. Turn the dough over to grease the top. Cover with a towel or cloth and let it rise in a warm place until doubled, about 1½ hours.

5. Shape the dough into a round loaf and place in a round pan greased with a little olive oil (I prefer a cast-iron pan for this). Let rise about 1¼ hours.

6. Bake at 375 degrees for about 1 hour.

YIELD: 1 ROUND LOAF

Mulsum

Honeyed wine was usually served at the beginning of a Roman meal, and Apicius has a recipe for spiced honey wine that calls for ground peppercorns, mastic (a sort of resin), bay leaf, saffron, and dates. Trying to emulate this recipe would be a daunting undertaking. I prefer to make the Mulsum, or honey wine, by combining the honey and the wine. Some folks, like the Romans, like their Mulsum spiced. If you desire, you can add some peppercorns to it.

The question is: What honey to use? I prefer using pure, unprocessed honey. The type sold in health food stores, the lighter the better.

½ cup honey
1 bottle medium-dry red wine

1. Heat the honey in a small saucepan. Do not boil. Remove from the heat and let it cool.
2. Mix the wine and honey in a ceramic jar or pitcher and serve at cool room temperature. The wine and honey can also be mixed in a bowl and served in a decanter.

Yield: 4 to 6 servings

ARTICHOKES, OIL, AND MINCED EGGS

I like the following recipe because of its simplicity. Yes, even Apicius could come through with something simple and tasty for a meal starter. The recipe calls for artichokes, garum, oil, and minced eggs. That's it.

16 artichoke hearts
4 eggs, hard boiled and finely chopped
⅓ cup olive oil
⅓ cup nuoc mam fish sauce*

1. Wash the artichoke hearts under cold running water and pat dry with paper towels. Arrange the artichoke hearts on a serving platter.
2. Sprinkle chopped eggs atop the artichokes.
3. Drizzle with olive oil and fish sauce.

YIELD: 4 SERVINGS

*Nuoc mam fish sauce can be found in Asian markets.

Roman Sauce for Boiled Meat

As mentioned, the Romans liked strong flavored sauces. This rendition, a simple sauce for boiled meat, is not that hard to make. Here, Apicius uses the simplest of ingredients plus dates to produce a sauce with a sweet-and-sour affect not unlike modern Chinese sweet-and-sour sauce. This sauce is very tasty over boiled chicken.

    2 dozen dried dates, washed, pitted, and minced
    ½ cup coarsely chopped fresh parsley
    ⅔ cup nuoc mam *fish sauce**
    2 tablespoons red wine vinegar
    1 large shallot, peeled and minced
    1 tablespoon olive oil
    ½ teaspoon freshly ground black pepper

1. Combine all of the ingredients in a medium saucepan. Bring to a boil, lower heat, and simmer, covered, for about 20 minutes.

   Yield: 4 servings

    *Nuoc mam *fish sauce can be found in Asian markets.*

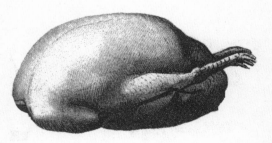

ROASTED RABBIT

For some odd reason, Americans have a thing about rabbits. Most of my acquaintances would be repelled at the idea of a good rabbit dinner. The ancient Romans had no such qualms. Hare, or rabbit, has been a staple in the Mediterranean region for centuries, as this Apician classic nobly attests. Here Apicius instructs that the rabbit should first be "soaked" or "precooked" in hot water, then roasted in oil, and, finally, seasoned in, among other things, celery seed, silphium, and garum.

> *1 3-pound whole rabbit, separated into 4 leg and thigh joints and 2 loin*
> *pieces*
> *Salt and ground black pepper to taste*
> *½ cup olive oil*
> *¼ teaspoon ground black pepper*
> *1 teaspoon dried savory*
> *1 medium red onion, peeled and finely chopped*
> *2 teaspoons dried rue**
> *1 teaspoon celery seed*
> *3 tablespoons* nuoc mam *fish sauce**
> *A pinch of* hing*
> *1 ¼ cups dry red wine*
> *2 tablespoons olive oil*

1. Preheat oven to 375 degrees.
2. Wash the rabbit pieces under cold running water and pat dry with paper towels.
3. Place the rabbit pieces in a pot or saucepan. Add water to cover. Bring to a boil, and cook, uncovered, for about 3 minutes.
4. Drain the meat and place in a roasting pan. Sprinkle with salt, pepper, and olive oil. Season the pieces well, and bake for 1 hour.
5. Meanwhile, in a bowl, combine ¼ teaspoon black pepper, savory, onion, rue, celery seed, fish sauce, *hing*, wine, and oil. Add this sauce to the baking pan and continue cooking the rabbit for another 40 minutes, basting frequently with the sauce.

6. When the rabbit is done (the meat will give easily when pierced with a fork), transfer to a serving platter and keep warm. Pour the remaining sauce into a saucepan and bring to a boil. Lower the heat and reduce the sauce slightly, stirring constantly.
7. Pour the sauce over the rabbit pieces and serve.

YIELD: 4 SERVINGS

*Dried rue can be found in health food stores or herbal shops, nuoc mam *fish sauce can be found in Asian markets, and* hing *in Middle Eastern markets.*

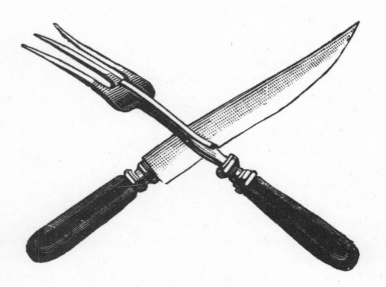

There are meals that change history. The Roman emperor Claudius has a penchant for mushrooms, and it's poisoned mushrooms that do him in— and Nero takes over. Marco Polo is served a noodle dish at the court of Kublai Khan, and, next thing you know, the Italians develop a voracious appetite for pasta. Ever wonder what Cleopatra served Mark Antony on that barge going up the Nile? They had a great feast but no written records remain. We can imagine the beauteous queen served her Roman general all the delicacies that reminded him of home plus lots of Falernian wine, or maybe vintage Opimian. What we know is that after plenty of food and drink, the noble Marcus Antonius threw in his lot with the Egyptian queen and turned on Rome—with dire consequences for both.

One such meal that influenced world history occurred in the Roman province of Judea, early in the first century of the Common era. On the fourteenth day of the Hebrew month of Nisan, a Jewish mystic and his disciples gathered in the upper room of a house in Jerusalem to celebrate the traditional Passover feast. How do we know it was a Passover meal? The gospels tell us that they "prepared the Passover" (Luke 22:13) after their master had instructed them, "Go and prepare the Passover for us, that we may eat" (Luke 22:8).

What they were commemorating was a Seder, the traditional Passover week dinner celebrating the exodus of the Hebrews from Egyptian bondage over three thousand years ago. As such, Jesus and his disciples most likely partook of the traditional dishes served at a Passover Seder: *maror* (bitter herbs), *karpas* (vegetable), *chazeret* (bitter vegetable), *charoset* (apple, nut, spice, and wine mixture), *zeroa* (shank bone), and *beitzah* (egg).

But what else did they eat? It's obvious there were bread and wine. This has become the basis of the Christian ritual called the Eucharist, a solemn rite in which the bread and wine symbolize the communion of the body and blood of Christ (Matthew 26:26-28).

Among the disciples of Jesus were fishermen from the Galilee. Seafood was plentiful in the area; so they probably ate fish, like the simple roasted fish that follows.

*1 whole fish (such as carp, trout, pike, fluke, etc.), about 3 pounds, cleaned
and scaled but with head and tail still attached*
6 whole black peppercorns
2 cloves garlic
1 teaspoon dried oregano
¼ cup olive oil

1. Preheat the oven to 400 degrees.
2. Wash the fish inside and out under cold running water and pat dry
   with paper towels.
3. Crush the peppercorn, garlic, and oregano in a mortar.
4. With a sharp knife, make 3 to 4 vertical slits on both sides of fish. Rub
   the seasoning thoroughly into the skin.
5. Place in a baking dish and pour olive oil over the fish.
6. Bake, uncovered, for approximately 30 minutes or until the fish flakes
   easily when tested with a fork.

YIELD: 4 SERVINGS

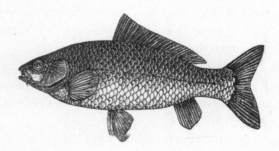

THE PHARAOH'S FEAST

TIROPATINAM

In his cookbook, Apicius describes a custardlike dish called Tiropatinam. The dish reminds me of a soufflé, except that there are no beaten egg whites here. Instead, it's whole eggs and milk, sweetened with honey, cooked on low heat, and sprinkled with pepper. Apicius was partial to pepper, even in desserts.

2 cups milk
¼ cup clear unprocessed honey
6 eggs
Dash pepper (optional)

1. In a medium saucepan, combine the milk with the honey.
2. Add the eggs and stir to mix until smooth.
3. Cook on low heat, stirring, until thickened.
4. Pour into four ½-cup size dessert dishes, sprinkle with pepper, if desired, and serve.

YIELD: 4 SERVINGS

SIX

MEDIEVAL EUROPE

HERB FRITTERS, NEW PEAS FOR A MEAT DAY,
NEW PEAS FOR A FISH DAY,
GRILLED PIKE IN WINE SAUCE,
CAMELINE SAUCE, ROASTED LOIN OF PORK,
PEARS COOKED WITHOUT COALS OR WATER

During my tenure at Wagner Junior High, Mr. Friedman, the history teacher, always drummed into our thick skulls that the time between the collapse of Roman civilization and the rise of the Renaissance was known as the Middle Ages, i.e. the medieval period or the Dark Ages. There's a reason why they were called the Dark Ages. A civilization had gone into the sink.

Historians date this period from the toppling of Romulus Augustulus, the last Roman emperor in the West, in 476 of the Common era, to about 1500. Some experts push this time back further to the death of Emperor Diocletian in 395. Either way, the Middle Ages began after the barbarian invasions, a time when people deserted towns and cities and settled in the countryside. From the fifth century onward, this newly rural population gave rise to a rural diet about which little is known. History seems more interested in the kings, queens, aristocrats, and theologians, not the average joe. The peasant diet, most likely, consisted of root crops, bread, salted pork, the occasional hen or rabbit, and, if they were lucky, ale. The spices that long had dominated Mediterranean cooking were no longer available—no garum, no silphium, no liquamen. People had to make do with what they had—which, in some cases, wasn't much.

Throughout much of Europe, especially north of the Alps, dining consisted of what the locals could scavenge and put in a cauldron or the stockpot that became ubiquitous in every hut, house, or castle. This cauldron became the centerpiece of the medieval kitchen. It usually hung over a roaring fire and was complemented by a pan or two, a ladle, a trivet, and a spit—a long pole on which meat could be secured and roasted. In the castle manor, a rich landowner would have a kitchen staff, and the kitchen would be set apart from what was called the great hall, where banquets and special functions were held. The kitchen itself would be constructed of stone or wood and it would be connected to the great hall by an enclosed passageway to prevent wind and drafts from getting the food cold. The pots used for cooking might be made of iron, bronze, copper, or clay. Those to the manor born could also boast a wine cellar and, if there were no cellar, then the wine could be stored, along with the ale, in a special spot in the kitchen. The manor also included a bakeshop where bread, not only for the lord but also for the peasantry, was baked.

The poor weren't happy campers, but living was good for the landowners, abbots, and monarchs. This was their time. Peasants paid tribute to the king and the monastery. This was due to duty (upkeep on the manor) and devotion (religious mandate) —or so medieval scholars tell us. The rise of a feudal system, of lord, vassal, and fief meant that there were taxes and tithes imposed and collected. Such as that decreed by Charles the Bald of France who in 844 ordered that a bishop "at each stage of his pastoral progress" could collect fifty loaves of bread, ten chickens, fifty eggs, and five suckling pigs. The cliché of the plump abbot, a la Friar Tuck, may not be too far off the mark.

In Northern and Western Europe, the truly Dark Ages were the ninth and tenth centuries when famine ravaged the population and Viking raids instilled a sense of fear on the continent. It wasn't until the eleventh century, with a revival of trade and reawakening of urban life, that commercial activity began anew. As towns began to flourish, the demand for commodities increased. This re-awakening in trade was to be given an unexpected lift by that enterprise known as the Crusades.

The crusaders were motivated by two things: Christian zeal and the prospect of enriching themselves by conquering other lands. European trade with the East was channeled through Venice to Constantinople. And Venice was more than happy to transport crusaders and pilgrims on their way to the Holy Land. Italian merchants began importing silken cloths, sugar, and spices on the ships back to Italy. Luxury goods again became available in the southern part of Western Europe. But more important, returning crusaders brought back a taste for foods and spices that had all but been forgotten in the West. How best to impress the lord of a rival fiefdom than by displaying all the exotic ingredients from the East at one of your banquets.

For the many, the medieval kitchen remained relentlessly monotonous. Most of the food had to be preserved by salting or drying, especially in the north where long winters made it difficult to keep farm animals around. Cooking techniques were abysmal, by our standards. The few surviving cookbooks of the period don't offer much help when it comes to surveying the cooking scene. Most do not refer to exact quantities of ingredients used or even how to prepare a dish except by the most general of assertions like "soak in several changes of water," or "chop forth with raisins of Corinth." Most of these tomes refer to the kitchen of the noble households or royalty. In fact, salt meat and dried fish are rarely mentioned in the cookbooks since it stands to reason that royal households would have some kind of fresh meat, game, or fish available.

The common man and woman are scarcely represented at all. But if you were poor, how would you cook the salted fish or meat? Two ways: by soaking it in water and, if there were no local stream or well available, by cooking it with something that would absorb the salt, like bread or dried beans. Again, the rich would smother the dishes with flavored sauces made from cardamom, ginger, or cloves. Whereas the peasant would make do with dark bread and whatever was available in the stockpot. The aristocrat would avail himself of several different courses, each consisting of different dishes. Not like today's formal dinner of appetizer, soup, salad, fish, meat, and so on. After the meal, what were known as "confections" or "jellies" were served. The drink of choice for the rich was, naturally, wine. Even in a nation of ale drinkers like England, after the Norman Conquest, wine was increasingly in demand.

For diners, even of the highest rank, plates were not common. Only someone of the highest stature might have his own plates and drinking vessels. Instead, they ate off trenchers. A trencher was a flat, thick slice of bread, several days old, that acted as a kind of absorbent plate. The guest would eat his trencher at the end of the meal; or maybe toss it as a scrap to the dogs running around in the castle. It was customary to keep an extra pile of trenchers on hand for those who needed them during dinner. The food itself consisted of roasts (pork, venison, or game), frumenty—a milky jelly that was made by soaking husked wheat in hot water for a day or so—soup and brewet—fish, meat or, poultry in a thin creamy sauce. Pies and fritters would also grace the banquet table of a rich lord. But, rich or poor, they ate with their fingers. There were spoons, but forks would not come into habitual use until the eighteenth century. Every guest had a knife, usually his own, for cutting and carving meat.

Napkins were another oddity. By the sixteenth century they were in vogue. But, if in the fourteenth century, or earlier, you were invited to dinner, your shirtsleeve was your napkin.

One would think cleanliness would have been a concern while dining. Dipping your fingers into shared platters would mean you had better have clean hands. As one commentator of the time, Giovanni della Casa admonished, "Washing of the hands which is done before sitting down to dinner . . . should be done in full sight of others, even if you do not need to wash them at all, so that whoever dips into the same bowl as yours will be certain of your cleanliness." Della Casa, who became Archbishop of Benevento and Papal Nuncio to Venice, wrote on courtesy, manners, and deportment. He advised servants who wait on gentlemen to not, under any circumstances, "scratch their heads—or anything else—in front of their master when he is eating . . . They must keep their hands in sight and out of suspicion, and keep them carefully washed and clean. . . ."

But these were not the hygienic times we have now. There was sewage in the streets and livestock running around the house, both in town and in the countryside. Public cook-shops, open air markets, and slaughterhouses harbored grime and germs. Lice were a constant problem. The refuse, the rotting carcasses of animals, the household garbage, all gave rise to an ever increasing population of black rats that, by the thirteenth century, infested every community. The lord of the manor may have been well fed, but so were the rodents. The rats carried infected fleas, which in turn infected humans. Under such conditions, it's not hard to imagine how an epidemic like the bubonic plague or, as it was called, the Black Death, could ravage medieval Europe—as it did from 1347 into the 1600s.

Every artistic endeavor has what I call the downer phase—the mediocre second act, that slump in the seventh inning of a good ball game, that sag in a good story. I guess, in this treatise, medieval cooking is it. Yet we can see that the medieval cook showed a certain sophistication under rather trying conditions. They had to rise above their circumstances, and sometimes they did. Cooking with salted and dried foods meant you had to be innovative. You could soak the meat in water, but what if there was no readily available water? (Remember, there was no indoor plumbing.) Suppose there were no root plants or vegetables about? You could pour bread crumbs into the cauldron but, if there were no bread, then what? You might use some particular spices and, if they weren't available, maybe some fruit to decrease the salt content. You might invent some creamy sauces, or even add sugar or honey to the mix. You might add rice and almond milk to come up with something like *blank mang* or *blamanger*, a thick mixture of shredded chicken combined with rice, almond milk, and sugar, and garnished with anise; or mortrews—boiled meat or fish, to which bread crumbs, stock, and eggs were added, then reduced to a stiff paste that was garnished with ginger. It was called mortrews because the ingredients were pounded in a mortar. The medieval chef became a master at dressing up a mediocre meal.

Yes, in this case necessity was indeed the mother of invention. The medieval period was the interlude before the dawn—a dawn which would transform society and cooking in general.

HERB FRITTERS

Le Ménagier de Paris (The Goodman of Paris) came out circa 1395. It is prefaced as *A Treatise on Moral and Domestic Economy by a Citizen of Paris*. That's a quite a mouthful; and the book does contain numerous recipes from the period including various Parisian menus consisting of three courses, with numerous dishes per course. Fritters are served in a first ("Beef Marrow Fritters") and second course (just plain "Fritters"), most likely batter fried as in the recipe given—which comes from another cookbook of the time, *Forme of Cury*, which is English in origin. The late middle English of the period is something to behold. For instance, the recipe is titled a *Fryto of Erbes*. And it calls for "grynde gode erbys and medle hé w flō and waī a lytel zeft and falt, and frye hē 1' oyle, and ete hē w clere hony." Translation: Grind the good herbs with flour and water, and a little yeast and salt, fry them in oil, and eat them with honey.

> *1¾ cups lukewarm water*
> *1 package active dry yeast*
> *½ teaspoon salt*
> *¾ cup, washed and rinsed, chopped green herbs such as parsley, basil, dill,*
>   *marjoram, thyme, etc.*
> *2 cups all-purpose flour*
> *½ cup, or more, vegetable oil*
> *2 tablespoons honey*

1. Place ¼ cup of lukewarm water in a large bowl. Sprinkle in the yeast and stir to dissolve.
2. Dissolve the salt in the remaining water and add it to the yeast. Add the herbs and slowly stir in the flour. Blend well to make a smooth, stiff batter. Cover with a towel or cloth and let rise in a warm place until the dough has doubled, about 1½ hours.
3. Heat the oil in a large frying pan or skillet. Cook the batter by dropping spoonfuls into the hot oil and frying until golden brown.
4. Drain on absorbent paper towels, place on a serving platter, drizzle with the honey, and serve.

YIELD: 4 SERVINGS

New Peas for a Meat Day

Religion was of paramount importance to medieval man and woman. They accepted the teachings of the Christian church without question; and as long as you atoned for your sins, you could still find salvation. This devotion to faith even impacted the daily diet. According to the religious calendar, there were fish days, meat days, festival days, and Lent, the fast of forty days that was observed annually from Ash Wednesday until Easter—for the truly devout a period of fasting and penitence could occur at any time of the year. Recipes of the time include *Frutowr for Lentyn* (Fritters for Lent) and *Frumente yn Lentyn* (Frumenty in Lent). This devotion applied to such simple items as peas. *Le Menagier de Paris* gives instructions on how to cook peas for a meat day and a fish day.

> *1 pound fresh young green peas, shelled*
> *4 cups beef broth (what medieval cooks refer to as a Gode Broth)*
> *2 bunches fresh parsley leaves, rinsed and chopped*

1. Wash green peas under cold running water.
2. Heat the broth in a medium saucepan. Add the peas and parsley, and bring to a boil.
3. Reduce the heat and simmer gently, covered, for 30 minutes or until the peas are tender.
4. Drain the peas and serve.

YIELD: 4 SERVINGS

New Peas for a Fish Day

1 pound fresh young green peas, shelled
4 cups milk
1 teaspoon freshly grated ginger
¼ teaspoon crushed saffron threads

1. Rinse the peas under cold running water.
2. Place the milk in a medium saucepan and heat to a slow simmer.
3. Add the ginger and saffron, and stir to blend.
4. Add the peas and cook, covered, over very low heat for about 40 minutes or until tender.
5. The peas may be served drained or in whatever liquid is left in the pan.

Yield: 4 servings

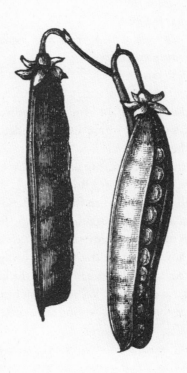

GRILLED PIKE IN WINE SAUCE

The Forme of Cury contains a recipe for cooking pike in a wine sauce, *Pykes in Brafey* (Pikes in Brasey). The sauce contains *gode wyne, powdō gyng* (powdered ginger), and salt. As noted, in the fourteenth century, sauces, whether thin or creamy, were the mainstay, especially for the rich, in order to "dress up" a dish or make it more palatable. By this time, in the city of Paris, professional sauce makers had become a familiar sight. By the sixteenth century you had recipes, like one given in *The Good Huswives Handmaide,* where fresh salmon was simply "seeth" or poached in beer and vinegar. Things had improved somewhat, cooking wise. The Grilled Pike in Wine Sauce is not that daunting. The instructions are simple: boil good wine, ginger, sugar, and salt in an earthen pot, and serve over roasted fish.

> *4 medium sized pike or carp, cleaned, scaled, with head and tail still attached**
> *2 cups red wine*
> *1-inch piece of fresh ginger root, peeled and finely chopped*
> *1 tablespoon sugar*
> *Salt to taste*

1. Preheat the grill or broiler to medium.
2. Wash the fish, inside and out under cold running water and pat dry with paper towels.
3. With a sharp knife make 3 shallow cuts on each side of the fish and arrange the fish in a broiler pan.
4. Grill or broil the fish for 5 minutes. Remove the broiler pan from the heat and, using a spatula, turn the fish over. Grill or broil for another 5 to 6 minutes or until the fish flakes easily when tested with a fork.
5. Meanwhile, make the sauce by bringing the wine to a boil in a medium saucepan. Lower the heat, add the ginger, sugar, and salt. Stir until the sugar is dissolved. Remove from heat.
6. Place the fish on a serving dish and pour the wine sauce over the fish.

YIELD: 4 SERVINGS

  * Any variety of freshwater or even saltwater fish can be substituted for the pike or carp. You can substitute trout, whiting, whitebait, herring, or any small to medium-sized fish, fresh or frozen.

CAMELINE SAUCE

Le Viandier de Taillevent, compiled in 1375 by Guillaume Tirel, chef to Charles V of France, contains a recipe for Cameline Sauce. *Le Viandier* is one of the first cookbooks in modern European history. But even here, direct instructions as to quantities, preparation, and cooking technique are missing. One must infer that, in the few surviving cookbooks, it was assumed that the professional cook or housewife would instinctively know how much of a condiment or ingredient to use when cooking. Cameline Sauce is a case in point. Monsieur Tirel states simply: "Grind ginger, a great deal of cinnamon, cloves, grains of paradise, mace, and if you wish, long pepper; strain bread that has been moistened in vinegar, strain everything together and salt as necessary." In recreating the recipe, the only difficulty lies with the grains of paradise, which are hard to find. A good substitute is cardamom. *Le Menagier de Paris* alludes to a "cameline meat brewet," in which the sauce is served over meat. I would recommend beef or pork.

   1 cup cider vinegar
   1 cup water
   ¼ teaspoon ground ginger
   ½ teaspoon ground cinnamon
   ¼ teaspoon ground cloves
   ¼ teaspoon ground cardamom
   ¼ teaspoon ground mace
   1 cup unseasoned bread crumbs
   Salt and ground black pepper to taste

1. In a medium bowl, combine the vinegar and water.
2. Add the spices while mixing thoroughly with a whisk.
3. Add the bread crumbs, whisking thoroughly until blended to desired consistency.
4. Add salt and pepper and stir to blend.

   YIELD: 2 CUPS OF SAUCE

   NOTE: Depending on the consistency of the sauce, one can use fewer or more breadcrumbs, as needed.

ROASTED LOIN OF PORK

We've noted that roasts were a popular staple in the Middle Ages among the gentry. *Cormarye*, or roast loin of pork, is from *The Forme of Cury*. It instructs to "Roost loyne of pork" in a sauce made of *colyaundre* (coriander), *caraway fmale gronden* (caraway), *powdō of pep* (pepper), *garlee ygronde* (garlic), and *rede wyne* (and red wine). I find that this recipe works well with pork shoulder, so you can substitute that in place of pork loin if price is an issue. Of course, the cooking time will vary depending upon the size of the roast.

2 boneless pork loin roasts, center cut, about 1½ pounds each
8 whole black peppercorns
2 cloves garlic, peeled
1 teaspoon salt
½ teaspoon caraway seeds
1 teaspoon ground coriander
2 cups red wine
½ cup chicken broth
½ cup water

1. Wash the pork under cold running water and pat dry with paper towels.
2. In a mortar, crush the peppercorns, garlic, salt, and caraway seeds. Add the coriander and mix. In a bowl, combine this mixture with the wine.
3. With a sharp knife make various slits in the pork loins and place in a roasting pan. Pour the wine over the meat.
4. Preheat the oven to 325 degrees.
5. Roast the meat, basting frequently for 2½ hours, or until the meat is thoroughly cooked. When cooked, the pork should be golden brown.
6. Remove roasts from the pan and keep warm. Pour whatever drippings remain in the roasting pan into a saucepan. Add the chicken broth and water. Bring to a boil, lower the heat and simmer, stirring constantly for about three minutes.
7. Slice the roasts to desired thickness and serve with the sauce poured over the meat.

YIELD: 6 TO 8 SERVINGS

Pears Cooked without Coals or Water

Master Chiquart Amiczo, chief cook to Duke Amadeus of Savoy, had a novel way of cooking pears: he would put them in an earthenware pot, cover the pot with hot coals, and bake the pears. Baked pears and apples were usually served at the end of a feast along with other confections. In this instance, the pears would be cooked in all their purity; and this was good since pears were considered to have medicinal properties. Amiczo stated that when they are cooked, the pears should be put into fine silver dishes before "they are borne to a sick person." In 1420 he compiled his culinary expertise in a treatise known as *Du Fait de Cusine.* It includes this recipe. It's interesting to note, though he instructs that the pear receptacle be covered with coals to provide heat, he calls the recipe "pears cooked without coals or water."

4 pears, washed and cored

1. Preheat the oven to 400 degrees.
2. Place the pears in a greased baking pan and bake for 45 minutes until browned and tender.

YIELD: 4 SERVINGS

SEVEN

THE ARAB WORLD

ISFANAKH MUTAJAN,
GAZPACHO CON AJO BLANCO, BURAN, THARID,
ZIRBAYA, HAIS, SEKANJABIN SIMPLE

While Europe was in the doldrums, the Islamic world was at the height of its glory. Europeans were dining on roasted rancid meat. The Arabs were dining on savories cooked with spices from India and China, apples from Syria, olives from Palmyra, raisins from Jerusalem, rice from the valley of the Jordan, exotic fruits from Central Asia—such as pomegranates, apricots, and lemons—fatty mutton from Palestine, and pigeons raised in special fattening towers, and using rosewater in their cooking.

Thundering out of the Arabian Desert, the message of Islam ranged far and wide. Fifty years after the death of the prophet Muhammad in 632, Islam had spread to three continents. From southern Spain to the western borders of China, the Islamic empire ruled a multitude of communities and peoples, modifying and adapting to varied cuisines.

The capital of this empire, militarily, politically, and gastronomically, was Baghdad. In the seventh century, the Arabs had moved their capital from Damascus in Syria to Baghdad, the heart of the former Persian Empire they had conquered. Here the transition began. The desert Arabs had subsisted on sheep's milk, barley, mutton, and fresh and dried dates. This spare diet changed with their expanded realm. A banquet for a desert Arab would have been a slaughtered camel drained of blood and roasted on an open fire. In contrast, the caliphs of Baghdad enjoyed truffles from the Arabian Desert, cakes from Egypt, and steamed couscous from the Mahgreb. Not only that, there would be poetry recitations and gastronomic discourse praising the sumptuousness and quality of the meal. Such as in the tenth century banquet given by Caliph Mustakfi, in which all the guests had to, not only philosophize on the food, but also recite poetry alluding to each dish. Guests recited lines such as those written by Ibn al-Mu'tazz, in which he describes a tray of hors d'oeuvres:

> Here capers grace a sauce vermilion
> Whose fragrant odors to the soul are blown . . .
> Here, too, sweet marjoram's delicious scent
> With breath of choicest cloves is richly blent . . .
> Here pungeant garlic meats the eager sight
> And whets with savor sharp the appetite . . .

The Muslims took their cuisine seriously. Men of learning were expected to have more than a passing interest in the fine art of cooking. It was not unusual for royal princes to write cookbooks, or for philosophers as well as kings to be as well versed in the culinary arts as in everything else. This was not self-indulgence; this was required conduct. As witness another caliph, al-Mu'tasim who required his *nadims,* or boon companions (as his festive friends were known), to cook various dishes for a banquet and who assigned an unfortunate guest the task of judging their taste and quality. I'm sure the caliph's preferences were echoed by the judge. After all, who would contradict the boss.

Muslims don't eat pork and scavenger fish (shell fish). Their holy book, the Koran, deems pork to be impure. Alcohol is also prohibited. There are various schools of thought as to how this came about. Early on, the Arabs did indulge in fermented drinks. Taverns were a common sight in the Arab world. So why give up the booze? One theory ascribes this to the fact that on the eve of a battle the prophet Muhammad found some of his soldiers dead drunk. Another theory, just as colorful, states that the Prophet and his followers were feasting one night in the city of Medina, and enormous quantities of wine were consumed. One of his lieutenants ostensibly made an offensive remark about the citizens of Medina. And one of the citizens present took umbrage, grabbed a shank bone, and hit the offender over the head. Bedlam ensued. The Prophet repaired to his quarters where he prayed to God for guidance as to how to resolve the mess. He received a succinct answer as noted in Surah 5:91 of the Koran: "The Shaitan (Satan) only desires to cause enmity and hatred to spring in your midst by means of intoxicants and games of chance, and to keep you from the remembrance of Allah and from prayer. Will you then desist?"

That's all the Prophet needed to hear. Hereafter alcohol was banned to believers. Water, tea, and juices became the predominant drinks at table.

The ban on pork was a minor dietary sacrifice to the Arabs. Even in their nomadic days, meat to them meant mutton, fat and rich, especially after their conquest of Persia. In Persia, tender young lamb was cooked in slices or chunks. The tougher goat meat was used as ground meat for meatballs. Likewise, the Persians liked sweet and sour sauces, especially those flavored with powdered almonds, walnuts, and pistachios. Persian cooking had an impact on Arab cooking, especially during the golden age of the caliphate. This influence can be seen in such a popular dish as *harisa,* in which grilled kid or lamb was stewed in a sauce of ground almonds and nuts.

There were other influences as well. From India, they adopted recipes for cooking rice in milk. From tropical Asia, they learned to cook eggplant in a layered dish similar to moussaka, from Egypt they learned about pastries and cakes, from the nomadic tribes of Central Asia they adopted milk products like curds and yogurt.

The Arabs ruled over restive populations, and they wisely learned from earlier civilizations, incorporating elements of these cultures into their own and forming a unique world view. This was a golden age of unparalleled intellectual activity in science, literature, technology, and linguistics. It was the Muslims who preserved classical Greek and Roman sources, translating it into Arabic and transmitting it back to a Western world that had largely forgotten it.

This intellectual curiosity included the preparation of foodstuffs.

How did they cook? They remained true to their nomadic heritage in at least one area—most cooking was done in a single pot. Even the most complicated dishes were prepared this way. The earliest cookbooks, dating from the thirteenth century, reflect this. For example, in a cookbook written by a gourmet known as al-Baghdadi (the whole name is Muhammad ibn al-Hassan ibn Muhammad ibn al-Karim al-Katib al-Baghdadi), some of his "simple and sweet dishes" go on and on, with frying, mincing, boiling, straining, and stewing, all in one pot. The Persian influence can be seen not in the method but in the manner of cooking: the dishes are full of spices from the East and the recipes themselves, whether cooked in one pot or not, usually involve many steps and are time-consuming.

What was the cooking oil used? Here it gets interesting—the fat-tailed sheep had an asset that was to be protected at all costs: its enormous tail. The fat rendered from the fat-tailed sheep yielded a cooking oil called *alya*. Even for his simple recipes, al-Baghdadi almost always instructs the reader to "Cut meat into middling pieces: dissolve tail and throw away the sediment." Afterward, "Put the meat into this oil and fry lightly. . . ."

Arabs knew that proper diet was a vital key to health. The precept was simple: a balanced diet can enhance life. As simple and appealing a concept as it was then, it is now. Central to this concept was the principal of the "four humors" —a theory first expounded by Empedocles in Greece in the fifth century B.C.E., and then enhanced by Galen, the Greek physician and philosopher. The theory states that a person is made up of the same four elements that make up the cosmos: air, fire, water, and earth. They manifest themselves in the human body in the "four humors": blood, bile, phlegm, and black bile. Some humans suffer from an excess of one or more of these elements. If you have an excess of one humor then you should decrease the use of that element. This is where proper diet comes in. A person of hot (bile/fire) temperament should not eat hot foods, but should eat cool or moist foods. An elderly person, who is assumed to have a phlegmatic temperament, should eat warm foods.

This odd mix of myth and diet was transported back to Europe late in the eleventh century where it remained dogma until the end of the sixteenth century and, in some cases, right up until the nineteenth. But this wasn't the only contribution that transformed the diet of Medieval Europe. The first crusaders set foot in the Holy Land in 1099. What they discovered amazed them. Here was a culinary paradise few had known. The local produce was enough to start them salivating—figs, lotus fruit, coconut, licorice root, citrus fruit, and luscious grapes that would make superb wines. They succumbed to the pleasures of the East and soon were using the many spices and ingredients they had found. Those who returned to Europe could only marvel at the wonders they had seen in this strange and fascinating land. The Muslims were light years ahead, not only in cooking but in other areas—they built the world's first astronomical observatory, developed the astrolabe, introduced new breeds of livestock; and would introduce into medieval Europe such comestibles as plums, artichokes, apricots, fennel, squash, pumpkin, eggplant, the date palm, sugarcane, and new strains of wheat. The European Renaissance would come, a new flowering, and the exotic cooking that so fascinated the crusaders, would re-establish itself at the Western table.

Isfanakh Mutajan

The vegetable recipes I've come across in early Arabic cooking are by and large highly complex in terms of the spices, some of which are difficult to find. There are recipes for vegetables such as lentils and eggplant, which include sumac, taro, murri, "Egyptian beans," and coriander juice. That's why I find this recipe so endearing: it's simple. It's from al-Baghdadi, and here he doesn't go to town with numerous ingredients and cooking techniques. Found under the heading of "relishes," this dish is nothing more than lightly boiled spinach seasoned with sesame oil, garlic, cumin, coriander, and cinnamon.

2 to 2½ pounds fresh spinach, stems removed, washed, drained, and
chopped
Salt to taste
2 tablespoons sesame oil
2 cloves garlic, peeled and finely minced
¼ teaspoon ground cumin
¼ teaspoon ground coriander
½ teaspoon ground cinnamon

1. Parboil the spinach for 1 to 2 minutes in a large pan of boiling salted water. Drain and squeeze dry.
2. Stir in the sesame oil, add the garlic, and mix.
3. Transfer to a serving dish, sprinkle with cumin, coriander, and stir to mix.
4. Sprinkle with cinnamon and serve.

Yield: 4 servings

GAZPACHO CON AJO BLANCO

In 711 the Muslims of Northern Africa, known as Moors because of their mixed Berber and Arab lineage, invaded Spain. Sailing across the Strait of Gibraltar, they soon conquered most of the Iberian Peninsula. Their occupation was to last over seven centuries. It wasn't until 1492 when the last of the Moors were expelled from Spain. But their influence has lasted to this day, particularly in the provinces of Andalusia and Valencia. Not the least, in their cuisine. The extensive use of nuts in Spanish cooking can be attributed to the Moors, especially in the use of almonds and pine nuts, which are used in sauces for fish, meat, and eggs. One of the most famous of Spanish dishes, gazpacho, evolved from an Arabic dish. Some etymologists suggest that the word, *gazpacho*, derives from the Arabic word for *soaked bread*. Others say that it may have come from the Mozarab word *caspa*, which means *residue* or *fragment*—as in the residue or fragments of bread used in the original gazpacho soup. Mozarab, by the way, comes from the Arabic *must'arab*, or "would-be Arab," alluding to those Spanish subjects who were allowed to practice their religion while still pledging loyalty to the Arab rulers.

Andalusia is renowned as the home of gazpacho. It probably originated as a soup of soaked bread, olive oil, and garlic. Today, the Spaniards would call this an *ajo blanco*, or garlic soup. In Malaga, a province in the region of Andalusia, they boast a garlic soup that dates from Moorish times. Their *ajo blanco* includes crushed almonds and is served garnished with fresh grapes. The province of Cordoba claims an even older version of gazpacho made with bread, garlic, and water. For a time, in Spain, the most common gazpacho was made of bread crusts soaked in water and mixed in a sauce of anchovy bones, crushed garlic, vinegar, sugar, salt, and olive oil. So how did we get to the chilled tomato concoction of today? Simple: Christopher Columbus and the introduction of the tomato to the European continent. With the addition of tomatoes, gazpacho became a dish of international renown. As early as 1824, American cookbooks included recipes for this kind of gazpacho.

Today, Andalusian gazpacho is made with ripe tomatoes, bell peppers, cucumbers, garlic, moistened bread, olive oil, vinegar, and ice water. I've gone back to the original gazpacho as derived from its Moorish influence.

1 cup untrimmed fresh bread, cubed
3 cloves garlic, peeled and finely minced
½ teaspoon salt
½ cup olive oil
Cold water

1. Soak the bread in water. Drain and squeeze to extract excess moisture.
2. In a mortar (preferably earthenware), pound the garlic until crushed.
3. In a wooden bowl, mix the garlic, bread, and salt, and stir in the olive oil.
4. Add cold water as desired, to get the smoothness of a soup. Serve at room temperature.

YIELD: 4 SERVINGS

NOTE: You can modify this recipe for Malaga-Style Gazpacho by adding ⅔ cup crushed peeled almonds and ½ teaspoon red wine vinegar before adding the cold water.

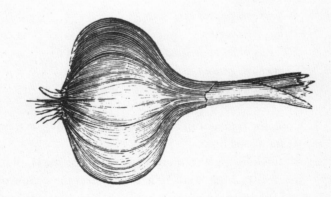

BURAN

Al-Baghdadi's lamb recipes are nonpareil. He cooks lamb with rice, with chickpeas, even with noodles. Buran, the following recipe, contains lamb kabobs served with fried and mashed eggplant.

Al-Baghdadi, as would most cooks today, recommends that the eggplant be boiled in salted water and then dried for one hour or more to remove excess moisture and bitterness. I've always cooked eggplant without this procedure. I find no difference in taste whether the eggplant is prepared in this way or not. But then, I'm a philistine, so what do I know? In this recipe I shall be true to al-Baghdadi and do as he suggests. He also recommends sesame oil for frying the eggplant and "melting fresh tail" for frying the lamb kabobs. In place of this sheep-tail fat I shall use regular vegetable oil.

1 medium-sized eggplant, about 1 ½ pounds, peeled and cut lengthwise
into ½-inch slices
1 pound ground lamb
¼ cup sesame oil
½ cup vegetable oil
Salt to taste
¼ teaspoon ground coriander
1 cup plain yogurt
2 cloves garlic, peeled and finely minced
½ teaspoon ground cumin
1 teaspoon ground cinnamon

1. Cook the eggplant in boiling salted water for 5 to 6 minutes. Drain and let stand one hour.
2. Meanwhile, use wet or oily hands to shape the lamb into small meatballs (about 20 to 30 kabobs). Heat the sesame oil in a large skillet and fry the meatballs over medium-high heat until well browned (about 10 minutes). Cover with water, bring heat to low and simmer until most of the water has evaporated and only some of the oil is left. Set aside and reserve.

3. Heat the vegetable oil in a large skillet (or use the same skillet from before), and fry the eggplant over medium heat until golden on both sides. The frying may have to be done in several batches with more oil being added as needed. As each slice is ready, remove and drain on paper towels. Place the eggplant in a bowl and mash with a ladle or large spoon. Add salt, coriander, yogurt, garlic, and mix well.
4. Transfer the eggplant to a serving dish, arrange the meatballs on top, sprinkle with cumin and cinnamon, and serve.

Yield: 4 servings

THARID

This dish is from another gourmet of the period, Ibn al-Mabrad (or Ibn al-Mubarrad). The dish is called *Tharid*, and the recipe states: "Meat is boiled and bread is moistened with broth. Yogurt, garlic, and mint are put with it and the meat is put with it. Likewise there is a Tharid without meat."

> *2 pounds boneless lamb stew meat, cut into small pieces, about ½-inch-thick cubes*
> *4 cups water*
> *½ cup bread crumbs*
> *6 cloves garlic, peeled and finely minced*
> *10 sprigs fresh mint (leaves only), rinsed and chopped*
> *1 cup yogurt*

1. Wash the lamb under cold running water and pat dry with paper towels.
2. In a medium saucepan, bring the water to a boil. Add the lamb, lower the heat, and simmer, uncovered, until the liquid is reduced to about 1 cup (approximately 30 to 40 minutes).
3. Remove the lamb to a platter or serving dish, and set aside.
4. Add the bread crumbs, garlic, mint, and yogurt to the broth in the saucepan. Stir to mix, and serve this sauce over the lamb.

YIELD: 4 SERVINGS

Zirbaya

The chicken dish that follows is from an anonymous Andalusian cookbook of the thirteenth century that was translated from the original Arabic into Spanish. It calls for cooking a "young clean hen" with various spices, then adding crushed almonds, sugar, and rosewater. The author states the dish is very nutritious and good for the stomach and the liver. He adds, it is "good for all temperaments," and it can also be made with pigeons, doves, or young lamb meat.

1 medium stewing chicken, about 2 ½ pounds, cut into serving pieces
Salt to taste
5 whole peppercorns
1 teaspoon ground coriander
2 teaspoons cinnamon
⅛ teaspoon crushed saffron threads
2 tablespoons red wine vinegar
2 tablespoons olive oil
½ cup crushed almonds
½ cup pure cane sugar
⅓ cup rosewater*

1. Wash the chicken pieces under cold running water and pat dry with paper towels.
2. Put the salt and peppercorns into a mortar and pound until the peppercorns are crushed.
3. In a large pot, Dutch oven, or heavy iron casserole, place the chicken pieces along with the spices, vinegar, and olive oil. Bring to a boil, lower heat, and simmer, covered, for about 40 minutes. Be sure to stir occasionally to keep the chicken pieces from sticking.
4. In a medium bowl, combine the almonds, sugar, and rosewater and stir to make a gooey paste. Add this to the chicken, slowly bring to a boil, and cook until the sauce thickens, about 6 to 8 minutes.

YIELD: 4 SERVINGS

*Rosewater can be found in Indian and Arab stores.

HAIS

Hais is a dessert, although it can also be served as an appetizer. Take your pick. It's from al-Baghdadi again, and I get a kick out of the measurements he uses in most of his recipes. He says take a *ratl* of this or two *uqiya* of that, and so on. As close as it can be figured, a *ratl* is equal to 14.328 ounces (.8955 pound). The *uqiya* is equal to approximately 1.19 ounces. *Hais* consists of a *ratl* of fine dry bread, three quarters of a *ratl* of fresh or preserved dates, three *uqiya* of ground almonds and pistachios, and two *uqiya* of sesame oil. I find that in transcribing the recipes, good old horse sense is all that's needed, and constant experimentation.

> *2¾ cups dry bread crumbs*
> *1 pound pitted dates, finely chopped*
> *⅓ cup ground almonds*
> *⅓ cup ground pistachios*
> *½ cup sesame oil*
> *Pure cane sugar to taste*

1. In a large bowl, mix the bread crumbs, dates, almonds, and pistachios.
2. Stir in the sesame oil, and blend well.
3. Use wet or oily hands to form 1-inch balls. Place on a serving dish, dust with sugar, and serve.

YIELD: 4 SERVINGS

SEKANJABIN SIMPLE

Today, in Iranian restaurants, a popular concoction served with meals is *sekanjabin* (or *sekanjebin*). This is a drink that goes back a long way. The anonymous Andalusian cookbook gives a variety of syrup-flavored drinks for medicinal purposes, among them a *Jarabe de Sakanyabin Simple*, or Simple Sekanjabin Syrup, which can be served hot or cold. The recipe calls for simmering a pound of vinegar with two pounds of sugar until it forms a syrup. It should then be taken when fasting at the ratio of one ounce of syrup to three ounces of hot water. The author claims it is beneficial for phlegmatic fever and jaundice. The modern equivalent would be served cold with grated cucumber. Modern recipes also include fresh mint and suggest dipping lettuce into it. In this case one can serve it as a dessert as well as a tonic.

2 cups pure cane sugar
1¼ cups water
½ cup red wine vinegar

1. In a medium saucepan, dissolve the sugar in the water.
2. Bring to a boil, and stir in the vinegar.
3. Lower the heat and simmer, covered, until it becomes a syrupy blend (about ½ hour).
4. Remove from the heat and let cool.
5. Serve by diluting the syrup in cold water, normally 5 parts water to 1 part syrup (the ratio can be adjusted depending on individual taste).

YIELD: ABOUT 1½ CUPS
NOTE: The syrup need not be refrigerated.

EIGHT

THE CHINESE KINGDOM

STEAMED CHICKEN, CANTONESE STYLE,
BASIC STIR-FRIED VEGETABLES,
LOBSTER CANTONESE A LA LARRY QUAN,
SZECHUAN STYLE NOODLES, SZECHUAN SQUID,
SPICY BEAN CURD, HUNAN LAMB, SMOKED
DUCK, SWEET AND SOUR FISH, LION'S
HEAD, MONGOLIAN HOT POT, NORTHERN
(PEKING-STYLE) DEEP-FRIED BEAN CURD

All your household have come to do you honour: All kinds of good food are
ready:
Rice, broom-corn, early wheat, mixed all with yellow millet;
Bitter, salt, sour, hot and sweet: there are dishes of all flavors
Ribs of fatted ox cooked tender and succulent;
Sour and bitter blended in the soup of Wu;
Stewed turtle and roast kid, served up with yam sauce,
Geese cooked in sour sauce, casseroled duck, fried flesh of the great crane;
Braised chicken, seethe tortoise highly seasoned, but not to spoil the taste;
Fried honey cakes of rice flour and sugar-malt sweetmeats;
Jadelike wine, honey flavored, fills the winged cup;
Ice cooled liquor, strained of impurities, clear wine, cool and refreshing.
Here are laid out the patterned ladles, and here is sparkling wine.

The preceding is from a third century B.C.E. Chinese poem, *Chao hun.* ("The Summons of the Soul.") It, more or less, sums up what the upper strata of China was eating at the time. The Chinese kitchen, whether high class or low, had evolved further by this time than its western counterpart. To the Chinese, cooking was not only an art—it was a science.

Early on, the Chinese sought balance in their cooking, defined in the principle of *yin* and *yang*—which says everything should be balanced, even between equals and opposites. The same holds true for food—the flavors should be in harmony as much as is possible. Essential to this is the concept of the five flavors. The fourth line of the poem alludes to this—"Bitter, salt, sour, hot and sweet: There are dishes of all flavors." As the poet-narrator strives to show, the essentials of cooking are embodied in the contrast of these five flavors.

This concept of the five flavors appeared early on in Chinese cooking. The idea, for its time, was revolutionary. It can be traced back as early as the Shang dynasty (c. fifteenth to eleventh century B.C.E.) when, legend has it, the scholar Yi Yin came up with the idea of the harmonization of foods. He related the five flavors concept to the nutritional needs of the five major organ groups in the body: heart, liver, spleen, pancreas/lungs, and kidneys. This gave rise to the belief of the medicinal value of food. Many of the ingredients used in Chinese cooking, such as fresh ginger root, scallions, garlic, dried lily buds, tree fungus, and so on, were considered to have properties that would prevent and alleviate various ailments.

When did Chinese cooking, as we have come to know it in the West, evolve? No one knows for sure. We can't rely on literary sources simply because there were none before the first millennium B.C.E. The earliest Chinese text is the *Shih ching, The Book of Songs*, a compendium of traditional ballads and fragments on feasting and farming in the northwestern highlands of Shensi sometime after 600 B.C.E. The work contains no recipes as such. It tells of men hunting in the winter, farming in the spring and summer; rice wine being fermented in the tenth month of the working year; and a village feast that includes the sacrifice of a young lamb cooked on aromatic southernwood— "As soon as the smell rises / God on high is pleased: / What smell is this, so strong and good?"

Some point to Confucius as an early source of Chinese cuisine. In *The Analects*, or *Lun Yu*, a collection of his sayings, Confucius expounds on all aspects of life, including eating food, and even clothing. When preparing to make a sacrifice to the spirits of his ancestors, one must eat rice only "of the finest quality," and the meat must be "finely minced." Among the prohibitions are: "Rice affected by the weather," "fish that is not sound," and one must not eat "anything discolored or that smells bad," anything that is "overcooked" or "undercooked," "out of season," or "any dish that lacks proper seasoning."

Good sound advice for any epoch.

My favorite among these early tomes is the *Li-Ki*, a manual of ritual behavior compiled during the Han dynasty (202 B.C.E. to 220 C.E.). It contains recipes for the pounded delicacies, among them ox, sheep, elk, and deer, which were prepared for nourishing the aged. There is a steeped delicacy, which is beef, cut into small pieces, "steeped in good wine," and eaten with pickle, vinegar, or the juice of prunes. The standout recipe is for a whole suckling pig, stuffed with dates, roasted, deep fried, and steamed on a bed of herbs. Of course, other delicacies include the liver of a dog roasted in a casing of its own fat. Dog meat, which is said to have high protein content, is still a common dish in parts of China and other parts of East Asia as well.

But, again, here we are stuck with the food of the rich and the mighty, of the mandarins of the Middle Kingdom and the emperors of "all the heavens and all the earth." What about the poor joe down in the rice paddies? And we may owe more to that poor joe and jane than we think. Consider stir-fry. A peasant and his family living on the plains of the Yellow River had limited resources. They would have to depend on wood or charcoal for cooking, and these were hard to get. In tough times, even dry dung might be used as a source of fuel. They had to develop a cooking style that required a minimum of time and effort. What better method than to cook thin strips of meat or millet, or whatever vegetables were available, in as quick a time as possible, in as little oil or fat as possible. And to do it in a pot or conveyance ideally in a conical shape that would provide more depth and frying surface. Here you have the wok, that great innovation. When did it appear? That information is lost in the mists of time.

The successors to the Han dynasty may have dined on fried honey cakes and steamed dumplings but the average "one of the many" probably didn't know where his next meal was coming from. He had to improvise. He or she had to make use of whatever was available, whether animal, vegetable, or other. If you were near the coastline, there was fish—sturgeon, sea bass, carp. Of vegetables, there were onions, bamboo shoots, and greens such as bok choy. If you were lucky, you might have some pork now and then. Otherwise, the mainstay of the poorer classes was bean curd.

The soybean has been a part of Chinese culinary history since it was introduced into southern China in the second century B.C.E. In the West, we naturally think of soy sauce. But in China the soybean has always had versatile uses, either as a soy milk product, curd, sauce, or meat supplement. To a poor peasant, a cake of bean curd, eaten with cabbage, was a sumptuous meal.

The peasant diet was dependent on local conditions and manifested differently throughout China. The diversity of climate and vegetation made for a diverse and complex cuisine. The term *Chinese cooking* means more then it seems. There is not one type of Chinese cooking. The variations or styles prevalent in the cuisine are influenced by geographical area. Naturally, all these cooking styles evolved through time. Chinese dishes began to be separated by southern and northern regional taste during the Spring and Autumn period (c. 770 to 476 B.C.E.) and the Warring States period (c. 475 to 221 B.C.E.). In the Tang (618 to 907 C.E.) and Song (960 to 1279 C.E.) dynasties the medicinal and nutritional values of foods began to be categorized. In time the four main regional cuisines: Northern (Beijing), Sichuan ("Chuan" dishes), Southern (Cantonese or "Yue" dishes), and Huaiyang (Yangzhou food) evolved, after the Tang and Song dynasties, into the eight types known as Szechuan (Sichuan), Cantonese, Shandong, Yangzhou, Beijing, Anhui, Zhejiang, and Hunan.

Before and during the growth of all these cooking styles, the techniques used by the poor left a lot to be desired. Food was lightly cooked or not at all. Marco Polo, in his travels through China in the thirteenth century, observed that in Yunnan, "The natives eat flesh raw—poultry, mutton, beef, and buffalo meat. The poorer sort go to the shambles and take the raw liver as soon as it is drawn from the beasts; then they chop it up small, put it in garlic sauce and eat it there and then. And they do likewise with every other kind of flesh." Those of the learned upper classes looked down upon this habit. "People of the present time eat fish and vegetables mostly uncooked," complained the Buddhist traveler I-ching. Naturally, they did not have to worry where their next meal was coming from or where to get fuel for the fire.

Both rich and poor shared a passion for edible exotics. This ensured that anything that could be cooked landed on your plate. The poor ate not only frogs and geese, but snakes ("brushwood eels"), grasshoppers ("brushwood shrimps"), and rats ("household deer"). In Hupei, one of the most popular dishes was "white flower snake"—a type of viper. A rich table might be graced with such unusual dishes as roasted snails, smoked sea cucumber, shark's fins, and bird's nest soup, which is still popular today—if you can find the rare type of seaweed that Chinese swallows use to make their nests and that produces the gelatinous ingredient that gives the soup its delicate flavor. This yen for unusual edibles has survived to the modern day, as any visitor to some markets in Hong Kong will attest, where can be found anything that can be cooked, from lizards to insects.

The street vendor in thirteenth-century China sold fresh honey fritters, cakes, and candied fruits. By contrast, the street vendor in Medieval Europe sold dried fish and stale bread. A fourteenth-century European traveler to Canton, Friar Oderic de Pordenone was awed by what he found: "And this city hath shipping so great and vast in amount that some of it would seem well nigh incredible. Indeed all Italy hath not the amount of craft that this city hath. And here you can buy three hundred pounds of fresh ginger for less than a groat. The geese too are bigger and finer and cheaper than anywhere in the world. . . . And the geese are as fat as fat can be, yet one of them well dressed and seasoned you shall have there for less than a groat. And as it is with the geese, so also with the ducks and fowls; they are so big that you would think them perfectly marvelous."

An imperial banquet would be something to behold. The meal would consist of different dishes, up to 150 offerings or more of stir-fried, grilled, and roasted meats, seafood and vegetables; different flavored rice dishes;

fruits and sweetmeats. And each dish would incorporate the proper season-ings, correct ingredients, and proportions. These dishes were aesthetically pleasing, combining not only the five flavors, but contrasting colors and aromas. One course might consist of a dozen or more dishes with numerous refreshing drinks to cleanse and cool the palate between courses. There would be rice wine, and wine from the special vines planted in the imperial palace park. The question is, who could eat so many courses? My guess is that some protocol had to be observed. Each guest would be seated according to his rank and status and would be expected to sample those dishes to their liking. Only a glutton would try to sample everything in sight—and with the emperor at the head of the table, you had better watch your manners.

The one thing missing from the imperial banquet was noodles—that fabled product that Marco Polo is reputed to have brought back to his native Venice. Whether this tale is true or not, that's open to question. We do know that in the Indian and the Arab world, noodles were eaten regularly. The Arabs called their noodles, *rishta*, a Persian word for *thread*. The Chinese seem to have cooked and enjoyed noodles since as early as the third century B.C.E., when they began grinding wheat into flour instead of cooking it whole. This came about through crosscurrent trade between the Han dynasty and the Roman Empire, when merchants along the Silk Road brought grind-stones into China. The ground flour was cut into strips, boiled, and steamed. So now, they not only had noodles, but made dumplings, pancakes, and steamed buns—what came to be known as *ping*, the generic word for all their pasta products. Some scholars attest that, even though noodles may have been prevalent in the peasant kitchen, up until the sixteenth century they were regarded as food fit to be eaten by only the coarse and vulgar masses. They were disdained by the educated and refined palates of the elite, which favored millet over wheat products.

Apart from rice wine, of which fifty-four different varieties were recorded in Marco Polo's time, the other great drink known to Chinese cuisine is, of course, tea. According to legend, Emperor Shen Nong was taking a stroll one summer day in one of his gardens in the year 2737 B.C.E. The emperor had a habit of drinking boiled water as a hygienic precaution. A leaf from a nearby bush fell into his cup. The emperor noticed that the leaf had infused the water with a brownish tinge. He tasted this liquid, and liked it. Thus tea was born.

In time, tea consumption became an integral part of Chinese society. It was a refreshing drink, but it was also believed to have medicinal properties.

Among other things, tea was considered a beneficial concoction for alleviating fever, headache, stomachache, and pain in the joints. Tea in China became a ritual drink, as it would later on in Japan. It would become a drink not only of social interaction and medicinal value, but also a drink to enhance meditation. Lu Yu, a scholarly Buddhist monk, wrote the *Ch'a Ching*, the first definitive book on ancient tea cultivation and preparation in the year 800 of the Common era.

Tea was enjoyed among royalty and commoners alike. There were green teas, black teas, and herbal teas—which were the medicinal teas created from varied flowers, seeds, roots, and berries. Keemun is the most famous of the black teas. Another favored tea was oolong, originally grown in Fukien province. Oolong is actually a cross between green and black teas, and today the best quality oolong (formosa oolong) is grown in Taiwan.

Now we come to that greatest of all questions: why did the Chinese, then as now, use chopsticks? I remember back in my salad days when my family would go to New York's Chinatown for an "authentic" Chinese dinner. Let's categorize that—as authentic as Chinese-American food was then (or is today). Among our crowd would be my Uncle Phillip, of late memory, who was a classic iconoclast and not very politically correct. Throughout the dinner I would try to impress him with my knowledge of Asian history, recounting how in the Middle Ages, when Western man was in the dumps, China had one of the most advanced societies. And he would always retort, as he struggled with his chopsticks: "If they were so damn smart why the hell didn't they invent forks?"

The Chinese have been using chopsticks since at least the fourth century B.C.E. The popular theory is that people cooked their food in large pots, which held heat for a long time. The would-be diners would then break twigs or branches off trees and bushes to get at the food. As we have noted, fuel for cooking was hard to come by, so food was chopped into small pieces so it would cook more quickly. You don't need a knife and fork for small morsels of food. In time, the twigs became chopsticks, and they were made from a variety of materials. Bamboo is still the most popular material for making chopsticks since it is readily available and inexpensive. But other materials were also used: sandalwood, teak, pine, animal bone, and even precious metals such as gold and silver. The latter were especially popular in dynastic times during the Middle Ages since it was thought that silver chopsticks would turn color if they came in contact with poisoned food. Good insurance (if you buy the theory) for some aristocrat who may have incurred the emperor's wrath.

By 500 C.E. the use of chopsticks had spread to Vietnam, Korea, and Japan.

Uncle Phillip's protestations aside, if you consider it logically, chopsticks are an ingenious invention. They are quick and efficient, and well suited to their task—once you master their use. Francesco Carletti, an early European visitor to China, marveled at their use by the locals: "They can pick up anything, no matter how tiny it is, very cleanly and without soiling their hands. For that reason they do not use tablecloths or napkins or even knives, as everything comes to the table minutely cut up and brought to them in certain square lacquered trays on which they put the plates and bowls full of rice and of food. . . . When they want to eat it, they bring the bowl it is in close to their mouth and then, with those two sticks, are able to fill their mouth with marvelous agility and swiftness."

Marvelous agility and swiftness. Not only with the implements used but in the cooking. This is what came out of the Middle Kingdom and the great classical age of China. A view of cooking as a science, not just a craft. It can be summed up in the words of the Taoist sage, Lao–tzu: "Governing a great nation is like cooking a small fish—too much handling will spoil it."

Let me state that most of the recipes that follow are contemporary and not historic in nature, mainly because Chinese cuisine, despite the myriad influences, has remained constant in terms of the cooking techniques. The main differences in Chinese cooking are regional. For example, rice is the main crop in the subtropical south, and wheat is grown in the colder northern areas. This means that noodles have become a staple in the northern regions. But in each case, the cooking styles, relative to each area, have remained the same since time immemorial.

STEAMED CHICKEN,
CANTONESE STYLE

Speak of southern Chinese cuisine and what comes to mind is Cantonese cooking. For most of us in the United States, Cantonese cooking was our first exposure to Chinese cooking. In my part of the world it is still the most popular type of Chinese cuisine. And that leads us to that old canard: Chinese-American cooking. It wasn't until I was an adult that I discovered that what I considered authentic Chinese cooking all those years that I had ventured to Chinatown was really an American variant of the original. You may get arguments from some quarters, but chop suey, chow mein, and egg foo yung did not originate in China. They were invented in the U.S.A. To be blunt, order a poo-poo platter in a restaurant in Beijing and I'm sure you'd be surprised at what you're going to get. The best illustration of these American creations is chop suey. There are many apocryphal stories concerning its origin. My favorite is the one regarding a Chinese immigrant cook who, during the California Gold Rush, was accosted by a drunken miner in a San Francisco restaurant. The miner was loud, obnoxious, and hungry. This pissed off the Chinese cook, who went into the back of the restaurant, took whatever leftovers were in the garbage, mixed it in a broth and served it to the miner. Rather than being insulted (and because he didn't know any better), the miner loved the dish and came back again and again to order the chop suey (chopped sewage). Before long, everyone in town was eating the stuff.

Large-scale immigration from Canton to the U.S. in the 1800s assured that this Americanized version of Chinese cooking would take hold. The Chinese immigrants who flooded to California to work on the Pacific Railroad were constrained by the lack of authentic ingredients and vegetables that had represented their diet back home. They had to make do with what was available. Not only that, if they went into the restaurant business, they had to make their dishes palatable to Western tastes. It's amusing to think that someone from the Chinese mainland would come to this country today and go in search of genuine American chop suey and chow mein.

Authentic Cantonese-style cooking is something to behold, with dishes artistically presented and properly garnished, using a wide range of ingredients that must be as fresh as possible. Unlike its Americanized version, it is not corrupted with soggy vegetables overflowing with cornstarch, overcooked fish or poultry, and every dish swimming in heavy seasonings. In genuine Cantonese cuisine the emphasis is on preserving the natural flavors of the food. Seasonings are used sparingly. As much as possible, foods must retain their natural taste. This has led to such cooking methods as stir-frying, roasting, and steaming—including this simple steamed chicken dish.

Before we start, a note on steaming. A wok with a cover and steamer rack is perfect for this. If you have a bamboo steamer, then you are way ahead of the game, especially the type that comes with a series of interlocking trays that can be placed in the wok. Another advantage to this type of steamer is that two or three dishes can be cooked at the same time, so you can have a vegetable such as broccoli or cauliflower cooking on top while the chicken is steamed in the bottom tray. Whether using the wok by itself or the bamboo steamer, only a small amount of water is needed for the process. The water should not touch the food, the rising steam will cook the ingredients. Just make sure that if using the wok or steamer you have a secure lid that will cover the apparatus so that the food will cook evenly and no heat will escape. If you don't have a wok or steamer, then a big cooking pot will do. Put a can or high plate in the bottom of the pot, and put the chicken dish on top. Put enough water in the pot to cover the bottom up to about two inches. Once the water reaches a fast boil, cover the pot and steam the chicken.

For those not familiar with the wok, let me repeat, it is a marvelous cooking utensil. It is ideal for any type of cooking, especially deep frying and stir-frying. Woks come in varying sizes and are made of various materials, from copper, to aluminum, to stainless steel. Iron woks are the most commonly used. There are families who have used the same wok for generations, rendering it with that distinctive black color from constant use. Be aware that if using an iron wok, it first has to be seasoned. This is a simple enough procedure: after washing the wok with hot water and soap and drying carefully, coat the inside of the wok with peanut oil. Heat the wok over high heat for a minute or so, and rinse with hot water. Repeat the procedure again, oiling and heating the wok, rinse with hot water and dry it over low heat. The wok is ready for use. Never use harsh abrasives or detergents to clean the wok. Just rinse it with very hot water and scrub with a plastic scouring pad or bamboo scrubber. Dry over low heat, coat it with a light film of oil, and store. The iron wok will blacken with use. That's what you want; that's what makes it distinctive.

1 fryer or stewing chicken, about 2 ½ pounds, cut into bite-sized pieces
2 tablespoons light soy sauce
1 teaspoon corn starch
1 teaspoon sesame oil
1 tablespoon rice wine or dry sherry
½ teaspoon sugar
1 teaspoon grated fresh ginger

1. Wash the chicken pieces under cold running water and pat dry with paper towels.
2. Place the chicken on a plate that will fit tightly in the wok or steamer.
3. Combine the remaining ingredients in a small bowl and pour over the chicken pieces. Mix well.
4. Place the plate in the wok or steamer, bring the water to a boil, cover and steam on high heat for approximately 15 to 20 minutes, or until tender.

YIELD: 4 SERVINGS

NOTE: This recipe can be modified slightly with the addition of sea salt. Salt the chicken pieces generously with sea salt, place in a covered pan or container, and let it rest in the lower shelf of the refrigerator for 2 to 3 days. Remove, rinse carefully with cold water, wipe dry, and steam as instructed. This dish can be served hot or cold, and it makes great sandwiches.

BASIC STIR-FRIED VEGETABLES

Stir-frying is one of the Cantonese marvels. And a wok is especially suited for this. If you don't own a wok, then a skillet is the second best choice. Otherwise, use a shallow frying pan with a depth of less than two inches. Sliced meats as well as any seasonal vegetable can be stir-fried.

In most Chinese dishes peanut oil, a golden oil pressed from peanuts with a light and fragrant nutty flavor, is preferred for stir-frying or deep frying. It smokes only at extremely high temperatures and therefore is very well suited to wok cooking. If you are worried about the cholesterol, then any good vegetable oil will do.

> *2 pounds any mix of vegetables in season: broccoli, cauliflower, carrots,*
> *   onions, mushrooms, tomatoes, spinach, cucumbers, etc.*
> *2½ tablespoons peanut or vegetable oil*
> *1 clove garlic, peeled and crushed*
> *1 small slice of fresh ginger*
> *1 teaspoon salt*
> *1 tablespoon rice wine or dry sherry*
> *2 teaspoons sesame oil*

1. Wash vegetables under cold running water and cut into bite-sized pieces. For example: if a tomato, cut it into eight wedges; if an onion, slice into ⅛-inch thick layers; if a green pepper, dice into 1-inch squares. Separate any stems from leafy parts, and cut up the leafy parts. If the stems are thin (collards) or tough (celery), slice on an acute diagonal.
2. Heat the oil in the frying pan or wok until very hot. Add the garlic and ginger. Cook until the garlic is brown and the oil is infused with the ginger. Discard the garlic and ginger.

3. Stir in the salt, and add the vegetables in sequence with those taking the longest time to cook, added first. As each vegetable is added, it is dropped into the oil and stirred around the sides of the wok or fry pan, forming a well. The next ingredient will fall into the bottom of the well and be cooked accordingly for a minute or so until it changes color.
4. Add the rice wine or sherry and stir-fry for 1 to 2 minutes more.
5. Garnish with sesame oil and serve.

YIELD: 4 SERVINGS

Lobster Cantonese
a la Larry Quan

I belong to a group that is affectionately known as the Gang of Five. We are friends who have known each other for twenty years or more, and we gather every month, guys only, no wives or girlfriends, for a dinner in our favorite restaurant in New York's Chinatown. On birthdays and Chinese New Year's Eve the whole family is invited to partake in the festivities. One of the dishes we enjoy at these banquets is Lobster Cantonese. Fish and shellfish such as squid, lobster, and prawns are prominent in Cantonese cuisine. This recipe is from one of the Gang of Five, my dear friend, Larry Quan.

1 live lobster, about 1¼ pounds
2 tablespoons olive oil
¼ pound ground pork
1 teaspoon light soy sauce
1 teaspoon black bean sauce
1 tablespoon dry sherry or rice wine
½ cup chicken broth
1 teaspoon cornstarch
Salt and ground black pepper to taste
1 egg, beaten
1 scallion, washed and finely chopped

1. Plunge a knife into the place on the lobster where the tail and body meet. This will kill it instantly. Break off the claws, and cut the tail into three sections crosswise. Remove and discard the tough sac near the eyes. Set the lobster parts aside until ready to use.
2. Heat the oil in a wok or skillet. Add the pork and stir-fry with a wooden spoon, cooking the pork on a high flame until brown. Add the soy sauce, lobster pieces, and black bean sauce. Stir in the wine and chicken broth, cover and cook on high heat for about 1 minute.

3. Remove the cover and add the cornstarch. At this point, depending on how thick you want the sauce, you may add a little water and more cornstarch. Season to taste with salt and pepper.

4. Bring to a boil and slowly pour in the egg. Stir-fry for about 10 seconds. Remove from the heat. Place the lobster with its sauce on a serving platter. Garnish with scallions and serve.

YIELD: 2 SERVINGS

NOTE: The ingredients can be doubled for 4 servings.

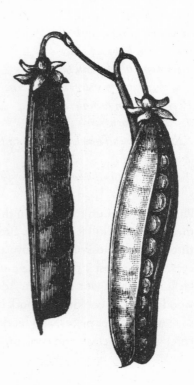

SZECHUAN-STYLE NOODLES

It's only recently that Szechuan food has caught on in the West. I had never heard of it until it started popping up in Asian neighborhoods. I was impressed, not by the spiciness of the food, but by the subtle use of hot spices within the food. Szechuan dishes are not simply hot, they contain many flavors—sweet, sour, bitter, salty, fragrant, and aromatic. They not only stimulate the palate, they make us more sensitive to these flavors. After years of eating bland Cantonese-style food, this was a revelation. I was hooked.

What does give the hot component to Szechuan cuisine is its use of chili peppers. But initially, chili peppers were not utilized in Szechuan cuisine. The Chinese had their own milder variety, *faraga*, also called Chinese pepper or Szechuan pepper. The cuisine became even more peppery when Portuguese and Spanish traders introduced chilies to the region during the sixteenth century.

1 pound fresh noodles (Chinese thin noodles are the best, otherwise, angel hair pasta is a good substitute)
3 tablespoons peanut or vegetable oil
½ pound shredded barbecued pork, store bought or home made*
½ cup bok choy, washed, drained, and cut into bite-sized pieces
½ cup carrots, cut on the diagonal into ½-inch pieces
½ cup broccoli florets
½ cup snow peas
1 onion, thinly sliced
1 cup chicken broth
1 teaspoon cornstarch (or as needed)
2 tablespoons light soy sauce
2 tablespoons hoisin sauce
1 teaspoon sesame oil
½ teaspoon sugar
1 teaspoon Chinese chili paste with garlic (can use more or less depending on taste)

1. Parboil the noodles in a pot of boiling water for three minutes. To insure noodles do not stick, loosen up the noodles with chopsticks as they boil.
2. Heat the oil in wok or large frying pan. Add the pork, bok choy, carrots, broccoli, snow peas and onion, and stir-fry until the vegetables are crisp-tender, about 2 minutes. Remove the vegetables to a platter.
3. Add the remaining ingredients, stirring until thickened. Add the pork and vegetables and stir well until the mixture comes to a boil. Taste and adjust seasonings as desired. Serve.

YIELD: 4 SERVINGS

You can substitute a chicken breast, cut into strips, for the barbecued pork. In that case, stir-fry the chicken first until nearly done. Remove the chicken from the wok and continue as directed in the recipe, adding the chicken and vegetables to the sauce as the last step.

THE PHARAOH'S FEAST

SZECHUAN SQUID

It is said that in Chinese cooking anything that walks, swims, flies, or crawls is a candidate for the pot. Squid is a case in point. It is one of those edibles that make people either salivate or turn up their noses. This Szechuan version makes a case for the former. I'd suggest serving this tasty squid with boiled rice.

2 pounds squid, fresh or frozen
2 tablespoons light soy sauce
1 tablespoon rice wine or dry sherry
½ teaspoon sugar
½ teaspoon sesame oil
½ teaspoon salt
3 tablespoons cornstarch (more or less, as needed)
3 to 4 cups peanut or vegetable oil for deep frying
¼ teaspoon ground red hot chili pepper, without seeds
1 tablespoon chopped fresh ginger
1 clove garlic, peeled and minced
1 teaspoon ground Szechuan peppercorn
½ cup bok choy, washed, drained, and cut into bite-sized pieces
1 carrot, cut on the diagonal into ½-inch pieces
3 stalks scallion, washed and finely chopped

1. If using fresh squid, wash under cold running water and cut off the tentacles. Remove and discard the mouth, which is located in the center of the tentacles. Under running water, using your hands, rub off the purplish outer skin from the body of the squid. Hold the closed end of the body (also called the mantle) in one hand and with the other squeeze out the innards, pushing out the viscera, head, and translucent backbone. Turn the body inside out, discard the head, viscera, and bone. Wash the inside of the body thoroughly. Lay the body on a flat surface and slice down the center from top to bottom. Spread open and cut the body lengthwise and crosswise and then cut it into diamond-shaped pieces about 1-inch long. Cut the tentacles into 1-inch rounds. If using frozen squid, wash under cold running water and cut the squid into the necessary pieces.

2. In a small bowl, combine the soy sauce, wine, sugar, sesame oil, and salt. Reserve.
3. Sprinkle the squid pieces evenly with cornstarch.
4. Heat enough oil in a wok or frying pan to deep fry the squid until the squid curls up (about 1 minute). Remove and set aside.
5. Drain the oil from the wok and clean it out with a paper towel. Heat about 3 tablespoons of fresh oil in the wok, making sure that it coats the sides. Add the chili pepper, ginger, garlic, and Szechuan peppercorn. Add the bok choy and carrot and stir-fry for 1 to 2 minutes. Add the squid and sauce, and stir to mix well. Garnish with scallions.

YIELD: 4 SERVINGS

SPICY BEAN CURD

Bean curd is used in many Szechuan recipes. It is often an item that shares the pot with other ingredients, For instance, in hot-and-sour soup the bean curd is mixed with pork, bamboo shoots, and Chinese mushrooms to produce a delicious stew. In this recipe bean curd is the prime ingredient.

¾ cup chicken broth
1 teaspoon cornstarch
1 tablespoon soy sauce
4 tablespoons peanut or vegetable oil
1-pound container fresh bean curd, preferably extra firm, patted dry, and cut into ½-inch cubes
1 tablespoon hot soybean paste*
1 teaspoon ground red hot chili pepper, without seeds
½ teaspoon ground Szechuan peppercorn
1 clove garlic, peeled and minced

1. Combine the chicken broth and cornstarch in a medium bowl and stir until the cornstarch dissolves. Mix in the soy sauce, and set aside.
2. Heat 2 tablespoons of oil in a wok or heavy skillet over high heat. Add the bean curd and stir-fry until golden brown (about 4 minutes). Transfer the bean curd to a platter using a slotted spoon.
3. Add the remaining 2 tablespoons of oil to the wok and set over high heat. Add the bean paste and stir-fry one minute. Add the chili pepper, Szechuan peppercorn, and garlic, and stir-fry until fragrant (about 1 minute).
4. Stir in the broth mixture and bring to a boil, stirring constantly. Remove from the heat, pour the sauce over the bean curd and serve.

YIELD: 4 SERVINGS

*Hot soybean paste can be found in Asian markets. If it can't be found, a good substitute is fermented black beans.

HUNAN LAMB

So you think Szechuan cooking is hot? Are you in for a surprise. Hunan cooking is less well-known than its Szechuan cousin. It is often lumped with Yunnan in the south as representative of China's western regional style of cooking. But there are differences. Hot and sour and sweet and sour are popular flavor combinations in Hunan. Like its neighbors, Hunan does employ stewing and sir-frying techniques along with simmering and steaming. But Hunan cooks are fortunate that they have more ingredients and materials to work with and thus can do more and be more innovative with the ingredients prior to cooking. For example, a classic dish such as orange beef does not only contain dried orange peel but the beef is marinated overnight, washed, and marinated again in egg white, wine, and pepper, then cooked twice in a wok, and then cooked again with fresh chili, ginger, and the orange peel. Another classic dish, General Tso's chicken, has the chicken marinated in a mix of egg, salt, and pepper, and uses a sauce, prior to cooking, that has garlic, ginger, sugar, rice vinegar, rice wine, chili peppers, and scallions. Hunan lamb is not so outlandish or complicated, but it does taste good. Serve with boiled rice.

2 tablespoons dark soy sauce
2 tablespoons rice wine or dry sherry
2 teaspoons cornstarch
1 teaspoon rice vinegar (or white wine vinegar)
½ teaspoon sugar
¼ cup water
2 tablespoons peanut or vegetable oil
4 small dried hot chili peppers
1 teaspoon fresh shredded ginger
1 clove garlic, peeled and minced
1 stalk scallion, washed and thinly sliced on the diagonal
1 pound boneless lamb meat, sliced into thin strips (can use boneless lamb leg, lamb shoulder, or stew meat)
1 teaspoon sesame oil

1. In a medium bowl whisk together the soy sauce, wine, cornstarch, vinegar, sugar, and water. Reserve.
2. Heat the oil in a wok or heavy skillet over high heat. Add the chili peppers, ginger, garlic, and scallion, and stir-fry for about half a minute.
3. Add the lamb and stir-fry until the lamb is no longer pink. Add the sauce mixture and cook, stirring, until slightly thickened (1 to 2 minutes). Stir in the sesame oil, remove from the heat, and serve.

Yield: 4 servings

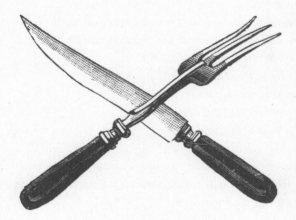

SMOKED DUCK

Hunan cooking, like Szechuan, has dishes featuring smoked meats, including ham and pork. This Smoked Duck recipe is a typical example. The only problem with this recipe is that traditionally it calls for deep frying a whole duck. Trying to do this in a wok is a messy endeavor. If you have a deep fryer big enough for a duck, then you're in luck. Those of us who don't have these conveniences are stuck out in left field. I've modified the dish by cutting the duck into small pieces prior to frying.

1 duck (4 to 5 pounds)
Salt to taste
1 tablespoon ground Szechuan peppercorn
Aluminum foil (as needed)
½ cup black tea leaves (not from tea bags but in bulk tea leaves, such as keemun black tea, pu-erh tea, or lichee black tea)
½ cup white rice (uncooked)
½ cup pure cane sugar
2 tablespoons light soy sauce
1 tablespoon cornstarch (or as needed)
½ cup peanut or vegetable oil

1. Wash the duck under cold running water and pat dry with paper towels. Rub generously inside and out with salt. Sprinkle inside and out with the ground peppercorn.
2. Wrap the duck in aluminum foil as airtight as possible. Place on a platter and top with a heavy weight (such as a large cast-iron skillet or even bricks). Place in the refrigerator and leave overnight.
3. The next day, remove the foil and place the duck on a steamer rack in a wok. If you don't have a wok large enough to accommodate the duck then place a deep plate or can inside a large pot and place the duck, in a dish, on top. Put enough water in the pot to cover the bottom up to about 2 inches. Once the water reaches a fast boil, cover the pot and steam the duck for 1½ hours.

4. Line the wok and wok lid with aluminum foil. Do the same with the pot if not using a wok. Be sure that no water remains in the pot. Arrange the bulk tea leaves, rice, and sugar in the bottom of the wok or pot, mixing the ingredients well.
5. Replace the duck, breasts side up, on the rack or pot. Cover tightly to prevent heat from escaping. A way to ensure this is to seal the wok or pot lid with additional aluminum foil.
6. Turn the heat high and cook the mixture until it starts to smoke. Smoke the duck for 10 minutes on high heat. Reduce the heat to medium and smoke for 10 minutes more. Turn off the heat and leave the duck inside the wok or pot for another 20 minutes.
7. Remove the duck to a cutting board. Once it has cooled, chop it into bite-sized pieces (a Chinese cleaver is perfect for this). Rub the pieces with soy sauce and sprinkle evenly with cornstarch.
8. Heat the oil in the wok or heavy skillet on high heat. Stir-fry the duck pieces until brown. Remove and drain on paper towels. Serve immediately.

YIELD: 4 SERVINGS

NOTE: For those who may want to bypass the deep frying part altogether, just smoke the duck. Once it has cooled, season inside and out with soy sauce. Brush with peanut or vegetable oil and roast in a 400 degree oven until the duck is brown. Turn the duck every 5 to 10 minutes and brush with more oil if necessary. To insure a quick brown color, a coat of soy sauce mixed with oil may be used for the last coating. In this instance, the duck can either be served whole and carved at the table or chopped into bite-sized pieces.

SWEET AND SOUR FISH

This fish recipe highlights the sweet and sour flavor combination so popular in Hunan. You'll note that one of the ingredients used is good old ketchup, an item often associated with Western food. Ketchup is, in fact, Chinese in origin. It was in the 1600s that Dutch and British sailors brought back a salty pickled fish sauce from China called *ketsiap*. At the time it was closer to soy or oyster sauce than the sweet, tomato-vinegar concoction we call ketchup. Westerners modified the sauce to suit their taste adding such things as shallots, pepper, white wine, lemon peel, and even mushrooms. It wasn't until the 1830s that Americans began adding tomatoes to the mix, and modern day ketchup was born.

2 tablespoons tomato ketchup
1 tablespoon light soy sauce
1 small dried hot chili pepper
1 tablespoon sugar
¾ cup rice wine or dry sherry
1 tablespoon corn starch dissolved in 2 tablespoons water
*1 whole fish (use a fish with very few bones such as cod, sea bass, or striped
    bass), about 3 pounds, cleaned and scaled but with head and tail still
    intact*
1 clove garlic, peeled and minced
1 tablespoon fresh chopped ginger
2 stalks scallions, washed and sliced on the diagonal

1. In a medium bowl, combine the ketchup, soy sauce, chili pepper, sugar, wine, and cornstarch. Reserve.
2. Wash the fish, inside and out, with cold running water and pat dry with paper towels. There are two ways to prepare the fish. One is to steam the fish in a covered wok or steamer for about 10 minutes. Remember to always start to steam the fish when the water in the steamer starts to boil. The second method is to cut 5 slits diagonally on both sides of the fish, rub it all over with salt, and dust with flour. Then deep fry the fish until dark brown and crispy.

3. Once the fish is done, remove it to a platter. Using the same wok or frying pan or, if steaming the fish, heat the wok with 1 tablespoon of cooking oil. Add the garlic and ginger and stir-fry over high heat for about 30 seconds. Add the sauce mixture and stir-fry for 1 minute. Add the scallions and stir to mix.
4. Pour the sauce over fish and serve.

YIELD: 4 SERVINGS

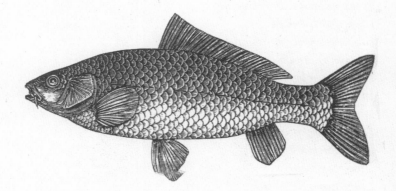

LION'S HEAD

Eastern China (Shanghai) cuisine is best known for it's "red-cooking" technique—a process whereby meat is stewed slowly in dark soy sauce. The meat is infused with a reddish tinge that is highly favored by connoisseurs—hence the name (as in such entrees as red-cooked chicken). But there are other popular dishes such as Lion's Head, which is a casserole with meatballs and bok choy and is traditionally cooked in a clay pot. If you don't have a clay pot, a good old wok or skillet will do. The name of the dish refers to the oversized meatballs.

1 pound ground beef or pork
1 teaspoon fresh grated ginger
3 stalks scallions, washed and cut into thin slices
½ cup minced water chestnuts
1 egg, lightly beaten
1 tablespoon rice wine or dry sherry
Salt and ground black pepper to taste
1 tablespoon light soy sauce
1 tablespoon cornstarch
¼ cup peanut or vegetable oil
1 pound bok choy, washed and chopped coarsely
2 cups chicken broth
1 teaspoon sugar
1 tablespoon cornstarch
2 tablespoons water

1. In a bowl, combine the meat with the ginger, scallions, chestnuts, egg, wine, salt and pepper, soy sauce, and cornstarch. Wet your hands lightly and form the mixture into balls the size of small tangerines.
2. Heat the oil in a wok or skillet over high heat. Lower the heat to medium and fry the meatballs, a few at a time, until golden brown. Drain on paper towels and remove to a warm platter.

3. Stir-fry the bok choy in the same oil. Place meatballs on top of the bok choy. Mix the chicken broth with the sugar and pour over the meatballs and bok choy. Cover and simmer on low heat for about 1 hour.
4. Remove the meatballs and bok choy, and arrange the meatballs on top of the bok choy in a large bowl. Bring the remaining stock to a boil and thicken if necessary, with the cornstarch dissolved in the water. Pour the sauce over the meatballs and vegetables and serve.

YIELD: 4 SERVINGS

MONGOLIAN HOT POT

Northern Chinese cuisine, also known as Beijing (Peking) cuisine is renowned for hot pot cooking (or fire pot cooking). You could say it's the Chinese version of fondue. Everyone gathers around a large communal pot and chooses from morsels of raw food to place in the pot for cooking. Once cooked, diners scoop out the food, dip it in a sauce, and eat. The hot pot (*huokuo*) hails from Mongolia and is commonly called Mongolian Hot Pot. It makes sense in a land of chilly winds and frigid weather. The hot pot or fire pot is made of ceramic or metal, with a base (ash receiver) in the bottom. The heat source is supplied by a fire pot section in the middle, equipped with a small chimney that provides air flow for the food to cook. It also has a valve for controlling the size of the cooking flame. Surrounding the fire pot is a removable bowl for dipping and cooking the food. In the old days the preferred fuel was charcoal. If you have a genuine hot pot you can use charcoal briquets for this purpose. Nowadays most people use gas or electricity to fuel their hot pots. If you don't have a genuine hot pot then a fondue pot will do.

The recipe given uses lamb as the main ingredient. Mutton is a popular dish in northern China. Sheep are raised there in abundance, and they tend to be large, rendering meat that is tender and less rank.

4 pounds boneless lamb, trimmed of all fat and sliced paper thin
1 pound bean thread noodles
1 tablespoon soy sauce
1 teaspoon sesame oil
1 teaspoon chili sauce
1 clove garlic, peeled and minced
1 tablespoon red bean curd (fermented) paste mixed with 1 tablespoon
*   cooking oil and 1 teaspoon sugar*
Chinese mustard
10 cups water
1 teaspoon fresh chopped ginger
1 bunch scallions, green part only, washed and cut into thin slices on the
*   diagonal*

1. Wash the lamb under cold running water and pat dry with paper towels. Wrap in cellophane or a freezer storage bag and store in the freezer until partially frozen. This will make it easier to slice the meat very thinly. Once the meat is sliced, place about 8 ounces for each guest in a small dessert-size dish.
2. Soak the noodles in a bowl of hot water. When the noodles have softened, drain and reserve.
3. Combine the soy sauce, sesame oil, chili sauce, and garlic, and place in a small saucer-size serving dish. Put the fermented bean curd paste in one dish and the Chinese mustard in another. Arrange the dips on the table with the hot pot in the center.
4. Set up the hot pot or fondue pot according to the instructions. Add the water, ginger, and scallions and bring to a boil. Use chopsticks to cook the lamb slices in the boiling water for a few seconds until the color changes. Then dip the meat into the desired sauces.
5. When the meat has been consumed, add the noodles to the water. Once heated, dish out the noodles and enjoy.

YIELD: 8 SERVINGS

NOTE: Some recipes call for using lamb or chicken broth instead of water in the hot pot. My Chinese friends insist on using plain water. The rationale is that after dipping platefuls of lamb in the water, it becomes as strong as a broth. Another custom is to add poached eggs to the water at the end of the meal.

Northern (Peking-Style) Deep-Fried Bean Curd

Another bean curd recipe. This one goes well with rice or noodles. It can be used as an entrée or as a side dish.

1-pound container fresh bean curd, preferably extra firm, patted dry and
*   cut into ½-inch cubes*
3 tablespoons cornstarch (more or less as needed)
Peanut or vegetable oil for deep frying (as needed)
1 tablespoon soy sauce
1 teaspoon sesame oil
1 teaspoon chili sauce
Sweet and sour sauce (see sauce recipe for Sweet and Sour Fish, page 126)

1. Sprinkle the bean curd evenly with the cornstarch.
2. Heat the oil over high heat in a wok or deep skillet. Add the bean curd and deep fry until golden brown. Depending on the size of the wok or skillet, you may have to do this in batches. Remove the bean curd with a slotted spoon and drain on paper towels.
3. Mix the soy sauce, sesame oil, and chili sauce.
4. Dip the bean curd in the soy sauce and sweet and sour sauce, as desired

Yield: 4 servings

NINE

THE NEW WORLD
MEETS THE OLD

LIMONIA, POACHED STURGEON, ZABAGLIONE,
DUXELLES, SAUCE POIVRADE, CAPON
ARMADO, IPOCRAS, VINEGAR GARLIC BEEF,
THE BEST PANCAKES, RICE PUDDING,
VEGETABLE TEMPURA,
TEMPURA DIPPING SAUCE

In 1492 Columbus sailed the ocean blue . . .

Those of us a certain age can remember that rhyme from grade school. Yes, Cristoforo Columbo did sail the ocean blue. Except, he went the wrong way and hit upon the Americas instead of India.

This all came about because Europeans wanted the spices from the East to season their food. The spice trade was a profitable endeavor. Early on, Venice and Florence were the ones who controlled the cartel. They traded with the Ottoman Turks at Alexandria and Damascus, and their middlemen exacted quite a profit from the trade. Venice alone brought back to Europe an estimated 2500 tons of a pepper a year, and nearly as much ginger. Any nation that could find a direct trade route to the East would be sitting pretty.

Fifteenth-century Spain had just expelled the last of its Moorish conquerors. They were itching to burst out on the world stage. So when Columbus proposed his daring voyage to "the Indies," Queen Isabella of Castille hocked her jewels, and we know the rest.

When the Great Admiral reached his destination he found no great riches, just simple natives agog at these white guys coming ashore.

The Portuguese had better luck. Vasco da Gama landed on the southwest coast of India in 1498. Thereafter, for twenty-five years Portugal held control of the spice monopoly.

This didn't deter the Spanish, nor the English, French, or the Dutch, from staking claims in the New World. There were lands to be conquered, heathens to be converted, and, not the least, gold to be found. Spices were okay, but the loot mattered more.

Pope Alexander VI Borgia, being a reasonable fellow, figured that there was enough plunder to go around—at least for the big boys. In 1494 he settled the matter of imperial rights to unclaimed territories by drawing a line from north to south through the Atlantic. Spain and Portugal hit the jackpot. Spain got all the new lands west of the line and Portugal all those east of the line.

The age of exploration was underway. The New World never yielded the great amount of Eastern spices that had propelled the exploration. But it would contribute new foodstuffs and ingredients that were to change the diet of the Old World. Such staples as tomatoes, pineapples, green peppers, red peppers, lima beans, potatoes, chocolate, tapioca, papayas, sweet potatoes, as chili peppers, and corn were to transform a pedestrian diet into something new to behold.

But the Old World gave something back in return. The Spanish brought to the New World chickpeas, wheat, barley, and sugarcane, as well as cattle and pigs. A few decades later the British were to introduce many of the same foods to North America.

Exploration was coupled with rising nationalism and imperial rivalries. Europe became aware, as never before, about national identity. The new foods helped to deepen and separate the individual characteristics of each country. An ethnocentric outlook took hold. Each country was viewed in light of its cuisine. And human nature being what it is, it became fashionable to praise your native cooking and dismiss everybody else's. As the Venetian ambassador to Paris pointedly commented about the French in 1577: "They ruin their stomachs and bowels by eating too much, as the Germans and Poles do by drinking too much."

One British traveler's complaints about Italian food began with the table-cloth: "The table-cloth is taken off neither here nor in France; nor, I believe, in any part of the continent: —their tables are made of the commonest wood, and are always dirty; —our tables are both handsome and clean, so we may use our pleasure." But, to this disgruntled traveler, the table setting was the least of it: "Butter, you will sometimes see as a side dish: it is a rarity, oil being commonly used in their kitchens. Raw ham, Bologna, sausages, figs, and melons are eaten at the first course. Salt meat, unless it be hams or tongues, is totally unknown. No boiled leg of pork and pease pudding. No bubble and squeak . . . In short, you must not expect good cookery in a country where all the servants are cooks."

Despite the grousing, in some cases, European cuisines did have a lot in common. Today we think of French cooking as being par excellence. But it wasn't always so. Up until 1533 French food had been stuck in the monotonous norm common to all Europe. It still was a throwback to its medieval heritage. Then it was contracted that Catherine de Medici of Florence would marry the French dauphin, the heir to the French throne. When she departed she took her entire kitchen staff with her, including her chefs and pastry cooks. A new style of cooking was introduced to the country with the addition of such Italian novelties as sherbet, quenelles, zabaglione, ices, and pasta. She even introduced the use of forks to the uncouth French. There is no historical evidence of the fact, but it is claimed that she also introduced spinach to the French court. To honor her birthplace, anything that henceforth contained spinach—especially with eggs, fish, or white meat—was referred to as "a la Florentine."

Later on, at the end of the century, it was Marie de Medici's turn to cement a political alliance when she was betrothed to Henry IV of France. Her kitchen staff introduced to the country such foodstuffs as artichokes, broccoli, and savoy cabbages.

The French learned quickly, adapting the Italian cooking style and, in time, developing their own. By the mid-seventeenth century French cooking had come of age, with sauces made from meat drippings, the choicest cuts of meat, vegetables cooked as a separate dish, and such delicacies as truffles and artichokes.

The Italians had led the way out of the morass of the medieval table with its reliance on sauces and whatever was available in order to hide what was on the plate. Spices had always been scarce in medieval Italy and even by the Renaissance they still remained a rare commodity. When Constantinople fell to the Turks in 1453, and three years later Athens followed suit, the eastern Mediterranean was closed off to trade. The Italians had to make do with what they had; and they adapted well. Their menu simplified, eschewing the heavy use of spices and relying on native edibles—sausage, fowl, fruit, cheese. A simplified menu meant a simplified presentation, accentuating the natural flavor of the dish.

Today, Italian cooking, especially Southern Italian, is know for its pasta. Marco Polo aside, it is probable that pasta may have been introduced to Italy as early as the eleventh century. Remember that Venice, Florence, and Genoa had been trading with the Arab world, which already had a history of eating noodles. Once established in these cities, it is conceivable that the product spread throughout Italy. By the sixteenth century it had become synonymous with Italian cuisine. Throughout Europe the most common name for pasta was *macaroni*, and this applied to the tubular as well as the flat type. In the eighteenth century it became a term of derision when English dandies were called *macaronis* because of their gaudy attire and hairdoes. So where did the word *spaghetti* come from? (What we use to call pasta back in the old days.) It derives from *spago*, the Italian word for string.

In Spain, by the time of the Renaissance, cooking had been transformed due to two major influences: the Arabs and the New World. From the New World they got two items that were to become staples of Spanish cuisine: the tomato and the capsicum—the large mild variety otherwise known as the pimento. The Arabs introduced the Spaniards to rice, a food that was to become an integral part of Iberian cooking. The Arabs were mutton eaters, and this led to an increase of sheep farming in Spain. They also gave the Spaniards a taste for sweetmeats, especially the almond-based ones such as nougat and marzipan.

There was another product from the New World that was to hook the Spaniards, and eventually Europe and the rest of the world. This was chocolate. All you chocoholics out there have the Spanish to thank—by way of the Aztecs in Mexico who made chocolate by roasting cocoa beans over a fire, then pounding them into a paste. Little cakes of this paste were mixed with water in a gourd until they frothed. The drink, *chocolatl*, was relished by the Aztecs, and then the Conquistadors. It is said that in 1519 Emperor Montezuma served *chocolatl* to Hernando Cortez and his lieutenants. After the conquest of Mexico the drink and method of production was exported to Spain—where it became the rage. Spain held most of the overseas colonies where the cacao tree grew. And for over a hundred years they zealously guarded both the production and consumption of this delicious drink, keeping it a secret from the rest of Europe. Chocolate was consumed mainly as a drink for almost three hundred years in Europe. It wasn't until the early nineteenth century that it was mass-produced into the solid eating block form of today. By the end of the sixteenth century, sugar was being added to the chocolate, and by the early seventeenth century the chocolate paste was being exported to Flanders and Italy. By this time Spanish monks had let out the secret as to how to process cocoa beans, and by 1659 the new drink was established in France. Two years before, the first chocolate house had opened in Great Britain.

France, Italy, and Spain led the way, establishing their own cuisines. The rest of Europe followed suit, with nation-states establishing their own culinary tastes. The principalities that were to become Germany relied on pork (especially sausage), cabbage, lentils, rye bread, and beer. Poland's diet consisted of veal, fermented milk, and pickled cabbage. Hungary was occupied by the Turks for most of the sixteenth and seventeenth centuries, and this foreign incursion was reflected in their cuisine in two major ways—the Turks introduced maize and the common red pepper (which furnished the condiment known as cayenne pepper). In Russia, the contrast between rich and poor was the most stark. The rich ate well: the Czarist court mimicked anything that was French by sending their cooks to France to learn about haute cuisine or by importing French cooks. The poor subsisted on black bread, boiled cabbage, and kasha (buckwheat groats cooked in water to make a porridge).

The Dutch delved early into the exploration game via their East India Company. As a result they complimented their fatty diet with all kinds of exotic fruits such as peaches, plums, cherries, oranges, and lemons. The English table consisted of boiled salted beef, mutton, fowl, pigs, rabbits, and pigeons. Some things never change.

Something else spilled over the culinary borders: distilled spirits. By the sixteenth century almost every country in northern Europe had begun to distill its own variant. First it was alcohol distilled from wine and later, distilled ales. In Germany distilled wine became known as *brandewin*. To the English this became *brandy*. The French had their wines, but they also had cognac made from the wines of the Charante. The Low Countries had their akvavit from fermented grains; and in England it was gin, derived from juniper berries. In Ireland and Scotland they had distilled a magic elixir from golden grains of malted barley, peat smoke, and rich brown water. The result was enshrined in the Gaelic *uisge beatha* (water of life). In time, the abbreviated *uisge* became *whisky*.

LIMONIA

This recipe is from an anonymous manuscript containing two different recipes sections, Book A and Book B. Published at the end of the fourteenth century or the beginning of the fifteenth, it was titled *Anonymous Southerner (Anonimo Meridionale)*, because the author used southern Italian expressions, especially those from Naples. Limonia, is from Book A, which contains 164 recipes. Limonia was a popular dish in medieval and Renaissance Italy. Different recipe collections term it *lumonia*, *limonia*, or *limonea*. It may have made its way to Europe via the Arab world. Arab texts as far back as the thirteenth century have recipes for *laymuwiya*, which are very similar to the one given here.

According to the *Anonymous Southerner*, to make Limonia, all one has to do is brown chicken in lard together with chopped onions and almonds. Stir in more pork lard and spices, and cook. Add lemon juice when it's done, and serve. This sounds very much like modern day chicken piccata, although I've never heard of almonds being added to it. In the original recipe, lard would give it the flavor. These days, olive oil is a healthier alternative.

I like this dish served over steamed rice.

2 to 3 tablespoons olive oil
1½ pounds boneless chicken thighs, cut into 1-inch cubes
Juice of one small lemon
¼ cup blanched almonds*
2 tablespoons butter
Salt and ground black pepper to taste

1. In a large skillet, heat the olive oil. Add the chicken cubes and cook until lightly browned. Reduce the heat to low and cook, covered, for a minute or two.

2. Using a wooden spoon, stir in the lemon juice and almonds. Stir well to dissolve brown particles in the bottom of the pan. Add the butter, blending it well into the sauce.
3. Season with salt and pepper, and serve.

Yield: 4 servings

*To blanch almonds, simply drop the shelled almonds (with their brown skin) into boiling water to cover. Boil exactly 1 minute. Drain. Press the almonds between your fingers until the almonds slip out of their skins, and pat dry.

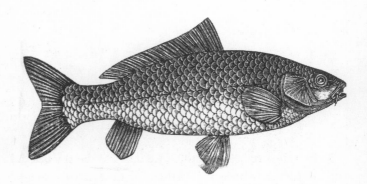

THE PHARAOH'S FEAST

POACHED STURGEON

Martino Rossi, nee Martino da Como, nee Martino de Rubeis, nee Giovanni Rosselli, was also known as Maestro Martino (Martino the Master), presumably because of his cooking prowess as shown in his four manuscripts known as *Libro de Arte Coquinaria*. This is an extremely important book in the history of cuisine. For once the recipes are somewhat precise and well organized. The book gained wide currency, printed in Latin in 1475, then in Italian, French, and English. It was a popular treatise well into the 1700s.

In this fish recipe, Martino suggests poaching a whole sturgeon in a pot large enough to hold it. "Any fish is better when it is cooked whole, rather than in pieces or in any other way."

Martino also gives a whole slew of sauces that could accompany the poached fish. I've suggested one here but feel free to use whatever sauce you desire.

The recipe calls for sturgeon but any good whole fish will do—like sea bass, striped bass, whitefish, etc.

> *1½ cups dry white wine*
> *½ cup water*
> *Salt to taste*
> *1 sturgeon (about 3 pounds), cleaned and scaled but left whole*
> *3 tablespoons butter, softened*
> *3 tablespoons flour*
> *Juice of one lemon*

1. In a large fish cooker, poacher, or Dutch oven, bring the wine, water and salt to a boil. Add the fish and simmer, covered, over low heat for about 15 to 18 minutes, or until the fish flakes easily when tested with a fork.
2. Very gently transfer the fish to a serving platter.
3. Strain the cooking liquid into a saucepan.
4. Blend the butter and flour. Bring the liquid to a boil and add the butter mixture, bit by bit, stirring constantly. When thickened and smooth, add the lemon juice and serve with the fish.

YIELD: 4 SERVINGS

ZABAGLIONE

In his magnum opus, Martino Rossi describes a dessert comprised of egg yolks, sugar, cinnamon, and sweetish wine. He calls it *Zabaglione* (roughly translated: eggnog). Today, Zabaglione is one of Italy's most famous desserts. Rossi says that the Zabaglione should be served when "it soils the spoon" (translation: when it is so thick it sticks to the spoon). Modern Zabaglione is made just prior to serving, usually in a copper sauce pot, and should be served immediately after it has thickened.

6 egg yolks
1 cup sugar
½ teaspoon cinnamon
¼ cup marsala wine
1 tablespoon white wine

1. Mix all of the ingredients in the top of a double boiler. Cook over boiling water, beating the mixture constantly until it warms and thickens.
2. Remove from the heat and continue beating until the mixture is fluffy. Serve in a serving bowl or individual cups. The Zabaglione, though thickened, should be soft, smooth, and light. One may have to add more or less sugar and/or wine depending on the consistency desired, some prefer it heavier, some prefer it lighter.

YIELD: 4 SERVINGS

NOTE: In some quarters, modern day Zabaglione is served over Italian macaroons (*amaretti*). Simply crumble the macaroons in the bottom of a serving bowl and pour the Zabaglione on top.

DUXELLES

Pierre Francois de la Verenne is recognized as the first great French chef of the modern era. He was the first to codify the Franco-Italian cuisine that had evolved from Catherine de Medici's famous trip. His cookbook, *Le Cuisinier Francois,* was published in 1650, and it is regarded as a landmark in the history of European cuisine. He was the first to describe stuffed mushrooms and Duxelles—finely chopped mushrooms cooked in butter with shallots and wine. Duxelle can be added to sauces and vegetables, and also makes a good filling for omelets, fish, or meat dishes.

> *1 stick butter*
> *2 pounds fresh mushrooms, washed, drained, and finely chopped (stems and caps included)*
> *2 shallots, finely chopped*
> *Salt and ground black pepper to taste*

1. In a medium saucepan or skillet, melt the butter over low heat (being careful not to burn it). Add the mushrooms and shallots, and cook over low heat, stirring constantly until the mushrooms give up their liquid and are black in color. Add more butter as needed.
2. Season with salt and pepper.

   YIELD: ABOUT 4 CUPS

   NOTE: Italians make Duxelles a little differently. If you prefer the Italian style, add 1 teaspoon of lemon juice to the shallots and mushrooms and cook 4 to 5 minutes over moderate heat. Add 3 ounces of diced boiled ham, cook 5 minutes more, add ¼ cup dry Madeira wine or brandy. Stir to mix until heated through.

SAUCE POIVRADE

La Varenne was one of the first to get away from the heavily spiced, thick, meat-and-almond sauces of his predecessors. He preferred simpler mixtures using vinegar, lemon juice, or stock. Sauce Poivrade is one of his creations: a peppercorn sauce made with beef stock, vinegar, onions, and carrots. Serve over any good beef or pork roast.

8 whole black peppercorns
3 tablespoons unsalted butter
1 small onion, peeled and finely chopped
1 carrot, peeled and finely chopped
2 cups beef stock
¼ cup cider vinegar

1. In a mortar, crush the peppercorns. Set aside.
2. In a heavy skillet or saucepan, heat the butter, add the onion and carrot, and cook over moderate heat until the vegetables are soft.
3. Add the stock and vinegar. Simmer, covered, on low heat for 10 minutes.
4. Stir in the crushed peppercorns and simmer for 10 minutes more. Strain the sauce through a fine sieve set over a bowl.

Yield: about 2 cups

CAPON ARMADO

In the mid fifteenth century Ruperto de Nola published his *Libre del Coch* or *Libro de Guisados, manjares y potages* (*Book of Stews, Foods, and Broths*). This book was re-edited several times during the sixteenth century with editions being published up to 1520. It gives us a snapshot of what well-to-do Spaniards were eating.

A popular dish in Europe at the time was capon. De Nola has a recipe for Capon Armado. It's basically capon or any large chicken roasted with bacon, then covered with an egg yolk sauce studded with pine nuts and almonds. I found you have to make the egg yolk sauce very thick so that the pine nuts and almonds will stick to it when roasting the capon.

1 6- to 7-pound capon or roasting chicken
Salt and freshly ground black pepper to taste
6 to 7 strips thin bacon
4 egg yolks
2 tablespoons sugar
¼ cup finely chopped flat-leafed parsley
¼ cup blanched almonds
½ cup pine nuts (pignoli nuts)

1. Preheat the oven to 350 degrees.
2. Remove the giblets and neck from the capon. Set aside for other use. Wash the capon under cold running water, drain well, and pat dry with paper towels. Season the capon inside and out with salt and pepper.
3. Arrange the bacon slices on top of the capon, using toothpicks to hold them in place, if necessary.
4. Place the capon in a greased roasting pan, and roast for one hour.
5. Meanwhile, combine the egg yolks, sugar, and parsley in a bowl, and beat with a whisk or wooden spoon until thickened. Stir in the almonds and pine nuts.

6. Remove the capon from the oven. Let it cool somewhat, and pat on the sauce so that as many almonds and pine nuts as possible stick to the bird.
7. Put the capon back in the oven and cook 1 hour longer.
8. Remove the capon and let it stand 10 to15 minutes before carving.

Yield: 6 to 8 servings

THE PHARAOH'S FEAST

IPOCRAS

Ipocras (or hiprocras) was a popular drink from the Middle Ages onward. It was a mixture of wine, cinnamon, sugar, and ginger. In some recipes nutmeg and galingale were also added. In the 1529 edition of his book, Ruperto de Nola gives this recipe for the drink.

> 1½ cups dry red wine
> 1½ cups dry white wine
> 1 teaspoon powdered cinnamon
> ½ teaspoon powdered cloves
> ⅛ teaspoon powdered ginger
> 2 tablespoons sugar (or more to taste)

1. Combine all of the ingredients in an enameled or heat-proof glass pot.
2. Bring slowly to a boil.
3. Once it starts boiling, remove from the heat. Strain though a cloth sieve set over a bowl. Serve at room temperature, or slightly cool, in mugs or (if you want to be fancy about it) wine glasses.

YIELD: ABOUT 2 CUPS

Vinegar Garlic Beef

The *Ein New Kochbuck* was published in Frankfurt in 1581. It's author, Marx Rumpolts, was one prolific guy when it came to recipes. In his section on preparing birds and game birds, he includes recipes for eagle, ostrich, swan, crane, peacock, snipe, woodpecker, turtledove, nightingale, magpie, swallow, not to mention the usual duck, goose, and turkey. For mutton alone he has forty-five recipes including ram testicles (yes, *ram testicles*).

His beef recipes are more traditional. He has eighty-three of them including this vinegar (or vinegary) garlic beef dish. This recipe requires a beef roast. I've tried the dish with boneless chuck as well as a bottom round of beef and tasted no perceptible difference in the finished product. So, if you're frugal like yours truly, then go with the boneless chuck. If coins are no problem, then go with the round roast.

Rumpolts adds that this dish is a good meal for Hungarian and Polish gentlemen.

1 bottom round roast of beef, or boneless chuck (4 pounds), well trimmed
½ teaspoon salt
1¼ cups water
1¼ cups white wine vinegar
8 whole black peppercorns, crushed in a mortar
½ stick butter

1. Place the beef in a bowl. Combine ¼ teaspoon of salt with the water and vinegar, and pour over the beef. Cover tightly and refrigerate overnight.
2. The next day, preheat the oven to 350 degrees. Drain the meat and reserve the marinade. Sprinkle the rest of the salt over the beef, place in a greased roasting pan, and roast for 3 hours or until tender, basting occasionally with marinade.
3. Remove the meat from the oven. Cover it with foil to keep it warm. Strain the marinade into a saucepan. Add the crushed peppercorns and butter. Slowly bring to a boil and cook for 1 to 2 minutes.
4. To serve, carve the meat and pour half of the marinade sauce over it. Serve the remaining sauce separately, if desired.

Yield: 4 to 6 servings

THE BEST PANCAKES

One of the earliest household cookery books was Gervase Markham's *The English Hus-wife*. It's exact title is *The English Hus-wife. Containing the inward and outward virtues which ought to be in a compleat woman; As her skill in Physicke, Cookery, Banqueting-stuffe, Distillation, perfumes, Wooll, Hemp, Flax, Dayries, Brewing, Baking, and all the other things belonging to an household.* Markham, a male, is editor and author of this noble work. He sought to acquaint middle-class and poorer ladies with the finer points of maintaining a household, not only in terms of cooking but in dairy work, spinning, weaving, dying, and even brewing and distilling. It was a popular work not only in England but in the American colonies as well. The recipes are very straightforward: no measurements, just general instructions. It was assumed the lady in question would know what she was doing. Markham has a recipe for making the "best pancakes"—which consists pretty much of eggs (with a "pretty quantity of running water"), cloves, mace, and wheat flour.

3 eggs, beaten
2 cups water
¼ teaspoon ground cloves
⅛ teaspoon ground mace
⅛ teaspoon ground cinnamon
⅛ teaspoon ground nutmeg
½ teaspoon salt
Whole wheat flour (1 cup or more)
5 tablespoons sweet butter
Light brown sugar to taste

1. Combine the eggs and water in a large bowl and beat together.
2. Add the cloves, mace, cinnamon, nutmeg, and season with salt. Add the flour and stir together, making the mix as thick as desired. The batter should remain somewhat lumpy.

3. Melt the butter in a griddle or cast-iron skillet. Using a ¼-cup ladle, pour the batter onto the griddle or skillet. Cook until bubbles appear on top, about 2 to 3 minutes. Turn over and cook 2 to 3 minutes on the other side. Serve immediately with brown sugar sprinkled on top.

YIELD: 4 SERVINGS

NOTE: The recipe states to "make it as thick as you think with fine wheat flower, then fry the Cakes as thin as may be with sweet butter." The amount of flour to use is a judgment call. If a thinner batter is desired, use less flour. If thicker, use more.

RICE PUDDING

The English Hus-wife suggests the following to make rice pudding: First soak the rice in milk overnight. Drain and boil with heavy cream. Then put in half a dozen eggs, pepper, cloves, dates, currants, sugar and salt, and a "great store of beef suet well beaten." Boil the whole thing and serve after a "day old."

I tried it, and it didn't work. The thing tasted awful. Thus I've modified the recipe somewhat, hoping to stay as close to the original as is possible.

½ cup uncooked white rice
2 cups milk
2½ cups water
½ teaspoon sugar
⅛ teaspoon salt
1½ cups heavy cream
1 egg, beaten
Dash of ground cloves
Dash of ground mace
1 tablespoon finely chopped dried currents
1 tablespoon finely chopped dried pitted dates

1. Place the rice and milk in a mixing bowl, cover tightly, and refrigerate overnight.
2. The next day, drain the rice and discard the milk. Combine the rice, water, sugar, and salt on top of a double boiler and place the pan directly on the heat. Bring to a boil, cover, and simmer until the water is absorbed and the rice is tender (about 40 minutes).
3. Add the cream, egg, cloves, mace, currents, and dates. Stir to mix well. Place the pan over simmering water and cook, stirring until the rice is thick and creamy (about 10 minutes). Serve warm or chilled.

Yield: 8 servings

Vegetable Tempura

Although the age of exploration may have centered on the New World, culinarilly, its crosscurrents were felt far and wide. The Portuguese were avid explorers and they were among the first to trade with the little known lands of the east. It wasn't just America that held their interest. They wanted worldwide commerce. It was in pursuit of this goal that in the sixteenth century Portuguese merchants inadvertently introduced to Japan two dishes that were to become among their best known. One of these was sukiyaki, probably the only dish known to America and the West prior to World War Two. The other was tempura—batter-dipped, deep-fried pieces of fish or vegetables. The Japanese observed that the Portuguese ate deep-fried dishes, usually seafood or vegetables during the Catholic holy days, the *Quattour Tempora*. In Japan, both sukiyaki and tempura were regarded as foreign dishes for over a hundred years. Only gradually were they to be accepted at the dinner table. By the eighteenth century the Japanese had adopted both as part of their national cuisine.

1 egg
1 cup cold water
1 cup all-purpose flour
Peanut or vegetable oil for deep frying
Vegetables for cooking: Any variety that is available—string beans, green
pepper, zucchini, mushrooms, eggplant, potato, etc., all cut into thin
strips. If using onion, peel and slice into thick rings. If using broccoli,
separate the florets.

1. Beat the egg in a medium-sized bowl. Add the cold water and flour, and mix. It is imperative that the water be ice cold to prevent the batter from absorbing too much oil. It also keeps the flour from getting sticky. Blend thoroughly but do not overmix.
2. Heat at least 1 inch of oil in a deep thick pan or wok. The oil should heat to between 340 to 350 degrees. To test the temperature, let a drop of water fall into the oil. If it sizzles, the oil is hot for frying. Another test is to drop a bit of batter into the oil. If the batter floats up right away instead of sinking to the bottom, the oil is hot.

3. Using tongs, a fondue fork, or chopsticks, dip the vegetables, a few at a time, in the batter, and drop into the hot oil. Fry until golden brown. Be aware that vegetables will cook rather quickly. Remove the vegetables with a slotted spoon and drain on paper towels.
4. Repeat, working in small batches, until all the vegetables are cooked. Serve with tempura dipping sauce (see page 154).

YIELD: ABOUT 4 SERVINGS

NOTE: To make Shrimp Tempura, prepare the batter as per instructions. Take one pound of fresh large shrimp and rinse under cold running water. Make a couple of incisions on the stomach side of each shrimp so that it remains straight. Deep fry as you would the vegetables.

TEMPURA DIPPING SAUCE

2 cups dashi soup stock*
¼ cup sake or dry sherry
2 tablespoons soy sauce
½ teaspoon sugar
1 tablespoon chopped scallions
2 to 3 tablespoons wasabi (Japanese horseradish)*

1. Mix all of the ingredients except the wasabi in a saucepan.
2. Bring to a boil on high heat.
3. Remove from the heat and serve at room temperature, along with the wasabi, in individual dipping bowls as dipping sauces with the vegetable tempura.

YIELD: 4 SERVINGS

*Dashi soup stock is a broth made with dried bonito tuna and seaweed. It's usually known as dashi no moto *and comes in a tea. All you do is boil the dashi in water for 2 to 3 minutes and use as directed. It is available in Asian and health food stores. Wasabi is a prepared radish condiment also found in Asian stores. As with the old saying, "Just a little dab will do ya," since it's hot and piquant.*

TEN

THE AMERICAS

GUACAMOLE, TAMALES DE VEGETALES,
AZTEC FRUIT CUP, POMME DE TERRE
A LA LYONNAISE, GERMAN POTATO SALAD,
CORN PONE, ROASTED VENISON

When Spanish explorers first came upon the peoples of the Caribbean, they were both fascinated and repelled by what the natives cooked and ate. They were bedazzled by the abundance of fruit, fish, and fowl; and some foods, like sweet potatoes, ground nuts, and root plants, they immediately accepted and enjoyed. Some other foodstuffs, like spiders and "white worms that breed in rotten wood, and other decayed objects," did not go down so well. Even the domesticated dog was considered a food item by the island tribes.

But two staples in particular were to capture the Spanish and, eventually, the European palate. One was cassava, the other was maize—what came to be known in North America first as *Indian corn*, and then simply, *corn*.

In the Antilles, cassava bread was made by peeling manioc root, grating it, pressing out the poisonous juices (it is a poisonous plant), sifting the pulp that was left, shaping it into flat bread, and cooking it on a hot plate. The bread could be hung up to dry and would keep for up to three years—a real convenience, especially on long voyages

That other great staple, maize, was boiled, roasted, or ground into flour. The Spanish took maize seeds back to the Old World, and soon thereafter it was grown throughout the Mediterranean. From Europe it was introduced to the Near East and Asia

The Portuguese get the credit for introducing manioc and maize into Africa during the sixteenth century. In an ironic twist, maize was a tool for the burgeoning slave trade of the period—it was stored as food in the slave ships.

From the Caribbean the Spanish spread northward, going their merry way, conquering and pillaging and, eventually, they hit upon Mexico in 1519. "We will embark upon the conquest of a new world" —or something to that affect, is the last line in a 1940s movie epic, *Captain from Castille*, starring Tyrone Power as a Spanish nobleman during the conquest of Mexico, and Caesar Romero as Hernando Cortez. I bring up this piece of trivia if only to underscore the mind-set of the time. Had Cortez and his crew spent more time savoring the tortillas, bean dishes, tomatoes, and tamales enjoyed by the Aztecs, things might have gone better for all concerned

In some ways Aztec cooking was way ahead of Spanish cooking. Bernal Diaz del Castillo, a Spanish soldier, noted the elegant dishes "cooked in their native style" that were served to King Montezuma in a typical dinner: "They cooked more than three hundred plates of food the great Montezuma was going to eat . . . pheasants, local partridges, quail . . . wild boar, marsh birds, pigeons . . . His servants brought him every kind of fruit that grew in the country . . . (and) two handsome women served Montezuma . . . with maize cakes kneaded with egg. . . .These maize cakes were very white and were brought in on plates covered with clean napkins." Diaz states that King Montezuma ended his meal with a frothing cup of chocolate brought to him in a cup made of pure gold

The Aztec diet consisted mainly of corn, tomatoes, beans, and peppers—the large sweet type and the smaller hot chili pepper. From chili pepper we get Tabasco sauce. We are also familiar with the dried hot chili pepper, and its powdered form (cayenne pepper). Pepper was used in everything. The Aztecs had at least forty varieties, and they incorporated them into soups, stews, meat, and fish

Corn was the main ingredient in tortillas and tamales. Dried kernels were boiled and the skin removed by rubbing with the fingers. A stone roller was used to crush the kernels, which formed a paste that was kneaded into a dough. This was shaped into thin cakes and cooked on a type of griddle called a *comalli*. The same tortilla dough could be stuffed with beans, tomatoes, meat, or fish. This was then wrapped in casings of cornhusks or leaves, and steamed. Once cooked, the cornhusks or leaves were removed and, voila, you had a tamale.

For breakfast there was boiled corn, which was cooked until it became a coarse porridge similar to cornmeal. This porridge was sweetened with honey or, if you were more adventurous, spiced with some red peppers

For some reason, dinner was at the hottest time of the day, sometime in the afternoon. Here, a bean dish might be added for variety. Beans were boiled, or combined with tomatoes and chili peppers. Initially Spaniards considered tomatoes to be weeds in the cornfields. Once they discovered the uses that the Aztecs derived from both ripe and unripe tomatoes, they became more interested in the lowly fruit. They took it back to Europe, where it was first known as "the Golden Apple" (because this type of tomato had a yellow color).

The meat consumed by the Aztecs consisted mainly of wild game—rabbit, hare, deer, duck. And little dogs.

Along with domesticated animals, the Aztecs seemed to enjoy certain other exotics that would turn the stomach of a European. They dined on insects such as the agave worm, a plump little critter also known as the maguey slug, and regarded as a delicacy in Montezuma's court. They also relished tadpoles, water fleas, winged ants, water larvae, white worms, and a peculiar type of newt called *axolotls*.

Apart from the dog, the other domesticated animal used for food was the turkey—which was regarded as the more superior of the two. It was not unusual in some meat dishes to put the cooked turkey on top and the cooked dog underneath. Also, this increased the meat quotient in the dish.

The dog no longer graces a banquet table in the Americas—it disappeared as an entrée once Europeans introduced cattle to the New World. The turkey is another story. The Spanish introduced it to Europe sometime in 1523-24. Here we get into the name game. In Italy it was known as the *galle d'India*. In Germany it was called *indianische Henn*. The French preferred *coq d'Inde* (Indian cock). By now you've probably guessed why all the *India* references. Remember, Columbus claimed to have discovered the "Spanish Indies." It was only natural to assume that the bird came from India. Besides, who could pronounce the Aztec word for it, *uexolotl?*

The English took it further by simplifying the whole concept. The fowl was brought to England shortly after its arrival in Europe. It was sold by merchants from Turkey whose stops along the eastern Mediterranean included the port of Seville. To the English these were "turkie-birds" they were buying. Eventually shortened, particularly in North America, to the simple *turkey*.

Turkeys, dogs, fat worms—to a certain extent a hard bitten conquistador might understand that to the Aztecs this was considered great eating. What they could not comprehend was Aztec ritual cannibalism. Mind you, the Spanish conquistadors were not Boy Scouts. They were as vicious and as bloodthirsty as anyone else during the era, in some cases, more so (witness the Inquisition). But to Europeans, cannibalism was way over the line. It's one thing to kill an opponent, even a heathen. It's another thing to eat him.

That's what the Aztecs did. A ritual sacrifice was made to the sun god. Captured prisoners from other tribes were used as the offering. The heart of the chosen victim was torn from his chest by a flint knife while he was still alive. Then the poor wretch was beheaded, the skull hung on a rack, and the body cooked into *tlacatlaolli*, or corn-and-man stew, which was served at a banquet to the family that had captured the prisoner. The nobles and the priests always got the choicest cuts from the body, say, the thigh. If the victim was a worthy opponent who had shown his strength in battle, then the banqueters got an added incentive since it was believed that you acquired your adversary's strength when you consumed his flesh.

So, further inflamed by such pagan behavior, the Spanish set about purging the Aztec empire and bringing them civilization. They did it with a pronounced Christian zeal. Within a generation almost all of the native people had been wiped out.

The Incas of Peru were considered more civilized since they frowned on eating dog and did not practice ritual cannibalism. It didn't matter. Francisco Pizarro was the counterpart to Cortez in Mexico. The Inca kingdom was rich in loot: temples lined with gold, precious stones everywhere—and rapacious conquistadors ready to pounce.

In the end, it wasn't the gold or the wealth of Peru that would have a lasting affect on Europe. It would be an insignificant little plant called the potato.

Like the Aztecs, the Inca diet was replete with corn, tomatoes, beans, and chili peppers. They also had squash, peanuts, cassava, and other tubers such as quinoa. In the mountain waters of Lake Titicaca, there were fish. The animals used for food were deer, llamas, bears, pumas, foxes, even guinea pigs and ducks. If you couldn't get a hold of wild game, then you could always try catching *vizcacha*, a large rodent native to the area. The Incas in the lowland valleys ate corn, which they prepared by grinding the dried kernels and boiling them into a porridge. But high in the Andes, above eleven thousand feet, corn would not grow. Instead, they ate *chuñu*, the dried potatoes of the Peruvian highlands, which the Spaniards called a "dainty dish." The Inca would spread a potato crop on the ground and leave it overnight in the cold air. The next day, all moisture was pressed out of the potato. The process was repeated for about five days. After drying in the sun to remove excess water content, the potatoes were stored. They could be cooked in a variety of ways and were popular with the locals.

Potatoes became the basic food for the slave workers in the Peruvian mines, and the main provision on the vessels carrying Peru's wealth back to Spain. From Spain the plant made its way to Italy, and then England. In 1586 Sir Francis Drake probably collected potatoes as supplies on the Columbian coast and carried them to English colonists in Virginia.

It took a while for the potato to be accepted in certain parts of Europe. Well into the eighteenth century the French thought the potato was poisonous. The Swiss thought it was responsible for such ailments as scrofula.

It wasn't until the 1800s that potatoes gained currency throughout most of Europe and cookbooks appeared with such recipes as Welsh rarebit and mashed potatoes.

The Spanish popularized another cooking technique from the Americas. In the north of Hispaniola, the cannibalistic Carib Indians were reputed to have cooked meat (whether human or not is open to question) over a frame of green wood. The Caribs called this process *boucan*. The Spaniards did the same with the pigs and cattle they had brought to the island. They called the greenwood frame a *barbacoa*. Today we know this as *barbecue*.

The Spaniards weren't the only ones exploiting the wealth, culinary and otherwise, of the New World. The Portuguese were no slouches in that area either. And they took advantage of whatever opportunities came their way. When the most Holy Pope Alexander VI Gorgia proposed the compromise with regard to who got what territories in the New World (see page 134), by a throw of the dice, Portugal won Brazil. Brazil was rich in sugarcane, and sugar production became a very profitable endeavor, especially when combined with the slave trade. When sugarcane juice is boiled, it produces molasses, which in turn is reduced to sugar crystals. The traditional European sweetener had been honey. But honey was time-consuming to produce and demand outweighed supply. Sugar, which became plentiful thanks to the proliferation of sugar plantations in the Americas, soon replaced honey. The European desire for sugar continued to grow, particularly when they discovered it could be used in making jam as a preservative for fruit.

In the fifteenth century, another Holy Pope, Nicholas V, condoned slavery when he exhorted Europeans to "attack, subject, and reduce to perpetual slavery the Saracens, pagans and other enemies of Christ southward from Capes Bajador and Non, including the coast of Guinea." It was on the west coast of Africa where the Portuguese plied the slave trade. Here they picked up African slaves that were shipped back to the sugarcane fields of Brazil.

This was a mutually profitable relationship, not only to the Portuguese but to the Arab merchants and African kings who were more then happy to sell their kinsmen into slavery in exchange for firearms, hardware, and rum.

Soon the Dutch, English, and French got into the trade when they began setting up sugar plantations on their own island possessions in the Caribbean.

Why the need for African slaves? Simple. Most of the native peoples had been decimated, which led to a labor shortage. It was thought that the

African workers could better endure the tropical heat and moisture. Prior to 1600 there were fewer than a million black slaves in the Americas. By the eighteenth century the figure had reached 7 million.

The Portuguese were to profit from another crop: coffee. It originated in Ethiopia but was to have a lasting effect on the world, old and new. As a beverage, coffee had been popular in the Near East since at least the fifteenth century. Its popularity spread from Aden to Mecca, then to Cairo, then to Damascus and, finally, Aleppo. From there it passed on to Constantinople, which had the honor of establishing the first coffee house in 1554.

The origin of the word, *coffee*, has been plausibly traced to *Kaffa*, one of the districts of the south Abyssinian highlands in Ethiopia, which seem to have been the original habitat of the coffee plant (*Coffea arabica*).

Coffee was imported by Italy in the sixteenth century, and by England in the seventeenth, where the first English coffee house appeared in Oxford in 1650. The stimulating new drink captivated the English. Soon, coffeehouses sprang up all over the country. As they did in Europe: Marseilles opened its first coffeehouse in 1671; and Paris the following year. The café had been born.

At first, the merchants of the Near East controlled the trade; and the English and Dutch East India Company got their supplies from them. This soon changed when in the 1700s the Dutch discovered that they could grow coffee beans in Java, and then in Ceylon. The English began growing their beans in the West Indies. The Portuguese discovered they could do the same in Brazil. The Spanish followed suit in Colombia. Fate intervened: a form of plant disease known as coffee rust appeared in Ceylon in 1870. This blight spread to Southeast Asia and by the end of the nineteenth century almost all the coffee plantations were gone. These areas started growing rubber and tea instead, and Brazil and Colombia became the main producers of coffee. In a roundabout way, coffee had made its way from Africa, to Asia, to Europe, to the Americas, and back.

In the early days of exploration, it was believed that a northwest passage could be discovered leading to the Pacific, and from there to the Spice Islands to the East. No such passage existed. In 1496 the English did discover the great cod-fishing banks off the coast of Newfoundland. The vast fishing fleets that grew out of this venture were to become indispensable to what would later be known as the New England colonies.

As early as the sixteenth century the English attempted to establish settlements in Virginia, without much luck. In 1607 they tried again with a settlement at Jamestown. This settlement would have perished were it not for the help of friendly North American Indians. The same would have applied to the gaggle of Pilgrims who landed on Plymouth Rock in 1620. The new land they settled was rich in venison, canvasback duck, wild geese, fish, and oysters. The Indians taught them how to grow maize and cook it in such variations as hominy, for which the grains were hulled and ground into a coarse consistency ("grits"), and succotash, which featured dried and fresh kernels cooked with beans.

European settlers began to import domesticated animals as soon as possible, and cattle and pigs added variety to a diet dominated by venison. Pork was so prolific that it became a mainstay of the diet, especially in Virginia. The North American Indians did get something from the settlers—they acquired a taste for pork.

The discovery of the Americas is synonymous with the Age of Exploration. Which brings up another topic: what did they eat during the ocean voyages? A passage from Europe to the Americas could take ten weeks or longer depending upon wind and crosscurrents. You needed enough food and water to sustain captain and crew. But you also needed storage space for guns and cargo. The solution was early "convenience foods" such as salted beef and pork, dried peas and hardtack, also called ship's biscuit—a dough baked and dried to such hardness that it could last for up to fifty years. As the voyage wore on, the hardtack became infested with weevils and other worms—which, oddly enough, helped because the perforations made by the weevils made it possible to chew the thing.

A sailor's diet mainly consisted of half-cooked salted pork and the hardtack. The only fire allowed aboard a wooden ship was in the cook's galley. This was alright when the weather was fine, but when the ship hit a storm or a squall, the fire had to be extinguished. Even in the best of times there wasn't much a ship's cook could do with oversalted meat and little fresh water to soak out the excess. There were no spices or seasonings, so you had salty and starchy food. Because the diet conspicuously lacked fruits and vegetables, the greatest threat to health and well-being was scurvy, and many a sailor died from it.

The best remedy against this disease is the vitamin C found in greens and citrus fruits. But it wasn't until the eighteenth century that the British Admiralty decreed that a fixed amount of lemon juice should be given to each sailor in order to combat scurvy. The lemon juice was mixed with the seamen's traditional rum ration. In 1795 this "grog" became a mix of rum, lemon juice, and water—too many men on duty were found "groggy" from the rum and lemon juice. In the mid-nineteenth century lime juice was substituted for the lemon juice. And American sailors, never missing an opportunity to razz their British counterparts, began calling them *limeys*.

GUACAMOLE

Among the many Aztec foods that intrigued the Spaniards was a pear-shaped pulpy fruit that rendered a tasty dish that was often served with the fat agave worm. The dish has come down to us as guacamole. The fruit is the avocado, also known as alligator pear. The Aztecs made guacamole with avocados, tomatoes, and peppers. Today guacamole is renowned as a snack, appetizer, and dip—and it is no longer served with a fat worm. For the health conscious it is good to note that, although high in fat, the avocado is also rich in protein and A and B vitamins.

In my family we prefer the Caribbean or Mexican avocados, the large ones with smooth green skin and texture, as opposed to the Haas avocado, which is smaller, darker, and has a rougher skin texture. Some say that the Haas has a better taste, others swear by the Caribbean variety. Use the one you like best, and serve it with corn chips or slices of jicama.

2 large ripe avocados
Juice of one lemon
1 medium-sized ripe tomato, finely chopped
1 clove garlic, peeled and minced*
1 fresh jalapeno chili, seeded and finely chopped
Salt to taste

1. There are two ways to peel the avocado. In the Caribbean the method is to cut the avocado into slices about ½-inch thick, peel the slices, cut them into chunks, and mash in a mortar (*pilon*) with a pestle. The Mexican method is to halve the avocados, scoop out the flesh, and mash in their version of a mortar and pestle (a *molcajete* and *tejolete*). If you don't own a mortar just scoop the avocado flesh into a bowl and mash with a fork.
2. Add the lemon juice, tomato, garlic, jalapeno, and salt. Mix till desired consistency. Serve immediately.

Yield: 2 to 2 1/2 cups

*If you prefer, you can omit the garlic and use 1 small red onion, peeled and diced.

Tamales de Vegetales

The Aztecs usually served tamales on special occasions. They complemented well the plain tortillas they ate almost daily. Today, many fillings are used to stuff a tamale, from pork to beef to fish. This version has a vegetable filling.

⅓ cup Crisco shortening
¾ teaspoon salt
1½ cups masa harina mix (cornmeal mix)
1 cup water
3 tablespoons olive oil
1 medium Spanish red onion, peeled and chopped
1 green bell pepper, chopped
1 red bell pepper, chopped
¼ jalapeno chili, seeded and chopped
2 cloves garlic, peeled and finely minced
1 medium ripe tomato, coarsely chopped
1 cup corn nibblets, drained
Salt and black ground pepper to taste
12 corn husks, fresh or dried
Kitchen string

1. In a large bowl, beat the shortening and salt until fluffy. Gradually beat in the masa harina mix alternately with the water until the mixture is light and fluffy. Set aside.
2. Heat the olive oil in a medium-sized pan or skillet. Add the onion, bell peppers, jalapeno, and garlic. Sauté on medium heat until the onion is translucent. Add the tomato and corn and season with salt and pepper. Cook for about 4 minutes. Set aside.

3. If using fresh corn husks, spread one husk at a time on a flat surface. If using dried corn husks, separate and soak in a sink filled with warm water for 15 minutes. Drain, pat dry, and spread on a flat surface. Using a tablespoon dipped in water, spread 2 tablespoons of corn dough in the center of each husk, forming a rectangle and spreading evenly. Spoon 1 tablespoon of the vegetable mixture in the center of the rectangle. Fold into a cylinder, then fold both sides as close to the center as possible. Tie with string.

4. Place the tamales in a closed steamer and steam in an upright position for 1 hour. If no steamer is available then you can use a 4-quart pot or Dutch oven with a 2-inch rack above gently boiling water. Arrange the tamales on top, cover with a lid, and steam.

5. The tamales are done when they are firm. To serve, cut the string and simply unfold the husk on a plate.

YIELD: 12 TAMALES

AZTEC FRUIT CUP

What would the Aztecs have eaten for dessert? Did they even have a dessert course? According to the Spanish sources, we know that when Montezuma was feasting, one of the courses included "every kind of fruit that grew in the country." In the Americas, fresh fruit abounded—there were papaya, mango, guava, pineapple, tamarind, and many other delectables. I can visualize an Aztec chieftain enjoying a cup of assorted fresh fruit.

2 mangoes, pitted, peeled, and sliced
1 ripe papaya, peeled, seeded, and cut into chunks
½ fresh pineapple, pared and cut into long wedges

1. Mix or layer the fruit into four dessert dishes or cups. The fruit can be served at room temperature or chilled.

Pomme de Terre
a la Lyonnaise

As noted, the lowly potato had long been a staple in the New World. Success in Old World France came at the beginning of the nineteenth century when pioneering chefs and gourmets finally convinced the gallic public that spuds were not harmful and were, in fact, a good nosh. Among these advocates was Antoine Viard who, in his *Le Cuisinier Impérial*, noted several potato recipes. The recipe given here is from *The Art of French Cookery* by Antoine Beauvilliers, another French lover of the spud.

> 1 ¼ *pounds potatoes*
> ⅓ *cup flour (or more as needed)*
> 3 *tablespoons vegetable oil*
> 3 *tablespoons butter*
> *Salt to taste*

1. Peel the potatoes, wash under cold running water, and pat dry with paper towels.
2. Slice into ⅛-inch rounds. Sprinkle evenly with flour.
3. In a large skillet, heat the oil and, when hot, add the butter.
4. Add the potatoes and cook, tossing and stirring, until soft and brown (20 to 25 minutes).
5. Remove from the heat. Drain on paper towels, sprinkle with salt, and serve in a very hot dish.

YIELD: 3 TO 4 SERVINGS

GERMAN POTATO SALAD

In the Pomeranian town of Kolberg in 1774 the citizens were starving due to famine. Frederick the Great of Prussia took action by sending the worthy citizens a wagonload of potatoes. They wouldn't touch them. They thought potatoes were poisonous.

Perceptions would change. By 1814 Beauvilliers included in his works a recipe for *maschepotetesse* (mashed potatoes). The Germans would develop a fondness for the tuber, and they would extol it in such dishes as German Potato Salad.

The recipe is supplied by Mrs. Virginia McDonagh, the spouse of one of the gang of give, Mr. Henry McDonagh. The recipe has been in her family for ages. And I included it here because it's a very old recipe, easy to make, and very tasty. Mrs. McDonagh insists that the recipe include a raw egg. That, and vinegar, is what gives it its unique flavor. Most of us are hesitant to use raw eggs in a recipe due to the possibility of salmonella. Although she has no scientific evidence to back it up, Ginger McDonagh swears that the vinegar counteracts whatever harmful agents are in the egg. If you're still bothered by it, then use one of the egg substitutes now on the market, the type that people use to prevent high cholesterol.

1½ pounds potatoes, either California white or waxy red potatoes
1 medium onion, peeled and thinly sliced
1 egg, lightly beaten, or equivalent egg substitute
2 tablespoons olive oil or vegetable oil
¼ cup white vinegar
Salt and black ground pepper to taste

1. Boil the potatoes in water until fork tender. Let cool, peel, and thinly slice.
2. Put the potatoes in a bowl, add the onion, egg, oil, vinegar, salt, and pepper. Toss well, cover and let it marinate overnight in the refrigerator.

YIELD: 4 SERVINGS

CORN PONE

Hominy and succotash were not the only grain foods of the early English settlers in Virginia. Another was "corn pone," a thick corn flat bread cooked over an open fire or on a griddle. Why is it called corn pone? One theory has it that among the several Algonquian words that found their way into the English language (including tomahawk and hominy) was *pone*—as in corn pone.

> *3 tablespoons Crisco shortening*
> *3 cups yellow cornmeal (preferably stone ground)*
> *2½ to 3 cups boiling water*
> *3 teaspoons salt or to taste*

1. Preheat oven to 350 degrees.
2. Melt the shortening over low heat in a 10-inch cast-iron skillet or baking pan. Swirl the fat to make sure it coats the entire pan or skillet.
3. In a large bowl combine the melted shortening with the cornmeal, boiling water, and salt. Stir to mix well. Transfer the cornmeal mixture back into a skillet or pan. Place in the oven and bake for about 50 minutes or until golden brown.

Yield: 6 to 8 servings

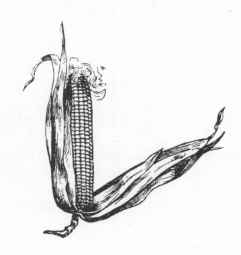

THE PHARAOH'S FEAST

ROASTED VENISON

No one holiday has influenced us more, as to what it is to be an American, than Thanksgiving. I was told by Ms. Robinette back in P.S. 81 that the first Thanksgiving feast was celebrated by the Pilgrims in Plymouth in 1621. They shared their bounty with all, including Native American guests. They had survived one harsh winter in the North American wilderness and gave thanks to God's favorable providence. Since that time we Americans have set aside this day to give thanks for all we hold dear and celebrate accordingly in glorious gluttonous wonder. And the holiday has spread beyond our shores—to the U.S. Virgin Islands and Puerto Rico, where it's called *El Dia de Acción de Gracia* (the day of giving grace).

It is my favorite holiday.

Still, fact and fiction converge in this singular event. What the pilgrims were most likely celebrating was a traditional autumn harvest festival, as was commonly done back in England. Once the harvest was in, the locals in a manor or village held a community-wide feast with whatever food was available. Historians say that the Pilgrims engaged in three days of feasting and festivities following the harvest at Plymouth. This was sometime between September 21 and November 9. I question this. And I have no basis other than a hunch. Would upright Puritan types have indulged in a celebration that lasted three days and invited non-Christian types like North American Indians? Even those who taught them how to grow corn and pick edible berries? We do know that Abraham Lincoln declared Thanksgiving a national holiday in 1863 after the Union victory at Gettysburg. Some of my southern friends claim it wasn't celebrated in the South until late in the nineteenth century. Whether it was a traditional English harvest celebration or whether the colonist invited Chief Massasoit of the Wampanoags and Chief Samoset of the Pemaquids and some of their tribesmen is beside the point. The event, and the celebration, has become part of the American psyche.

So, what was served at the "first Thanksgiving"? Historians can't agree, and most aren't sure. There is agreement that there would have been venison and wild fowl, since these were abundant in the New World, as well as fish, squash, beans, fruits, some sort of berries, and corn. No mashed potatoes, no apple cider, no gravy, no stuffing, no onions, and no pumpkin pie (though they probably served boiled pumpkin). Add to that, no ice cream, milk, butter, or cheese, since there were no cows aboard the Mayflower—

and probably no forks since the settlers, like most Europeans of the time, ate with knives and spoons. They probably ate from wooden plates and used large cloth napkins for wiping their hands and also picking up hot food.

What about the turkey with all the trimmings? Guess what, there probably weren't any at the Pilgrim's bash. In the 1600s *turkey* meant any bird with a featherless head. This could be anything from guinea fowl to pheasant, and even wild turkey. Ever try to cook a wild turkey? From acquaintances who have tried it, they say that the meat is so tough it cannot be roasted, and even after hours of boiling, it still comes out like stringy shoe leather. No doubt the Pilgrim fathers would ask themselves, Why serve this when you have all those great ducks and geese around?

It's safe to assume that a roasted venison dish like this one was served at the meal. This dish comes from the venerable cookbook, *The English Huswife*. Pilgrim housewives would most likely have known how to cook venison from experience back in their homeland.

In the recipe, the author says to stick the venison roast with cloves, smear it with mutton lard, roast in "a smoking fire," and then make a gravy with vinegar, bread crumbs, sugar, cinnamon, ginger, and salt. I've made one change—I've substituted olive oil for the mutton lard.

1 boneless venison roast, about 4 ½ pounds, tied with string
Olive oil
1 tablespoon whole cloves or more to taste
½ cup bread crumbs (or more depending upon desired consistency)
½ teaspoon sugar
¼ teaspoon ground cinnamon
¼ teaspoon ground ginger
Salt to taste

1. Preheat the oven to 425 degrees.
2. Rub the venison roast generously with olive oil.
3. Stud the meat with whole cloves all over the outside.
4. Place the roast, uncovered, in the oven and bake for 30 minutes. Turn once during roasting. The meat should have a golden brown color.
5. Reduce the heat to 350 degrees and continue roasting, basting occasionally. For medium rare it should be about 15 minutes more. Longer for well-done. To be on the safe side, insert a quick-reading

meat thermometer in the thickest part: 125 degrees for rare and 140 for well-done.

6. Remove the meat, cover with foil, and keep warm.
7. Discard all but 1½ cups of the drippings from the pan. Place in a medium saucepan, add bread crumbs, and cook over low heat, stirring constantly until the gravy has thickened. Season with sugar, cinnamon, ginger, and salt.
8. Serve the venison sliced, with the gravy.

Yield: 8 to 10 servings

Note: Some prefer to cook the gravy directly with the drippings in the baking pan. In that case, discard all but the needed amount of fat, add the bread crumbs, stir to thickened over low heat, and add seasonings.

ELEVEN

THE COOKING WORLD EXPANDS

MATAMBRE, JAMBALAYA, INDIAN PUDDING,
JOHNNYCAKE (OR HOE CAKE), INDIAN SLAPJACK,
RUM PUNCH, MINT JULEP

The first English settlers to North America had to adapt quickly to the vagaries of the New World. And this included a whole new way of cooking. Their English heritage was reflected in their culinary tastes. But this soon changed. Luckily, they were in a new land rich in fish, fur, timber, and produce. In time they would develop their own modes of speech, dress, behavior—and cooking style.

At first, the original thirteen colonies mirrored their English past. The colonial elite, north and south (inclusive of a good crosssection of the founding fathers), had their servants, their fine china, silverware, imported wines, soups, cheeses, white loaf sugar, coffee, and tea.

A prosperous eastern farmer with a large stable of farm hands could boast a similar lifestyle. The merchants and tradesmen of the eastern seaboard, even though most may not have had the luxury of servants or slaves, lived comfortably enough to get by in the cities.

The poorer farmer had a more demanding time of it. The crops had to be planted, the fields had to be tilled, livestock fed, and cows milked. Once the harvest was in, the family had to prepare for the winter by pickling and preserving food. The smokehouse had to be stocked with game and meat. Dried corn, potatoes, beans, apples, and squash had to be stored in the root cellar.

This lifestyle called for hardy simple fare. And usually, the farm wife didn't have many ingredients to work with. No refined table sugar here. Most likely she sweetened her pies and cakes with molasses and seasoned her stews with maple syrup and rock salt. The colonial elite may have eaten fine breads. The colonial farm wife fed her family cooked cornmeal mush. The only fish or fresh meat included what her husband or children could catch or hunt. Yet even if she had a well-stocked larder, preparation of the victuals was not easy. If her husband raised poultry, the farm wife had to kill the bird, pluck the feathers, and gut it. Fresh caught fish had to be scaled and cleaned. If she was fortunate in having some green coffee, this had to be roasted and ground. If she had flour, she could make bread. But if she added other ingredients such as nuts or raisins, then the nuts had to be shelled and the raisins seeded.

For the housewife, whether on the farm or in the city, the cooking tools left a lot to be desired. The fireplace was still the main conveyance for cooking food; and it was not until around 1728 that cast-iron stoves were sold in quantity in America. In Europe more sophisticated stoves were available earlier. Records show that a brick-and-tile stove was made in Alsace, France, as early as 1490. Early Swiss stoves were made of clay or brick, but without chimneys, and were built against an outer house wall with an opening to the outside through which smoke could escape. Early cast-iron stoves appeared in Europe in the late fifteenth century. They consisted of cast-iron plates that were grooved and fitted together in the shape of a box. In America, as elsewhere, the stove was regarded as an adjunct to the fireplace. It was simply a hollow stone square next to the fireplace with a stovepipe that led into the fireplace chimney. Swedish, Dutch, and German immigrants to New Jersey, Delaware, and Pennsylvania brought with them five-plate iron stoves (also called wall-jamb stoves). Though of German design, they were known as Dutch (from the German word for *German*, which is *Deutsch*) stoves, or less frequently, carved stoves since some had iron castings with highly decorative or artistic designs. Some of the new settlers also brought molds for casting the stoves, and as early as 1724, iron foundries began making the stoves en masse.

Early cast-iron stoves were difficult to use. Fueled with either coal or wood, the housewife had to set paper and kindling inside the stove, light the fire, and keep it going. Since there was nothing to regulate the stove's temperature (there were no thermostats), she had to keep an eye on the fire all day long. If the fire ebbed, then more fuel had to be added. Once the meal was cooked, the ashes from the old fire had to be removed. Then she had to gather all the ashes and cinders in a grate in the ash box and dump them into a pan. To cook another dinner she had to start the process all over again.

Cleaning the contraption was just as bad. She had to rub the stove with thick black wax to keep it from rusting. Worse, the soot and smoke from the stove blackened walls and stained drapes and carpets, which had to be cleaned by hand. In addition, the floors had to be scrubbed and the rugs had to be beaten. It was quite a Herculean task. Unless the housewife had servants, it was she and her daughters who did this grunt work.

Five-plate stoves were superseded by six-plate (or close stoves); and Benjamin Franklin improved on the overall design by inventing the Franklin stove (or Pennsylvania fireplace) in 1743. This was an iron stove that was used for heating. It was actually an improvement on the fireplace since it consisted of a downdraft iron fireplace set into or in front of the chimney.

Five- and six-plate stoves continued to be made until Revolutionary times. Around 1760, the English or ten-plate stove made its appearance.

This stove stood free of the wall and was larger than the six-plate version since it had four more plates that formed an oven and two hinged doors. It had openings on either side and smoke passed from around the oven and out a pipe. This stove could cook and warm at the same time. The added feature of an oven meant you could bake and cook inside the house, eliminating the need for a large masonry baking oven, which was usually situated outside.

For the majority, especially the poor farmer, the fireplace, or something close to it, remained the chief cooking device. It wasn't until the middle of the nineteenth century that the fireplace was replaced as the prime medium for cooking food.

But the farmer and his family had other things to worry about besides cooking their meals. What happened if the soil was poor or, worse, they lost the farm? Then they pulled up stakes and went in search of land. And this is what happened, especially after the Revolutionary War, when a new vision led countless thousands to settle a continent.

It took grit to venture into uncharted territory. The first to go west were the explorers and trackers. They had to travel light because their journeys were mainly on foot. If they were lucky, they might own a horse or a mule. If not, they were their own beasts of burden. Trekking up mountain trails and snow covered passes required sustenance that was portable, lightweight, and nourishing. Otherwise, food was scarce. Even if they encountered friendly Native American tribes, their food was strange to the European palate, as noted by this observer who tells how the Blackfeet Indians cooked a "few feet of a certain entrail" from the buffalo: "This Nat-ah-ki washed thoroughly and then stuffed with finely chopped tenderloin, and stuffed it in such a manner that the inside of the entrail became the outside, and consequently the rich fat was encased with the meat. Both ends of the case were then securely tied, and the long sausage-thing placed on coals to roast, the cook constantly turning and moving it around to prevent it burning. After about twenty minutes on the coals, it was dropped into a pot of boiling water for five or ten minutes more, and was then ready to serve. . . . The Blackfeet call this Crow entrail, as they learned from that tribe how to prepare and cook the dish."

When they could no longer rely on cooked buffalo entrails, possum, raccoon, and bear, they had to come up with something fast. That's where pemmican came in. *Pemmican* comes from the Cree Indian word for *fat*. It was well suited for a chilly northern climate. Preparation consisted of slicing lean meat from a large game animal, say a deer or elk, drying it over a fire or leaving it out in the sun. The meat was then pounded, shredded, and mixed with an equal amount of melted fat. For additional flavor, bone marrow and a few handfuls of wild cherries were added. Finally, the whole thing was packed in rawhide bags that were sewn up and sealed with tallow. Many a fur trader and explorer crossed the North American continent with pemmican as the basic provision. Its high fat content supplied the warmth and energy needed for an arduous journey.

Those who followed had to learn how to cook on the trail, as it were. You could live off the fat of the land for just so long. If you were crossing a vast desert or braving the frozen north then you stocked up on dried corn, salted and preserved meats, and, if you were fortunate to have them, a couple of containers of potted meat heavily sealed with fat.

Sheer necessity dictates innovation. That is why a few "portable" items came into being. One of these was "pocket soup." The next time you use a bouillon cube in a recipe, think of pocket soup, the bouillon cube's precursor. It was made from a stock cooked from veal or meat trimmings and pig's trotters. The stock was left out in the cold where it developed the consistency of solid glue. All that was required was to cut out a piece and let it dissolve in hot water to make a bowl of soup. What was good about pocket soup was that, like hardtack, it kept for years.

Another preferred item on the trail was the johnnycake (or jonnycake), which was nothing more than a dried cornmeal pancake. There are two theories on how the name *johnnycake* came about. It could be a distortion of *journey cake*, or the word hails from the Native American *Shawnee-cake*.

As the westward migration progressed, American cooking began to reflect the diverse cuisines brought over from other regions and countries. The new pioneers from Europe brought with them a taste of home and adapted their native cooking to reflect the new foodstuffs and ingredients available. This is one of the glories of what can be called "American cooking." We absorb and borrow from many sources and make it our own. The English brought us apple pie. From the French we got the fish dish *chaudier*—which became *chowder*. The Germans gave us sauerbraten and sauerkraut. The Dutch introduced us to *koolsla*—coleslaw. And what would an American breakfast be without that European specialty, waffles? The Swedes introduced us to meatballs. Black slaves on the Southern plantations gave us one of my favorites: "soul food." This was nothing more than the leftovers from the master's table: black-eye peas, ham hocks, turnip greens, and chitlins (*chitterlings*—for the more formal among us). A renowned delicacy (but not for everyone) made from the small intestines of a pig.

This amalgam came to be reflected in regional specialties: Boston baked beans, buffalo wings, Philly pepper pot, spoon bread, hush puppies, New Orleans jambalaya, Maryland chicken, country beans, Texas barbecue, New England hot toddy, and on and on . . .

Eighteenth-century America had another unique trait—it was a nation of drinkers. Never before or since have we been such inveterate imbibers. Why this was so is hard to say. Too much salt meat and fish? A lack of fresh water within human habitation? Yes, it was a nation of great rivers and streams. But once settlements and cities followed, the water could sometimes become undrinkable. The early colonists, as soon as they got here, had begun experimenting with fermented drinks. Pseudobeers were made from pumpkins and persimmons. The apple orchards of New England gave rise to apple cider and apple brandy. For the more hardy there was the highly potent applejack. Dutch and German immigrants began growing hops and barley in Pennsylvania.

By the eighteenth century, America was awash in booze. It had become a tradition, both social and even political. No less a personage than George Washington, when he first ran for the Virginia House of Burgesses in 1758, made sure to distribute among the voters seventy-five gallons of rum. It was the House of Burgesses that later sent him to the Continental Congress.

One could say liquor was the great equalizer. The colonial elite might sip their imported Madeira wine, toasting with cut crystal glass. The common man enjoyed his strong dark rum out of a mug at the local tavern. His wife might enjoy a bowl of rum punch at home. Upper-class preferences aside, rum was *the* drink of the ordinary masses in the American colonies prior to the Revolution. It is estimated that, before 1775, Americans were guzzling about 12 million gallons a year—that's four gallons per person. The best we can do today is 1.25 gallons a year per person for all liquors combined.

Needless to say, rum was a thriving business in the colonies, specifically with regard to the slave trade. This was that profitable triangular route where New England ship owners sailed with a cargo of rum to Africa. On the Slave

Coast they exchanged the rum for African slaves, who were taken back to the West Indies and sold to the plantation owners. The West Indies, being rich in sugarcane, provided molasses—the prime ingredient in making rum. Here the ship owners picked up a load of molasses to replace the slave cargo. The molasses was transported back to New England where it was distilled into rum. The sale of rum provided the capital for the next trip and the whole cycle started again.

What cut into rum's dominance was the American Revolution. In grade school we learned about the Boston Tea Party, during which a group of patriots dumped the British tea into Boston Harbor to protest a tax on tea. Some would argue that the tea tax was a mere sideline. The final break with the mother country was most likely due to the Molasses Act of 1733. This legislation imposed a heavy tax on sugar and molasses coming from anywhere other than the British islands in the Caribbean. New England merchants did not take kindly to any restrictions on the purchase of molasses. Not only did it impede the cycle of trade, but it also imperiled the rum supply.

During the Revolutionary War the British imposed an embargo on American goods, including molasses. Americans had to look elsewhere for their liquor supply. Scot and Irish settlers started experimenting with whisky distilling, but one prime ingredient was missing: peat. American whisky tasted nothing like the unblended whiskies from Ireland and Scotland, with their aromatic peat smoke and brown water. They developed their own version, rye whisky. But what set the standard was to follow at the end of the eighteenth century when corn-based Kentucky bourbon came on the scene.

Elsewhere, in Central and South America, the Spanish conquest had been completed. Now Spanish sheep and cattle roamed from Mexico to the east of the Andes. The criollo aristocracy that had arisen from the descendents of the Spanish conquistadors led very privileged lives, especially in the cities. They endeavored to maintain all the comforts of their former European homes, with good meat and good drink, horses to ride, draft animals to work their land, and European tutors to teach their children.

Wide open pastures for the free-range cattle made for prize-winning livestock. And ranchers took advantage of it, especially toward the southern part of the continent. One threat to the cattle breeders and owners came from that class of vagrants known as the gaucho. Today, especially in Argentina, this cowhand has been mythologized as much as the cowboy has been in the United States. The original gauchos were nothing more than cattle rustlers who preyed on the ranchers and farmers. They were part Spanish and part South American Indian. They roamed as mounted nomads, working outside of the law when it suited them, and subsisting on the cattle they stole. A far cry from Valentino strutting around in chaps with riding whip and ornate hat.

The indigenous people who survived the Spanish conquest found themselves on the bottom rung of the socioeconomic ladder. They cooked their food as they had for generations either over a communal fire, a clay hole in the ground inside their hut, or an outdoor stove made of stone. But at least they had sheep and beef to eat.

They also had *charqui*, which was to South America what pemmican was to North America. *Charqui* was a portable convenience food that may have originated in Peru. Initially it was a method of preserving game. When cattle came on the scene, beef was used. Made by cutting boned and defatted beef into thin slices and rubbing them with salt or dipping them in a strong brine solution, the meat was rolled up in cowhide and set aside for ten to twelve hours. This allowed the salt to be absorbed and some of the juices to be released. The meat was hung in the sun to dry and tied up in bundles that made it easy to carry. To eat it, they pounded the *charqui* between two stones and boiled it in hot water.

Charqui was a good food to carry on long journeys. It was perfect for the land traveler since it kept for long periods of time. The closest thing to it today would be jerked beef.

The other thing that kept a South American Indian going, especially in a harsh environment, was the coca leaf. Coca contains cocaine, a strong narcotic. The South American Indians would chew it mixed together with a small amount of ground lime. Its affect was to lessen fatigue and reduce hunger. It also made it easier to breathe at high altitudes—something that would go a long way in the Andean mountains. As one observer put it: "They say that chewing this leaf gives them strength and vigor, and such is the superstition and faith that they have in it that they cannot work or go on trips without having it in their mouths. And, on the contrary, having it, they work happily and walk a day or two without refreshing themselves otherwise or eating anything other than what they swallow of the saliva brought on by chewing the leaves."

This addiction to chewing coca became an integral part of South American Indian culture. Today we know that a steady diet of cocaine is not good for the bodily system. It can kill you.

Mutton and beef, particularly beef, would become the dominant meat consumed in South America. Outdoors it would be roasted on an open fire. People would tear off chunks and enjoy. This was not always that appetizing—as described by a European traveler to the Argentine pampas: "The pampas are so destitute of wood, that it is not thought of as fuel; the principal material, therefore, used as such is cow-dung, round which bones are laid, to keep it together, in a heap. The latter, indeed, do not burn—they serve to concentrate the heat; but they smell: and on this material, with its loathsome affluvia, another bone, with some flesh on it, is laid, and broiled; and if the gaucho is particularly disposed towards you, he takes the bone from the fire, knocks the cinders off his leg, tears off a morsal with his own teeth, to see whether if it well done; and you, as a polite gentleman say, with a sickly smile: 'Muchas gracias Senor'; and being indeed, as hungry as the most wretched cur, make your meal of it."

MATAMBRE

Gaucho cooking still fascinates the Argentines. Today they eat such dishes as gaucho steak and gaucho stuffed rib-eye steak. Gaucho cooking aside, one of the Argentine beef dishes that intrigues me is Matambre. Argentinians love this dish. It goes back a long way. The term *matambre* means "kill hunger" (or "hunger-killer") in Spanish. It is basically a stuffed beef roll.

A favorite drink served with this dish, or almost any Argentine dinner, is *yerba mata*, derived from the leaves of the *yerba* plant, an evergreen shrub related to holly. It is a drink similar to tea and is traditionally served as *yerba mate cebado*, where water is poured over the leaves in a gourd (*mate*). The leaves expand to fill the gourd and you sip the drink through a straw with a strainer made of silver (*bombilla*). *Yerba mata* is also popular as an aperitif.

1 large flank steak, about 2 pounds, butterflied (or see below)
½ cup red wine vinegar
2 cloves garlic, peeled and finely chopped
3 branches of fresh thyme or 1 teaspoon dried
1 bunch fresh spinach, washed, drained, and trimmed of stems
3 carrots, peeled and thinly sliced lengthwise
3 hard-boiled eggs, cut into quarters lengthwise
1 large onion, thinly sliced in rings
¼ cup fresh parsley, finely chopped
1 teaspoon cayenne pepper
1 teaspoon sea salt
3 cups beef broth or stock

1. If you don't have access to a butcher who can butterfly the flank steak, you can do it yourself. First, wash the meat under cold running water and pat dry with paper towels. Next, slice the steak horizontally to within ½-inch of the opposite side. Pound the steak between sheets of plastic wrap to flatten to about a ¼-inch thick. Trim all fat and sinew from the meat.
2. Place the steak, folded open, in a shallow dish. Combine the vinegar, garlic, and thyme in a bowl and pour over the meat. Cover and refrigerate for 6 hours, turning over once or twice.

3. Remove the meat from the marinade. Spread the spinach leaves evenly over the meat. Lay the carrots across the grain of the meat in rows **about** 3-inches apart. Place the egg quarters between the rows of carrots. Scatter the onion rings over the eggs and carrots. Sprinkle with parsley, cayenne pepper, and salt.
4. Preheat the oven to 375 degrees.
5. Carefully roll up the meat with the grain, jelly roll fashion. Tie the meat with kitchen string at 3-inch intervals, or secure with toothpicks.
6. Place the meat in a large roasting pan, casserole, or Dutch oven and pour the beef stock over and around it. Cover the pan with a lid or seal it tightly with foil and bake for one hour.
7. Remove the beef roll from the oven and place on a cutting board. Let rest for ten minutes. With a sharp knife remove the strings and cut the roll into ¼-inch slices. Transfer to a heated platter and serve, moistened with a little of the roasting pan liquid. This dish can also be served cold. In this case the meat is pressed under weights until the juices **drain off. The weight** could be anything as simple as a cutting board **with a big** book on top of it. The meat is then refrigerated and served as an hors d'oeuvre, cut into thin slices.

YIELD: 8 TO 10 SERVINGS

THE PHARAOH'S FEAST

JAMBALAYA

Jambalaya is a Cajun/Creole dish that originated in Louisiana. When I first encountered it, paella, the Spanish rice, chicken, and seafood dish, came to mind. Jambalaya has the same combination of meat and rice. The only difference is in the seafood: most recipes include shrimp. Could the dish have originated from the Spanish influence in Louisiana? Perhaps. There is a dispute as to which stock to use in the cooking. New Orleans Creole-style "red" jambalaya uses both tomatoes and chicken stock. Plain chicken stock is common in Cajun-style "brown" jambalaya.

We've opted for the tomatoes and chicken stock.

> *2 tablespoons olive oil*
> *1 medium-sized onion, finely chopped*
> *2 stalks celery, trimmed and finely chopped*
> *1 green bell pepper (pimento), seeded and finely chopped*
> *3 cloves garlic, peeled and minced*
> *1 10-ounce boneless chicken breast, diced*
> *10 ounces chorizo sausage, sliced into ¼-inch rounds (can substitute any smoked sausage such as andouille or chaurice)*
> *2 cups diced tomatoes*
> *½ teaspoon cayenne pepper*
> *½ teaspoon freshly ground black pepper*
> *½ teaspoon oregano*
> *2 cups long-grained rice, washed and soaked in cold water*
> *4 cups chicken stock*
> *2 bay leaves*
> *Salt to taste*
> *½ pound shrimp, boiled and peeled*

1. In a large saucepan or Dutch oven, heat the olive oil over medium heat. Add the onion, celery, and green pepper. Cook, stirring occasionally, until the onions are soft and translucent. Add the garlic and cook until it browns slightly.
2. Stir in the chicken and sausage and cook for another five minutes

3. Add the tomatoes, cayenne, black pepper, and oregano. Mix well and cook, stirring to break up the tomatoes (about 5 minutes).

4. Add the rice and chicken stock, stirring constantly. Add the bay leaves and salt.

5. Cover tightly and cook over low heat for 20 minutes. Add the shrimp and cook for five minutes more. The rice is done when it is tender and all the liquid has been absorbed. The jambalaya should be moist but not soupy.

Yield: 4 to 6 servings

THE PHARAOH'S FEAST

INDIAN PUDDING

Prior to 1796, the few American housewives who had access to cookbooks would have used European books published under an American imprint. In 1796 Amelia Simmons published *American Cookery*, a genuine American cookbook. This book featured some uniquely American recipes. Among them, recipes for pumpkin pudding and spruce beer. For the first time such words as *cookie* and *slaw* appeared in print.

Amelia Simmons was a self-described "American orphan." She worked as a domestic in the colonial period, which gave her the hands-on experience in preparing a good meal, from cooking roast beef to preparing stuffing for fowl. She lays out simple guidelines that are as applicable today as they were in her time. For example, to determine the freshness of fish, poultry, or meat, go by their smell. And in general use only the freshest ingredients.

American cuisine owes a lot to Ms. Simmons. Among the dishes that made their appearance in her book are three colonial favorites: Indian Pudding, Johnnycake, and Slapjacks.

Amelia Simmons gives three recipes for "A Nice Indian Pudding." Two recipes call for baking the Indian Pudding, and one advises to boil the ingredients for twelve hours in a "brass or bell metal vessel, stone or earthen pot." The publishers, at the time the book first came out, amended the boiling time to only six hours. This is noted in an Errata (corrections section) at the end of the book, just before the glossary.

I'll stick to the baking. Today Indian Pudding is usually served with whipped cream or vanilla ice cream.

4 cups milk
½ cup yellow cornmeal
⅓ cup dark molasses
1 teaspoon salt
3 tablespoons sugar
3 tablespoons butter
1 teaspoon ground cinnamon
1 egg, beaten
½ cup raisins

1. Preheat the oven to 300 degrees.
2. In a double boiler, or heavy saucepan, bring the milk to a rolling boil over high heat. Add the cornmeal, stirring constantly for about 3 minutes. Reduce the heat to low and cook, stirring often for another 15 minutes. The cornmeal should be softened but slightly thickened.
3. Add the molasses and mix well. Remove from the heat and stir in the remaining ingredients.
4. Butter or grease an 8- to 9-inch baking dish. Pour the pudding mixture into the dish and bake for about 2 hours. The pudding should be brown on top with a dark crust in the center. The pudding can be served hot, warm, or at room temperature.

YIELD: 6 TO 8 SERVINGS

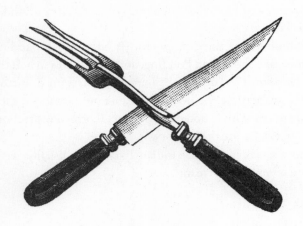

THE PHARAOH'S FEAST

Johnnycake (or Hoe Cake)

Johnnycake (Johny Cake, Johnycake, Jonnycake) is considered by **some** to be the precursor of the pancake. It is made with cornmeal, salt, boiling water, or milk. Some cooks swear by the water, others by the milk. Amelia Simmons gives both variations. Modern recipes often contain eggs, oil, and **baking** powder. The Johnnycake can either be cooked atop the stove or baked in the oven. I opted for the traditional fry-in-the-griddle method, using the boiling water rather than milk.

Serve these up with butter, maple syrup, or molasses.

> *1 cup stone ground white cornmeal (also called johnnycake meal, a rare*
> *   white flint corn found in parts of Rhode Island and Connecticut. If you*
> *   can't find it, then go with regular cornmeal.)*
> *1 teaspoon salt*
> *1 tablespoon dark molasses*
> *1¼ cups boiling water*
> *1 tablespoon butter or vegetable shortening*

1. In a large bowl, combine the cornmeal, salt, and molasses. Whisk in the boiling water and stir to make a moist but firm batter. Add a little more water if necessary but make sure the mix is smooth and thick.
2. Heat a griddle or heavy skillet (preferably cast iron) over medium heat. Add the butter or shortening to grease the pan.
3. Drop a tablespoon of batter at a time onto the griddle. Flatten them slightly with the back of a spoon or spatula and cook about 5 minutes per side. The johnnycakes should have a nice brown color, and they should be served while still hot.

Yield: 8 to 10 cakes

INDIAN SLAPJACK

In her recipe for Indian Slapjack, Amelia Simmons instructs the reader to beat together "one quart of milk, 1 pint of indian meal, 4 eggs, 4 spoons of flour, a little salt." She finishes by stating that the mix can be "baked on griddles, or fry in a dry pan, or baked in a pan which has been rub'd with suet, lard or butter."

I've modified the quantity of ingredients used. For greater authenticity, bake the slapjack in a cast-iron skillet.

2 cups milk
1 cup yellow cornmeal
2 eggs, beaten
2 tablespoons flour
½ teaspoon salt
2 tablespoons butter

1. Preheat the oven to 375 degrees.
2. In a large bowl, whisk together the milk and cornmeal.
3. Add the eggs, flour, and salt. Mix well.
4. Grease a 10-inch cast-iron skillet (or pie plate) with butter.
5. Pour the mixture into the skillet and bake for about 1 hour. Serve hot or at room temperature.

YIELD: 6 TO 8 SERVINGS

RUM PUNCH

In the American colonies, prior to the Revolution, no social function would be complete without a bowl of rum punch. But the popularity of rum was not only confined to the colonies, and the concept of the punch bowl could be taken to extremes, as shown in the following description of a rum punch bowl party in the West Indies in the eighteenth century:

"A marble basin, built in the middle of the garden especially for the occasion, served as a bowl. Into it were poured 1,200 bottles of rum, 1,200 bottles of Malaga wine, and 400 quarts of boiling water. Then 600 pounds of the best cane sugar and 200 powdered nutmegs were added. The juice of 2,600 lemons were squeezed into the liquor. Onto the surface was launched a handsome mahogany boat piloted by a boy of twelve, who rowed about a few moments, then coasted to the side and began to serve the assembled company of six hundred, which gradually drank up the ocean upon which he floated."

The recipe that follows will not serve six hundred. But it'll give you a buzz just the same.

1 cup pure maple syrup
2 cups lemon or lime juice
1 quart water
1 bottle (750 ml.) dark rum (I prefer Añejo)
Ground nutmeg

1. In a punch bowl, mix the maple syrup with the lemon or lime juice. Add the water and stir.
2. Add the rum and serve over ice in the punch bowl, with nutmeg sprinkled on top.

Yield: about 20 servings

MINT JULEP

Bourbon is America's native whisky drink. When they say "American whisky," that's what they're talking about. It is the only spirit sanctioned by an Act of Congress as being "a distinctive product of the United States." Why is it named after a French royal family? History states commercial distilling of the product began in 1798 at Georgetown, Virginia, later to be known as Kentucky. Georgetown was situated in Bourbon County, and the name has stuck. Bourbon has its roots in corn whisky, where in the eighteenth century enterprising Kentuckians were making the stuff. By the mid-nineteenth century Kentucky distillers were aging the whisky in oak barrels and developing that sweetness and softness that comes from the corn (by Federal law, Bourbon must be distilled from a mash containing at least 51 percent corn).

One bourbon drink that has come to signify southern hospitality is the Mint Julep. It's a mix of bourbon whisky, sugar, water, spearmint leaves (fresh mint sprig), and crushed ice. It can be served in a sterling silver julep cup or a tall highball glass.

Fresh mint sprigs
1 teaspoon superfine sugar
2 teaspoons water
Crushed or shaved ice
3 ounces bourbon whisky

1. Strip 10 or 12 leaves from the mint sprigs.
2. In a 12-ounce glass, dissolve the sugar with the water. Add the mint leaves and gently muddle the mixture, being careful not to break the leaves.
3. Pack the glass with crushed or shaved ice and add the bourbon. Stir gently until the glass is well frosted, adding more ice as necessary. Garnish with two sprigs of fresh mint and serve with a straw.

YIELD: 1 SERVING

TWELVE

THE INDUSTRIAL ERA

RICE CAKE, GLAZED AND ORNAMENTED,
FRAISES ROMANOFF, MULLIGATAWNY SOUP,
BEEF A LA MODE, POTATO PIE,
TOMATO OMELETTE, STUFFED EGGPLANT,
POULET A LA MARENGO,

The nineteenth century and the advent of the Industrial Revolution brought about many changes in the way we cook and prepare food. Such innovations as freezing, canning, and chilling gave more people more access to comestible products than ever before. But industry wasn't all for the good. The rise of industrial towns and massive urbanization produced major environmental problems that linger to this day and brought with it overcrowded slums and, at times, mass urban poverty. The food of the poor, both in Europe and America, still contrasted greatly with the food of the rich.

In industrialized England in the first half of the nineteenth century, the basic diet of the poor consisted of tea, bread, and potatoes; and, if there were money left over for a laborer who earned approximately sixty-two cents to five dollars a week, the family might indulge in a smattering of bacon or sausage purchased from a street stall or the local slaughterhouse. It is not what we know to be a healthy diet, but it was food on the table. In 1845 a main staple of this diet disappeared. All across Europe potato rot led to massive crop failure and famine. The British Isles were not spared, especially Ireland, where the results were catastrophic.

The Irish had come to rely on the potato mainly because it was convenient and easy to grow. A tiny plot could feed a whole family. Potatoes could be boiled, baked, or roasted, and with butter or even fatback, they constituted a meal. Once the potato famine hit, the destructive effect was unimaginable. Many died of starvation. A large proportion of those who survived would migrate to the United States.

But industrialization had another effect. It spawned a growing middle-class. Apart from common laborers who worked the factories and machine shops, there was also a need for factory foremen, clerks, managers, and administrators; investors were needed to supply the capital; bankers to supply the loans; insurers to guarantee functioning of the plant; shippers to distribute the product; engineers and architects to construct more factories. More housing was needed to accommodate the workers, which meant more schools and teachers to educate the young; more shops to sell everyday goods and more merchants to acquire stock; more policemen to safeguard the social order; more doctors and nurses to treat the sick and injured; more clergymen to minister to the faithful; and yes, more lawyers for litigation.

The middle-class did not eat as well the rich but, compared to the common laborer, they were better off. They had more disposable income, however slight, and more choices in what they could cook and eat.

This burgeoning middle-class created a growing market for goods and materials. In a sense, they were the vanguard for an expanding industrial society. Mainly they were town dwellers. They didn't have access to landed estates or farms to supply their vegetables and meats. Even the laboring class needed more food more cheaply. There was a need for quick land transport that could supply the beef and grain needed by the masses—and the railroad was one of the solutions. In the United States, the transcontinental railroads opened up the country, transporting cheap grain throughout the land. From the eastern seaboard, it was loaded onto ships bound for Europe. During the Civil War, canned food had been used by the Union Army. After the war, canned meat and vegetables were exported worldwide. In the 1880s beef from America could be shipped frozen to England. Eggs, dairy products, poultry, and fish could be packed in ice and transported across the Atlantic so that the worker in London and Manchester could avail himself of the same food as a worker in New York or Chicago.

The introduction of mass production techniques in the meat industry and agricultural sector made it possible for those in the towns to enjoy the same foods as those on the farm. Canning, freezing, and refrigerated transport meant you could cook and eat foods out of season, even tropical and subtropical items.

Mass production has its advantages. It inspires experimentation and change, which can be beneficial. But sometimes it can yield mixed results. A case in point is white bread. In the 1840s a new production method for milling flour was introduced. Iron rollers pressed grain in a new way so that the embryo or wheat germ was sieved off with the bran. This was thought to be good since oils from the germ turned the flour rancid in a few weeks. The new roller-milled flour kept for a longer time. Not only that, without the germ that gave the flour its distinctive yellowish color, it was whiter. This appealed to the growing middle-class since coarse brown bread was considered a staple of the underclass. But in discarding the wheat germ, the flour also lost its most nutritious component.

Rice is another tale in industrial experimentation and development. The thinking was, if white bread was good, so was white rice. By the end of the nineteenth century it was common to remove the outer sheath of the rice grain, so that you had "polished" or white rice. Again, the outer sheath contained the nutritious core of the rice. In a varied diet, this is no problem. But in a diet solely based on white rice, as was the case in most of Asia, this could pose a hazard. In the 1880s in the Dutch East Indies, natives who subsisted on a diet of white rice began to contract beriberi, a disease that attacks the heart, nerves, and digestive system. This was due to the fact that white rice lacked vitamins of the B complex, specifically vitamin B1.

Margarine is another mass-produced item with a long and checkered history. In the mid-nineteenth century, butter went rancid very quickly. As early as 1873, Hippolyte Mège Mouriés, a French food researcher, introduced an artificial butter product made from suet, cow's udder, and warm milk. In 1876 the Americans came out with a product of their own called butterine. In time, with the addition of vitamin concentrates, this became margarine. In the latter half of the twentieth century, this poor man's substitute for butter was touted for its health benefits as related to cholesterol. Over the past few years even margarine has taken a few shots with some proclaiming that butter may be better for you in the long run. The debate goes on.

What can we say about the quality of the cooking at this time? For the poor, not much. Living in an overcrowded slum, which normally was nothing more than a shantytown of wooden shacks or overcrowded tenements with no sanitation facilities, no running water, and no sewage system, didn't leave much time, money, or energy for the joy of cooking. The lady of the house didn't have much of a kitchen, maybe a primitive brick oven heated with coal.

The middle-class had it a little better. As early as the 1790s, Benjamin Thompson, also known as Count Rumford, had invented a closed-top stove with adjustable heat—a great innovation at the time. Adjustable heat made stewing, sautéing, and sauce preparation possible on a home range. In 1833 Jordan Mott invented the first practical coal stove. By today's standards, it would be considered primitive: a heavy cast-iron cylindrical apparatus with a hole on top, enclosed by an iron ring, complete with ventilation to burn the coal more efficiently. A Swede, Frans Wilhelm Lindqvist, came out with the first sootless kerosene stove in 1892. Unlike the solid-fuel stoves, this type was fueled with paraffin gas. By this time coal and gas heat were available in most homes, and gas stoves began to take over. Finally there was precision adjustment of heat.

Electricity brought about the next innovation: the electric stove, with patents as early as the 1890s. But it took some doing to convince people that the electric version was just as good as the gas stove, which by the early 1900s came equipped with top burners and interior ovens. It was not until the late

1920s that electric stoves became popular. To this day, some cooks still regard the electric stove with a wary eye—it is claimed that it heats too slowly, and it's difficult to adjust the heat when compared to the gas range. It's all a matter of taste and preference.

What made late nineteenth-century cooking unique was that for the first time the middle-class housewife could aspire to prepare the same dishes (within reason) as the rich or gentry. The gas range and the materials at hand made it much easier for her than for her predecessor from a generation before. Obviously, she would have a hard time preparing stuffed partridges in aspic, but she could prepare vegetables in season, scramble eggs and toast in the morning, a good hot broth at lunch, and meat, fish, or poultry, in whatever variety, at dinner. The big estates may have maintained their large kitchens and staffs with chefs on call, but the housewife (though not on par with a gourmet) could come into her own as an exemplary cook.

For the mucky-mucks in the upper crust of society, dining still involved a certain panache and pomp with its *service à la russe, service à la francaise, service à l'anglaise, service à l'Americaine,* service a la whatever.

This was the French influence with its six and eight courses and every-thing in-between. For the average household, a normal meal would be two courses and, maybe sometimes, three. No entremets, or the dainties served between courses (sweets, savories, vegetables, etc.). Yet the French influence was so pervasive that it could be found, even duplicated, in England as wit-ness one of the dinners given by King George IV when he was still Britain's Prince Regent. The meal began with four soups (going from foie gras to fish soup). Then came four fish dishes (everything from fresh water fish to sauced eel). Followed by four main dishes (*pièces de résistance*) surrounded by thirty-six entrees and five *assiettes volantes* (more side dishes like fillets of sole and fillets of wood grouse). Then came eight majestic mandatory or set pieces (some with pastry), four roasts (wild duck, chicken, hazel grouse), thirty-two entremets (truffles, lobster, pineapple cream, liqueur-flavored jelly, oysters, potatoes in Hollandaise sauce, scrambled eggs, Genoese cakes, etc.), fol-lowed by ten more *assiettes volantes* (potato soufflés and chocolate soufflés). The meal even included larks encased in toasted bread lined with a creamed chicken-liver mixture (*les petites croustades de mauviettes au gratin*).

Naturally, the meal was complimented by fine wine, liqueur, sherry, brandy, you name it.

This meal harkens back to classical French cuisine, to the great banquets given by Louis XIV, the "Sun King," and Louis XVI, the last pre-revolutionary king of France. French cooking, as my father would say, is a trip. After Louis XVI had his head chopped off, French cooking went into decline. But it re-emerged in the Napoleonic era and was supposedly more refined and elegant. This is widely attributed to Marie Antoine Carême, who in a series of books in the early nineteenth century documented all the culinary formulas and methods that went into French cooking. The meal described above was a Carême enterprise when he presided over the prince regent's kitchen. Carême had an impressive resume. At various times he was chef de cuisine to Talleyrand, Czar Alexander I, and the Rothschilds.

Carême was not the only professional chef to mark down his thoughts for posterity. Louis Eustache Audot did the same with his treatise, *Le Cuisinière de la Campagne et la Ville, ou la Nouvelle Cuisine Economique* (*The Cooker of the Countryside and the City or the New Economic Kitchen*). This book was aimed at the modest household and went through several editions up to the end of the century. My favorite among all of them is Charles Elme Francatelli, Queen Victoria's chief cook in ordinary. In 1845 he came out with *The Modern Cook*. This book was aimed at all classes and tastes. Besides recipes for such things as reindeer tongues, he also includes recipes for sheep's jowls and ox tongue with spinach. In this he was responding to the demands and needs of the middle-classe who clamored for cookbooks so they could impress their peers with the quality and variety of their table. But Francatelli went a step further. In 1861 he published *A Plain Cookery Book for the Working Classes*, which included such niceties as "Baked Bullocks Hearts," "Sheep Pluck," "Cow Meal Broth," and "Rice Gruel, a Remedy for Relaxed Bowels." He even included a section on how to brew your own beer.

A growing middle-class, fueled by the spread of industry and literacy is a good thing, especially if it leads to the publication of numerous cookbooks as occurred in the nineteenth century. Some of the cookbooks were specialized. There were cookbooks geared toward the housewife, the average working people, and even the laboring poor. But sometimes it could be carried to extremes—two cookbooks published during the siege of Paris in the Franco-Prussian War (1870-71) included recipes for cooking dogs and rats.

Rice Cake, Glazed and Ornamented

I find the recipes of Marie Antoine Carême to be daunting. Most are difficult to emulate, even in a modern kitchen. Case in point are his famous
chartreuse dishes such as *Chartreuse printuniere* (Spring Chartreuse), *Chartreuse à la parisienne, en surprise,* and *Chartruese de perdreaux,* which he called
"the queen of all entrees." These were molded dishes using an assortment of
vegetables, fowl, wild game, sausages, and a host of other stuff. His *Paris
Chartreuse* even has truffles, pullet fillets, forcemeat, and lobster tail all
baked in a cylindrical mold. I took one look at these recipes and said, No
way. It would take forever to do one of these things. But you have to give
credit to the man. His list of classic French dishes is exhaustive. With such
books as *L'art de la cuisine au dix-neuvième siècle* (*The Art of the Kitchen at the
XIX Century*) and *Le mâitre d'hôtel français* (*The Mâitre d' of the French Hotel*)
he not only discussed the preparation of the food, inclusive of ingredients,
garnishes and accessories, but he also took on such topics as the provision-
ing and organization of the kitchen. Today, Carême is regarded as the
founder of what is called *la grande cuisine Francaise,* the classic French style
of cooking, heavy on sauces, heavy on creams, heavy on decorations, heavy
on everything.

Here is a recipe of his that I can identify with, a Rice Cake Glazed and
Ornamented. I give it exactly as noted by Monsieur Carême.

Put 8 ounces of rice, boiled as usual, with the addition of a clove of
vanilla, in a semi-globular mold, buttered; then turn it on a dish, and
when cold, mask it all over with transparent apricot-marmalade.
Decorate the top and the sides, according to your fancy, with
pistachios, angelica, currants, *verjus* grapes, and preserved cherries.
Serve it up, either hot or cold.

YIELD: ABOUT 4 SERVINGS

NOTE: *Verjus* grapes are unripe, green grapes.

FRAISES ROMANOFF

Strawberries Romanoff was created by Carême for Alexander I, czar of all the Russias. I've seen the recipe in Russian as well as French cookbooks. The Russians call it *zemlyanika po romanovski*. In some versions the strawberries are served with *crème chantilly* (chantilly cream), where heavy cream is whisked in a bowl along with confectioners' sugar and vanilla extract. Some recipes even add crystallized violets as a garnish (violets dipped in sugar syrup, cooked to the point of crystallization and then dried). Carême would approve. I've kept it simple. The one caveat: pick fresh strawberries, preferably medium sized, and discard any that are bruised.

> *1 quart ripe strawberries*
> *½ cup orange-based liqueur such as Cointreau, Grand Marnier, or*
> *Curacao*
> *Juice of 1 orange (about ½ cup)*

1. Wash the strawberries under cold running water and pat dry with paper towels. Remove the stems.
2. Place the berries in a deep bowl with a lid and add the liqueur and orange juice.
3. Cover the bowl and refrigerate for at least 3 hours, turning the berries **over** gently once or twice. If the bowl does not have a lid, then foil or plastic wrap can be used as a cover.
4. Serve directly from the bowl (preferably glass), or in individual saucer-shaped glasses.

YIELD: ABOUT 4 SERVINGS

MULLIGATAWNY SOUP

I love thee as I love the swell
And hush, of some low strain
Which bringeth, by its gentle spell,
The past of life again.
Such is the feeling which from thee
Nought earthly can allure:
'Tis ever link'd to all I see
Of gifted—high—and pure!

The poem is by Eliza Acton (1799-1859). It wasn't poetry that brought Ms. Acton worldwide renown. A frustrated and unsuccessful poet, on the advice of her publisher she decided to try her hand at a cookbook—with good results. Ms. Acton was one of those maiden ladies who lived with her mother and never married. But she was a rebel of sorts who condemned processed foods. One of her pet peeves was store-bought bread, which she believed contributed to poverty and malnutrition. When *Modern Cookery for Private Families* first appeared in 1857, it became an instant best-seller. It is considered to this day one of the best cookbooks in the English language. Acton's book was well suited to the emerging middle-class in England. The recipes were usually simple and easy to prepare, with a minimum of ingredients. It was geared toward the housewife, not the culinary professional.

Mulligatawny Soup is one of the recipes given. This is the Anglicized version. Traditional Indian Mulligatawny Soup is a vegetarian curry-flavored pea and lentil dish, sometimes enhanced with coconut milk. As you will note, some English versions add rice, chicken, and other meats. I suggest serving this dish with hot boiled rice. As for the name, it's a British version of the Indian words for *pepper water—molegoo* (pepper) and *tunee* (water).

1 chicken, about 3 pounds, cut into small serving pieces
Flour
3 tablespoons vegetable oil
3 large onions, peeled and thinly sliced
3 tablespoons butter

8 cups chicken stock
2 tablespoons curry powder, mixed in ½ cup cold water and 2 tablespoons
  flour
Juice of 1 small lemon

1. Lightly flour the chicken pieces and set aside.
2. Heat the oil in a medium saucepan and gently fry the onions until a fine amber color.
3. Remove the onions and place in a deep stewpot or Dutch oven.
4. Into the original saucepan, add the butter and sauté the chicken pieces until brown.
5. Remove the chicken pieces with a slotted spoon or spatula and place on top of the onions in the stewpot. Add 6 cups of chicken stock. Bring to a boil and simmer on low heat, partly covered, for 45 minutes.
6. Remove the chicken pieces and strain the stock through a fine sieve or strainer set over a bowl. Press the stock and onions to remove as much of the liquid as possible. Place this stock in a clean pan and add the remaining two cups of chicken stock. Bring to a boil, and add the curry powder mixture.
7. Add the chicken and simmer on low heat, covered, for twenty minutes or until chicken pieces are tender.
8. Add the lemon juice just before serving.

YIELD: 4 TO 6 SERVINGS

BEEF A LA MODE
(ECONOMICAL)

There is no more fruitful source of discontent than a housewife's badly cooked dinners and untidy way. Book of Household Management

Mrs. Isabella Beeton's admonition would today be considered quaint. She was a product of Victorian society with its rules of etiquette and archaic forms of cookery. But there's more to Mrs. Beeton than meets the eye. In an avowedly male milieu she held a most unlikely profession; she was a journalist. And in 1861 she published her *Book of Household Management*, perhaps the best known English cookbook. It was a hit with the urban middle-class housewife who needed advice and guidance with such mundane affairs as how to run a household and how to organize a kitchen. Isabella Beeton included not only recipes in her book but preparation and cooking times, estimates on cost of ingredients, quantities, and precise measurements to be used.

Mrs. Beeton gives two recipes for *Beef a la Mode*, one economical, and one more elaborate containing many more ingredients. I've elected the economical version, which is far simpler.

3 pounds flank steak (Beeton states "3 pounds of clod or sticking of beef")
Flour
2 quarts water
¼ cup vegetable oil or shortening (She calls it "2 ounces of clarified dripping")
1 large onion, peeled and thinly sliced
12 berries allspice
2 bay leaves
½ teaspoons ground black pepper
Salt to taste

1. Slice the beef into small pieces, and roll the pieces in flour.
2. In a large pot, bring the water to a rolling boil.

3. Meanwhile, heat the oil over moderate heat in a heavy saucepan. Add the onion and sauté until translucent.
4. Add the beef pieces and cook, stirring, until nicely browned. Add boiling water to cover plus allspice, bay leaves, pepper, and salt, all the while stirring to mix well. Cover and simmer on low heat until the meat is tender (about 3 hours).
5. Discard bay leaves and serve.

YIELD: 6 SERVINGS

POTATO PIE

Miss Beecher's Domestic Receipt Book by Catharine Beecher (1846) is not just a cookbook, but also a treatise on household management. Miss Beecher, daughter of a prominent New England family, wrote on many social topics, including the championing of women's education and abolitionism (her sister was Harriet Beecher Stowe and her brother was Henry Ward Beecher). Her *Domestic Receipt Book* deals not only with recipes but general cooking techniques inclusive of such things as preparing tables for dinner parties and advice for cutting up a hog. Here is her recipe for potato pie, and I give it intact as noted in her cookbook since I do not presume to improve on it. This recipe is similar in some ways to modern shepherd's pie since it calls for layered potatoes with slices of meat in-between.

> Take mashed potatoes, seasoned with salt, butter, and milk, and line a baking dish. Lay upon it slices of cold meats of any kind with salt, pepper, catsup, and butter, or gravy. Put on another layer of potatoes, and then another of cold meat as before. Lastly on top put a cover of potatoes.

> Bake it till it is thoroughly warmed through, and serve it in the dish in which it is baked, setting it in, or upon another.

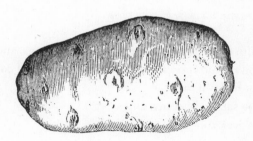

TOMATO OMELETTE

"There is no more prolific cause of bad morals than abuses of diet." Thus spake Mrs. Horace Mann in her 1861 work, *Christianity in the Kitchen*. Even the holy rollers got into the act in the nineteenth century. By their lights, some elements of cooking could be deemed immoral and un-Christian. Mrs. Mann, judging by her cookbook, firmly believed so. Extravagance in cooking was a no-no. One should be morally upright, even in the kitchen. Her book began with the dictum: "There's death in the pot." Pie crust made with butter or lard, pork, turtle soup, wedding cake, and wheat flour were bad for the digestion, which meant they were bad for one's individual character. I'm sure Tomato Omelette, the recipe here, would pass muster with Mrs. Mann—it's from her book, and it contains eggs. Mrs. Mann was a fan of eggs. For example, her Macaroni Pudding calls for four or five eggs; her Soft Custard recipe calls for eight eggs (plus a pint each of milk and cream); and her Italian Cream recipe calls for the yolk of eight eggs.

The number of eggs notwithstanding, the Tomato Omelette recipe struck a chord with me. It's not exactly an omelet as we know it where the eggs are folded over with some filling in the center. This is more like scrambled eggs and tomatoes cooked on a grill.

4 tomatoes, coarsely chopped
6 eggs, lightly beaten
2 tablespoons flour
6 tablespoons vegetable oil or butter
Salt and ground black pepper to taste

1. In a medium bowl, stir together the tomatoes, eggs, and flour. Mix well.
2. Heat the oil or butter on a griddle or frying pan and cook the eggs until they are set but still moist.
3. Season with salt and pepper, and serve.

YIELD: 4 SERVINGS

STUFFED EGGPLANT

There are some women, from a historical perspective, that I would enjoy spending a day with, just soaking in their knowledge and times. Among the group I would include Queen Elizabeth I, Katharine Hepburn, and Fannie Farmer. Fannie Merritt Farmer was director of the Boston Cooking School from 1891 to 1902. Her seminal work, *The Boston Cooking-School Cook Book* was published in 1896. It is considered one of the greatest American cookbooks. It was innovative in that it standardized kitchen measurements. No longer "the pinch of salt," "the measure of sugar," "the dash of pepper." Now you had the cupful of sugar, the teaspoon of salt, the tablespoon of butter. A precise measuring system liberated home cooks; they could follow the directions and get something closely resembling what the author described.

Fannie Farmer's instructions are simple and direct. For a century, *The Fannie Farmer Cookbook* has guided many incipient cooks through the rigors of American cuisine, from such commonly prepared dishes as Baked Cod, to continental adaptations such as *Veal à la Jardinière* (Loin of Veal). The recipe given is a favorite in many households, be it 1896 or the twenty-first century.

1 medium eggplant
1 cup soft stale bread crumbs
2 tablespoons butter
½ teaspoon finely chopped onion (or 3 slices of bacon)
Salt and ground black pepper to taste
1 egg, beaten

1. Cook the eggplant for 15 minutes in boiling salted water to cover.
2. Preheat the oven to 350 degrees.
3. Cut a slice from the top of the eggplant. With a spoon remove the pulp, taking care not to work too closely to the skin.

4. In a skillet, melt the butter. Add the onion and cook for 5 minutes. Or you can use the slices of bacon, using bacon fat in place of the butter. Add the chopped pulp and bread crumbs. Season with salt and pepper, and if necessary moisten with a little stock or water. Cook 5 minutes, cool slightly, and add the beaten egg.
5. Refill the eggplant shell, cover with buttered bread crumbs. Place in the oven and bake for 25 minutes.

YIELD: 2 SERVINGS

THE PHARAOH'S FEAST

POULET A LA MARENGO

Cookbooks for the middle-class were increasingly popular in the mid- to late nineteenth century. But there were also cookbooks aimed at the working poor. In the United States one of the leading exponents was Juliet Corson, who founded the New York School of Cookery in 1876. The following year she published fifty thousand copies of a pamphlet, *Fifteen Cent Dinners for Workingmen's Families*, which were distributed free to families earning $1.50 or less a day. In the pamphlet she gave advice on recipes, shopping, and suggested menus such as a one dollar Christmas dinner. She is credited with many other publications, including *Diet for Invalids and Children* (1886), and *Family Living on $500 a Year* (1886).

In this regard she was following the example of what came to be known as the British shilling cookbook. Charles Elme Francatelli led the way with *A Plain Cookery Book*. But the critics of the day were merciless in their reviews, citing that some of the recipes were rather elaborate for the working class. The most popular of the British shilling cookbooks was *Shilling Cookery for the People* published in 1855 by Alexis Soyer, who presided as chef of the Reform Club. The recipes in the book are practical and eschew elaborate kitchen utensils. By 1867 the book had sold a quarter of a million copies. Mr. Soyer had a social conscience—he was among the first to establish soup kitchens for the poor.

Even though his *Shilling Cookery* recipes were slated for a "new system of plain cookery and domestic economy," Soyer did include some fancified dishes such as *Poulet à la Marengo* (Chicken à la Marengo). This dish has an interesting history. Supposedly it was invented by Napoleon's chef after the first counsel's celebrated victory in Marengo, in Northern Italy, over the Austrian Army in June of 1800. The chef took whatever ingredients were available in the locale and gave it the Marengo moniker.

Soyer says that this dish is excellent served with a "few fried mushrooms" or "six oysters, with their liquor." A shilling could go a long way back in 1855.

*1 frying chicken (2½ to 3 pounds), washed, rinsed, and cut into eight
pieces
Salt and ground back pepper to taste
2 tablespoons butter or vegetable oil
1 cup dry white wine or ¼ cup vinegar
2 tablespoons ketchup*

1. Sprinkle the chicken pieces with salt and pepper.
2. Heat the butter or oil over medium heat in a large heavy skillet. Add
   the chicken pieces and cook until brown (10 to15 minutes), turning
   several times.
3. At this point the chicken can be served plain or, if a sauce is desired,
   remove the chicken to a warm platter. To the skillet add the white wine
   or vinegar and ketchup. Bring to a boil and cook until half reduced.
   Adjust the seasonings, pour the sauce over the chicken, and serve.

YIELD: 4 SERVING

THE PHARAOH'S FEAST

THIRTEEN

MODERN TIMES

PICKLED HERRING, CREAM VICHYSSOISE GLACEE,
FETTUCINE ALFREDO, CAESAR SALAD,
SPAGHETTI AND MEATBALLS, CLASSIC MEAT LOAF,
ROQUEFORT CHEESE BALLS AND MUSHROOM CAPS
FILLED WITH ROQUEFORT, BAKED FRANKFURTERS
WITH STUFFING, VICTORY PUDDING,
HAMBURGER STEAK, CALIFORNIA DIP, FILET OF
TURBOT MEUNIERE, CHEESE FONDUE, PASTA
PRIMAVERA, BRAN MUFFINS, MUSSELS A LA
TRIESTINA, STEAK AU POIVRE VERT, SAUTEED
SMOKED SALMON AND CARAMELIZED MANGO,
SAUTEED FRESH COD WITH PIGEON PEA STEW,
TROPICAL SALAD, RICH CHOCOLATE CAKE

Cultural historians would claim that the modern kitchen and, by effect, modern cooking began at the end of World War I when a slew of mechanical marvels came into the home. By this I mean the stuff that we take for granted today: electric mixers and blenders, slow cookers, coffee makers, waffle irons, can openers, toasters, and let us not forget the mechanical refrigerator. Add to that, easy-to-clean electric and gas ranges with automatic ignition. Advances in science brought about advances in the kitchen with new food preservation techniques and new ways of producing and packaging foodstuffs. The result: cooking became easier and more fun.

In the towns and urban areas of the nineteenth century, those who could afford it maintained domestic help. In the United States these were mainly young immigrant women who could help the lady of the house with the backbreaking chores of maintaining a home. In Europe it was mostly domestic help recruited from the countryside. But not everyone could afford to keep servants, and this is where the labor-saving devices helped—from apple corers, egg beaters, and clothes wringers to potato peelers. Also, with the coming of the modern century, middle-class women began to enter the work force, as did the hired domestics who found it more fruitful working in a factory or an office.

This is the prevailing view. I would submit, however, that the genesis of modern cooking as we know it began not after the Great War but before, in the previous century. The redoubtable A & P (Great Atlantic and Pacific Tea Company) was founded in the late nineteenth century. Peanut butter, baking powder, self-rising flours, canned deviled ham, saccharin and even margarine were products of that era. America's best-selling soft drink, that secret concoction known worldwide as Coca-Cola, was first sold in a drugstore in Atlanta in 1886. My favorite is Jell-O, invented by Paul B. Wait in 1897. Gelatin products had been around since the 1600s when it was discovered that the glutinous material from animal bones could be removed by the process of boiling. Mr. Wait added fruit syrup to the gelatin and his wife, May, called it Jell-O. The rest is, as they say, history—although, as with many things, it took a while before people accepted it.

Yet without a doubt, the twentieth century enhanced modern cooking. In the 1939 New York World's Fair, the masses were shown glimpses of the future with such things as flying cars and household robots. The General Electric Company featured what was known as "the kitchen of tomorrow." We are still waiting for flying cars and the robotic hired help, but most homes have dishwashers and garbage disposals—two of the wonders demonstrated in the kitchen of tomorrow.

Modern cooking continued to march inexorably forward. The 1904 St. Louis World's Fair introduced Americans to popcorn, puffed rice, ice cream cones, and meat burgers served on a bun. Three years before, at that storied baseball field known as the New York Polo Grounds, an enterprising merchant served a frankfurter on a heated bun and started the hot dog craze.

But 1904 was pivotal in other respects. It was the year that merchant Thomas Sullivan invented the tea bag, and iced tea was introduced at the St. Louis World's Fair; Campbell's soup came out with canned pork and beans; and Jell-O came out with its first recipe booklet including such favorites as Marshmallow Dessert, Paradise Pudding, and Raspberries Supreme.

And the list goes on. This time before the First World War was noteworthy in other ways: Kellogg's Corn Flakes went on sale in 1907; the Dixie Cup was introduced in 1908; by 1910 gas ranges had begun to phase out coal, wood, and petroleum stoves; the Morton Company introduced free-flowing granulated table salt; and Vitamin A was discovered in 1914, leading to what could be termed the vitamization of food products whereby the food production industry sought to convince housewives that vitamin-enriched foods were better for the health and well-being of the family. Fleischmann's Yeast Company advertised that eating four of its yeast cakes a day would provide enough vitamin B to "rid the body of poisonous wastes." Citrus fruit growers, flour millers, grape juice producers, almost every food producer jumped on the bandwagon. Among the most successful was the dairy industry. By the 1920s it could boast of canned milk enriched with vitamin D and soon thereafter, butter and fresh milk.

Another watershed year in the history of food and cooking was 1915: the first "self-contained" electric refrigerator was marketed by Frigidaire, and Corning introduced its first Pyrex baking dishes.

By 1918 the war "to end all wars" had ended. The twenties and the Jazz Age were in the offing. In the United States, we had Prohibition and the era of the flapper and the speakeasy. It also brought us enormous food conglomerates such as General Foods and Standard Brands that swallowed up smaller companies. The food industry expanded distribution networks, and utilized highly sophisticated promotion and advertising techniques. The home cook now had access to pamphlets and booklets put out by the food companies as well as popular women's magazines and journals all seeking to influence home cooks worldwide. A new guru, the home economist, came into being. Radio shows carried jingles advertising everything from new hydrogenated vegetable shortening to ballpark franks. Billboards appeared telling us what was good to drive or wear, but also what was good to eat.

As some of the cookbooks from the era show, it was a time when canned fruits and vegetables became a prominent part of our cooking. The house-wife was looking to save time. Many had entered the job market and it was easier to open the can.

In Europe, cooking was undergoing a similar evolution. Traditional diets, though still reflecting the nationalistic image, were changing. You now had oranges and tangerines coming in from Florida and California. Peanut oil and margarine were now competing with olive oil and shortening. Fresh vegetables and fruits were still preferred in southern Europe while in Eastern Europe the old standbys like potatoes and sauerkraut predominated in winter. Meat consumption increased among the urban population, along with increased consumption of milk and dairy products, especially in north-ern Europe. Consumption of alcoholic beverages also increased. The U.S. was to have its own day of reckoning with alcoholic beverages when the Eigh-teenth Amendment was passed banning the manufacture, transportation, and sale of alcohol.

What can one say about the twenties? It began with a bang and ended with a bang. It brought us quick-cooking oatmeal (1921), one of America's first convenience foods. It introduced the public to Kool-Aid (1927), and it also gave rise to the saying: "The greatest invention since sliced bread"— loaves of bread were first factory sliced in 1928.

The stock market crash and the start of the Great Depression came in 1929. Suddenly, industrial societies were beset by bread lines and soup kitchens. And everywhere cooking essentially became the same. It focused on familiar foods—meat and potatoes, rice and beans, fish and vegetables. What came to be known in the West as comfort food. It helped that food and sugar prices were low, at least in the beginning. Even so, in terms of cooking, the thrifty menu became the byword. This was reflected in one-dish meals and the inexpensive Sunday night supper. In America this was embodied by simple and homey fare: creamed chicken, corned beef, macaroni and cheese, salmon loaf, and that thirties favorite, creamed chipped beef served over toast, biscuits, or waffles. By World War II American GIs had their own name for this creation, "shit on a shingle."

The Great Depression was a worldwide phenomenon with lasting repercussions. In Germany inflation became so rampant that in some instances shoppers literally had to haul wheelbarrows full of deutsche marks to purchase a loaf of bread. The economic and social dislocations were to change society as we know it. In the U.S. the New Deal brought relief agencies and make-work projects, fueled by that hopeful saying that had become everyone's wish: "A chicken in every pot, a car in every garage."

Overseas it wasn't as benign. Italy became a Fascist state; Stalin intensified his murderous stranglehold on Russia; Hitler and his Nazi thugs came to power in Germany; the militarists took over Japan. In each case the would-be dictators promised their version of a chicken in every pot, a place in the sun, a return to the good times of a full dinner table.

In 1939 *American Home* magazine ran an add which read, "Hitler Threatens Europe—But Betty Havens' Husband's Boss is Coming to Dinner and *That's* What *Really* Counts." Leave it to Americans to figure out what's really important. Yet no number of fancy dinners or fancy cooking could dispel the gathering unease, or what Churchill would later term, *the gathering storm.*

The thirties left their mark on the food world with such New World innovations as frozen food (Bird's Eye line of "frosted foods"); my father's favorite, Twinkies, came on the market; free-standing sinks gave way to built-in sinks; General Mills developed Bisquick; Ritz crackers appeared on the shelves; American Airlines began serving meals aboard its twin-engine DC3s; *Woman's Day*, the first food-oriented supermarket magazine, was published; Teflon was discovered; and Cyclamate was approved as an artificial sweetener (later to be banned when it became a known carcinogen).

Changes to the cooking process were just as noteworthy—the electric range finally arrived; refrigerators become streamlined with exterior compressors ("monitor tops") built inside the appliance; flame resistant skillets and saucepans were developed with detachable wire handles; and copper bottomed pots and pans (Revere Ware) found their way into kitchen cupboards nationwide.

World War II ended the Depression. It re-energized the U.S. economy and put people back to work—the same way it had revitalized the economies of the belligerent nations when they put their people back to work building armaments. With the attack on Pearl Harbor in 1941, we were in it for the long run.

With war came food shortages, and rationing became the standard everywhere. In the U.S. not all foods were rationed. Poultry and game weren't so roast chicken, stewed hen and fricasseed rabbit were common at the Sunday dinner. Lesser cuts of meat weren't rationed, but prime rib, leg of lamb, and veal were in short supply. Commercially canned goods were restricted. Butter disappeared from the market shelves by the spring of 1942, as did sage from Greece and Yugoslavia, thyme from France, paprika from Hungary, and saffron from Spain. As countries fell under the onslaught of the Axis powers, foreign imports were curtailed. Stockpiles of East Indian peppercorn were depleted; and fats of all types were rationed. Olive oil in particular was hard to get. By 1943 it was selling for nine to eleven dollars a gallon.

Worldwide, everyone had to scrimp. Without canned goods, people started growing and home canning fruits and vegetables. In the U.S. there were the more than 25 million so-called victory gardens. In Europe, when times got bad you still had the vegetable garden or strawberry patch out back and, hopefully, you got to it before an enemy army trampled it underfoot. The juicy cuts of meat were a thing of the past, but now you made do with fish and innards, the things known as offals (liver, heart, feet, head, tail, etc.) In the U.S., margarine grew in popularity as did salad oils made from sunflower seeds or corn. Whether in America or overseas, honey, corn syrup, or molasses were good substitutes for sugar.

Making a little go a long way became the rallying cry. The esteemed Betty Crocker put it best in her wartime pamphlet, *Your Share:* "MAKE THE MOST OF MEAT! Use small left-over bits, diced or ground, in scrambled eggs, omelets, soufflés, hash. Simmer bones or trimmings an hour or two; use stock in soups, gravies, meat sauces. Fry out fat, render it and save for cooking."

It would stand to reason that the war years were not renowned for fine cookery. Although it did result in some innovative foods. Instant coffee is a product of the war years. What we know today as Minute Rice began as an experiment for creating an "instant rice" for C-rations. Another innovation was dehydrated food. It suited the war effort perfectly. Packaged dehydrated food was light in weight and small in size. Tons of it could be shipped to every theater of war. In the Allied armies there was dried powdered milk, dried potato flakes, dried tomato juice cocktail, dried spinach, powdered eggs, and dried meat shreds. On the home front, dried soups, instant mashed potatoes, and dried pudding mixes were popular. After the war dehydrated food went into a decline, and it wasn't until the microwave came on the scene that dehydrated food rebounded.

Of course, no culinary rendition of the war years is complete without that miracle of miracles, SPAM. No less an authority than Dwight D. Eisenhower proclaimed that the two things that won the war for the Allies were Spam and the Jeep. Hormel industries introduced Spam in 1937. This "new miracle meat in a can," a mix of pork shoulder, ham, and gelatin, was shipped and fed to every GI in every battlefield. Nikita Khrushchev said it was what saved the Russian troops from starvation on the eastern front. Though GIs complained about having to eat it every day, after the war they continued to do so. When I was a kid, my mother use to cook it all the time, and, guess what, we still love it. The English never lost their taste for this wartime treat. Today, outside of the U.S. it is sold most in the United Kingdom (and South Korea).

What's curious about the war years is that Americans ate more food, in total per capita, than they ever had before. And this despite the rationing, the shortages, and the "meatless Tuesday" campaign to stop Americans from eating meat just one day a week. The rest of the world was not as fortunate. One statistic is very telling. Despite meat rationing, Americans were allotted an average of roughly six ounces per day during the war. At the same time, their English allies had a meat allowance of sixteen ounces per week.

The war ended in 1945. The rest of the world was suffering from the after-effects. Most of Europe and Asia lay in ruins. But in America the good times had come. In 1946 Tupperware arrived; and the casserole decade of the fifties was just around the corner (even the renowned James Beard got into it when in 1955 he published *The Casserole Cookbook*). The U.S. economy was humming; the suburbs were growing, new appliances began to fill the home; Uncle Miltie was on TV; and the Kraft Television Theater began airing commercials showing how-to cook demonstrations. It was time to get back to the steaks, the chops, and the roasts, the cheese and the eggs.

The republic was undergoing a transformation. Women, who during the war had manned the factories and war plants, were now back in the kitchen. The plain, nondescript cooking that had fed the GIs during the war became the standard plain cooking at home, except that now there was more of it. Radio shows, TV, and magazines catered to the new housewife who was instilled with the value of time-saving devices, mixes, salad oils, dried soups and instant coffee, frozen waffles for breakfast, and frozen TV dinners while watching *I Love Lucy*. This was the time of processed food and instant haute cuisine. Mix a can of clam chowder, a can of chicken gumbo soup, a package of light cream, and you had a quick Creole clam bisque. Want to make a good cheese sauce?—use Velveeta processed cheese ("It melts to perfection"). Modern, convenient, and fast.

Former GIs now had a chance to own their homes with the help of low-interest federal mortgages. And the homes needed new kitchens with all the conveniences. A full-page ad that appeared in the July 8, 1949, edition of the Long Island *Star Journal* was a harbinger of things to come. The ad informed prospective buyers that they could select from five slightly different model homes for the new Levittown, and all for fifty-eight dollars a month. The ad guaranteed "Practically everything you can think of is included in that price. Refrigerator, range, Bendix, Venetian blinds, General Electric oil, legal fees, appraisal changes—yes sir, the whole works are in." For the modern house-wife this meant the latest appliances in decorator colors ranging from canary yellow to turquoise green. For this was the woman's domain. Hubby's domain was the lawn with the new lawn mower and the backyard barbecue.

The recipes and cookbooks from the fifties are a goof. The cookbooks themselves tell the tale. You had such titles as *Poppy Cannon's Can-Opener Cook Book* (1951). I guess it's no worse a title than *The I Hate to Cook Book* by Peg Bracken, which came out in 1960 and was a best-seller. You had *Pyrex Prize Recipes* published in 1953 by the Corning Glass Works; and Ruth Rosen's *Pardon My Foix Gras* (1956) with its reassuring dictum to the housewife, "you can gradually build up a repertoire of fine French dishes, without loss of time, temper, or tears." In most publications the recipes themselves are straightforward, such as the popular Three Bean Salad that appeared in a 1955 recipe booklet titled *Let's Eat Outdoors*. It calls for combining a can of red kidney beans, a can of yellow wax beans, plus a can of cut green beans mixed together with, among other things, sweet pickle relish and cider vinegar. Or the Duck with Wild Rice recipe that appeared in a 1953 *House & Garden* article, "20th Century Short Cuts to Old-Fashioned Dishes"—it called for canned wild rice and canned duck ("drained and juice reserved"). Even those adventurous cooks who strove for snob appeal could try to emulate French haute cuisine at home with the gourmet-from-cans concept. You wanted to impress your friends, you made a big show of preparing Lobster Thermidor. Instead of fresh, you added frozen cooked lobster meat; and for the béchamel sauce, you substituted a can of condensed cream of mushroom soup.

The fifties also gave rise to that singular American innovation, fast food. This is a trend that, for ill or good, was to affect our way of cooking and eating. It took cooking outside the home completely or relegated it to quick heating and paper plates. Americans love instant gratification, be it instant entertainment, instant purchases, or instant food. We work fast, we move fast, we eat fast. This was accelerated in the fifties when eating on the go, whether at the office, cafeteria, or drive-in, became sacrosanct. Eating interrupted the more important aspects of life: making money and getting ahead.

The fast-food chain had been with us since at least 1916 when the White Castle hamburger chain was founded by J. Walter Anderson of Wichita, Kansas. In the fifties, leading franchises began to establish outlets on major highways, in urban centers, and in shopping malls (another American innovation). Greater mobility and America's love affair with the automobile provided the perfect environment. By 1950 The A&W Root Beer Company had established a drive-in restaurant chain nationwide. Ray Kroc began franchising McDonald's in 1955; Kentucky Fried Chicken became a fast-food concern in 1956. It was in the fifties that former Marine Glenn Bell applied McDonald's techniques to serving Mexican food at his Taco Tia outlets. Eventually this would lead to the Taco Bell chain.

Pizza came in vogue in the late fifties. America's first pizzeria had opened in New York's Little Italy in 1905. This Neapolitan specialty remained largely the province of corner shops in immigrant enclaves. In 1943 Ike Sewell and Ric Ricardo (yes, that's the real name) had created deep-dish pizza at their Pizzeria Uno on Chicago's North Side. But it was American-style pizza that would take the nation by storm. A new technology had been developed where pizza could be prepared in advance, stored in metal containers, and refrigerated until it could be put in the oven. This technique was perfected by the Wichita-based company Pizza Hut and American-style pizza became a true fast-food giant.

The fast-food mania spread nationwide into the sixties, on to Europe in the late seventies and early eighties, and on to conquer much of the world. If Burger King could serve "a complete meal in fifteen seconds" to a customer in the U.S., it could do the same overseas.

Fast-food mania aside, for the rest of the world, cooking had remained more or less the same, depending on regional tastes and differences. In France hearty country cooking co-existed side by side with the upper gastronomic echelons of classic cuisine. Auguste Escoffier was the successor to the illustrious Carême. Unlike Careme, Escoffier espoused "tasteful simplicity." He streamlined the art of decorating food, reduced menus to something manageable, and organized his kitchens more efficiently, first at the Hotel Bellevue in Nice, then the fashionable Le Petit Moulin Rouge restaurant in Paris, and then at a string of luxury hotels worldwide from Lucerne to New York. Escoffier invented scores of new dishes, among them, Melba Toast (a grilled piece of toast split through the middle and cooked a second time until it was browned on each side). Escoffier died in 1935. By then countless former pupils had spread this concept of the new classic French cuisine far and wide.

In the early 1950s Fernand Point took up the mantel. His restaurant, the Pyramide, in Vienne, was regarded as the finest in the world at the time; and Point trained many of the country's outstanding chefs, including such heavyweights as Bocuse and Troisgros. Though trained in the classic style at the Hotel Bristol in Paris, Point nevertheless maintained a great appreciation of French provincial cuisine. Thus he combined them, and it was not unusual for a menu with caviar and brioche de foie gras to also include such regional favorites as crayfish, cassoulet, and bouillabaisse.

Culinarily the world was changing, faster in some places, slower in others. Electricity was gradually being installed in some rural areas in Europe and Asia. In other parts it was still nonexistent. Refrigeration was not universal and, in some cases, practically unknown outside of large urban centers. Most homes in the countryside had no ovens, and in most areas of the world, those who were fortunate enough to have one, did their cooking on a kerosene or charcoal stove. In a great part of the world rural cooking remained the same and the old cuisines prevailed, while in the cities modern influences were making inroads. To some degree in each country the cuisine retained strong ties to cultural and national norms.

That is not to say there weren't foreign overlays. Such crosscurrents as exploration and imperialism guaranteed a melding of cooking cultures. Thus you had the Portuguese influence on Brazilian cooking, the French influence on Haiti and the West Indies, the Mogul influence on Indian cooking, British and Danish on the cooking in the Virgin Islands, African influence on that of Guyana, and Chinese influence on the cuisine of such Asian countries as Cambodia, Vietnam, Laos, and Malaysia. The archetypal example of this blending of cooking would be in the Philippine's, which included a mix of Malay, Chinese, Spanish, Polynesian, and a touch of American.

Cooking was becoming multinational, which is a good thing. But in the developed world, something was amiss. Here and there one heard grumblings about the type and quality of food we were cooking. Major conglomerates were processing and marketing food to almost every part of the world, but was it nutritious, even edible? In the U.S. alone, in the 1960s, food companies were allowed to use 704 chemicals in the processing of food. Some were chemically produced, like Tang, which in 1965 became the official breakfast drink of the Gemini astronauts. Chemicals and pesticides abounded in farming production, and antibiotics were routinely added during meat production. Food and the environment were slowly inching their way to the top of the agenda. No less a source than *Newsweek*, in its July 17, 1961, issue, complained that the poor state of American gastronomy was due to dieting fads, working women, and the high cost of labor. But it stated also that "the principal villain is the refrigerator-freezer."

Critics had plenty to complain about not only with regard to cooking, but also the cookbooks that influenced the general palate. In America, the early sixties still harkened back to the gourmet-in-a-can cookbooks of the fifties. There were such distinctive titles as *Eating European Abroad and at Home* with recipes such as Baked Fillet of Sole with a shrimp sauce made from canned cream of shrimp soup; *Gourmet Meals for Easy Entertaining*— with a V-8 aspic; *What Cooks in Suburbia*, with a Tuna Tetrazzini recipe; and *The Fast Gourmet Cookbook*, with a Chicken Moutarde made from canned chicken, canned gravy, and canned grapes. The supermarket shelves were filling up with all the good stuff for the newly informed nouveau gourmet. It could and would verge on the ridiculous. In an October 3, 1964, *Saturday Evening Post* article, writer John MacPhee suggested that cookbook writers were using so much canned food that they were obviously practicing for life in a bomb shelter. He wasn't too far of the mark. The 1969 *Better Homes and Gardens Guide to Entertaining* featured a recipe, Bomb Shelter Chocolate-Cherry Delight Cake, whose main components were the ever-present canned cherry pie filling plus packaged devil's food cake mix and packaged dessert topping mix (or one could use Cool Whip).

Nika Hazelton put it in perspective when she wrote in a February 1966 *National Review* piece: "What our nouveaux gourmets apparently don't know or don't care about is that the secret of good food is in its utter freshness, both as a produce and in cooking." This new awareness of food and nutrition was just the beginning of a process that would reach its apotheosis in the late sixties with the advent of "health foods" and the increase in popularity of vegetarianism.

There were other lights on the horizon. One of them was James Beard who never tired of reminding Americans about the importance of fresh ingredients in cooking. Another was Julia Child. In 1961, along with Simone Beck and Louisette Bertholle, she published *Mastering the Art of French Cooking*. A chance appearance on Boston's WGBH public television station (where she had been sent to promote the book) led to *The French Chef,* her cooking show that was broadcast on more than sixty educational channels. After all these years I still get a kick out of watching Julia Child. On her show she would use the same wine bottle that went with the meal for rolling out the dough; things would drop from her hands and she would remain perfectly calm; she would liken a cut of meat to her thigh. But she made complicated things seem simple. She introduced many of us to fish poachers, charlotte molds, copper beating bowls, and chef's knives. She showed us that one need not be overwhelmed by such creations as Coq au Vin, *Boeuf à la Bourguignonne,* and Veal Orlaff. Like Beard, she insisted on the freshest ingredients that one could find.

On the cooking front, General Electric developed a self-cleaning oven in 1963, a boon to cooks and housewives everywhere. In 1967 Amana Refrigeration Inc. came out with a countertop microwave oven priced at $495. The microwave concept had been with us since the forties, but mainly for commercial use. In 1955 Tappan introduced a model for home use, but its $1,295 price tag made its cost prohibitive for most people. With a reasonably priced model, most consumers could not resist trying out the new appliance. Suddenly, microwave pamphlets and cookbooks abounded. The microwave promised to do everything. It did not. Americans soon discovered that defrosting and reheating were not the same as cooking a full meal. I'm sure some would think they got a better deal with the trash compactor which was unveiled by Whirlpool in 1969.

Vietnam, peace marches, flower children, free love—catchwords of the sixties. Fact was, it was the peacenik baby boomers who led the way. This progeny of the G.I. Bill, the Ozzie and Harriet generation, and TV began to question everything, not the least of it, food. The food establishment was the target with its mass-produced, mass-marketed products like white bread, white sugar, canned meals, and processed cheese. The bywords became *organic foods* and *unprocessed natural foods*. Adelle Davis's *Let's Eat Right to Keep Fit* and Rachel Carson's *Silent Spring* had struck a chord. Granola bars and tofu were in.

The food conglomerates did not take this lying down. Such halcyon institutions as the U.S. Food and Drug Administration and the American Medical Association said that the claims that organic foods were more nutritious than nonorganic foods were "nonsense." The September 1967 issue of *Good Housekeeping* said that health foods were "nutritional quackery." It was a battle that would continue for years to come with food producers finally co-opting the opposition in the seventies when they began remarketing their products with such catchwords as "natural," "farm fresh," and "nature's own."

What I remember about the 1970s is crock pot cookery. Suddenly everyone had to own a crock pot or pressure cooker. For a busy family, the crock pot saved time. Load and set it in the morning and come back to a fully cooked meal in the evening. Like most things, it didn't last. We moved on to the salad bar, which first arrived at R. J. Grunts in Chicago in 1971, and Starbucks which opened its first coffee shop in Seattle in the same year. More and more, in the U.S., we were getting away from cooking in the kitchen.

Then something happened, French chefs began experimenting with something called *la cuisine minceur*, which questioned the French classical canon. This new cooking called for more vegetables and shorter cooking times. It eschewed the flour-thickened sauces in favor of natural ingredients cooked in their own juices, with smaller amounts of butter, cream, and sugar. American chefs soon followed their lead, spreading the gospel of this "nouvelle cuisine" with such nouvelle recipes as green ravioli with ricotta and french herbs, scallop-vegetable terrine with tomato coulis (nouvelle tomato sauce), and that all time favorite, lobster with vanilla sauce. For me, nouvelle cuisine was a bust. Large, oversized plates with little twigs of greens and undercooked fish, meat, or chicken in the center may have been exciting for some, but for me and my crowd, it left us hankering for good solid fare.

The seventies was a decade of experimentation, and the U.S. led the way. It was the time of singles' bars, bell bottoms, group encounters, and LSD. For the youth of the time, it was the time for getting high and getting laid. This mind set was reflected in the music, the culture (mood rings, pet rocks, and platform shoes), and the cooking. The pimply preadolescents of the fifties had evolved into the long-haired rebels of the sixties and seventies. And the hippies' natural food movement flourished in this environment, eventually reaching segments of the mainstream population. The pressure would be on the food producing conglomerates. It's no accident that in 1969, bowing to consumer protest, major U.S. baby food manufacturers would stop adding sugar and salt to baby food—a product that had been with us since 1929.

All wasn't beautiful and natural in the age of aquarius. For the majority of the baby boomers, their taste and palate remained abysmal. The favored beverage at dinner was a soft drink. Even the wines popular at the time reflected a penchant for all things sweet—Lambrusco, Cold Duck, and Boone's Farm Apple Wine. The more prestigious "blush" wines, which appeared in the late seventies, still mirrored this Kool-Aid taste. The foods cooked at home tended to be creamy and gooey like quiche with lots of cheese and heavy cream filling, spinach salad smothered with Russian or French dressing, or moussaka with a creamy topping. If you were health conscious, you substituted granola (i.e. granola eggs benedict, granola quiche Lorraine, and granola fondue). Unfortunately, the granola bought at the supermarket came packed with honey, corn syrup, and brown sugar (reprising the sweet tooth) and packed with calories. Even yogurt, which came into its own in the seventies, came in an assortment of fruit flavors laced with sugar.

On this side of the Atlantic, one of the cuisines that became fashionable was Chinese—but not the old style "Chinese-American" cooking. This was something new. Szechuan and Hunan restaurants began appearing in metropolitan areas. Suddenly the chop suey joints had competition. And Chinese cooking moved into the home. Before, the only thing you could find in a supermarket was soy sauce. Now they were stocked with hoisin sauce, fresh ginger, bok choy, Szechuan powder, and hot soybean paste. Woks started appearing in homes, and all kinds—electric woks, ceramic woks, Teflon woks. . . . Chinese and Asian cookbooks proliferated, and stir-frying went from a fad to something ordinary.

Vegetarianism was on the rise—from lacto-ovo to vegan—first with the campus crowd, and when they graduated, it followed them into the home. The idea of Sunday brunch came into style, either at your favorite restaurant or at home, complete with eggs Florentine and the ubiquitous Bloody Marys and mimosas. It was a time of ridiculously named sweet drinks: Harvey Wallbanger, singapore sling, tequila sunrise. Even the traditional drinks like daiquiris and pina coladas now came frozen and in fruit flavors straight from the shelf. Traditional spirits like Scotch, bourbon, and rye became passé.

Other highlights? In 1973 the Cuisinart Food Processor made its appearance. Like the microwave it promised to do everything. Consumers soon discovered that chopping, shredding, and grating were not the only tasks for cooking. In mid-decade Doubleday, the same esteemed publishers that in 1962 founded the Cook Book Guild, came out with *The Doubleday Cookbook*, which, for the first time, gave a per-serving calorie count for each recipe. In 1978 *Food and Wine* magazine made its debut. The same year *Cuisine* (the Former *Sphere Magazine*) hit the newsstands. More and more publications were devoting themselves to food and cooking. The cooking scene had come a long way from 1955 when *Bon Appétit* appeared as a free promotional newsletter (distributed via liquor stores).

In the U.S., the seventies were christened as the me decade, and the eighties were the greed decade (remember Michael Douglas in the movie *Wall Street*, giving a speech on the benefits of greed?). The stock market was in a bullish phase, and hippies gave way to yuppies. In the old days it had been Daddy at the job and Mommy at home. Now both sexes were on the career track and "family" was put off to some time in the future. There was the two-income home and a lot of disposable cash. It was the time to spend—whether on new condos or cars, or kitchen items like the espresso maker, which everyone *just had to have.* And when you weren't at home trying out new recipes with a bizarre combination of flavors (smoked duck with maple syrup or raspberry vinegar), you were out at some flashy restaurant that extolled Chef Ramon and his new low-cal Southwest bistro-South Bronx-Rumanian-Asian cooking. But the hedonism of the seventies was giving way to more serious concerns. The baby boomers had begun to mature, and the times they were a-changing. The bottom fell out of the market in the late eighties and the age of AIDS was upon us.

In Western Europe, rebuilding and reconstruction had come after the war. This made it a prime target for food companies in America with an eye on expansion. As the standard of living began to rise, Europeans, just like Americans, saw the convenience of prepackaged and mass-marketed food. The same frozen foods, powdered mixes, and ready-made sauces could be found on the supermarket shelf overseas. This globalization of processed food ensured that pasteurized cheeses could be bought in Germany as well as the U.S., Corn Flakes could be on the English breakfast table, and Americans could start the day with Swiss muesli. But fast food posed another question. This "McDonaldization" of culture elicited opposition. During the Vietnam War, Swedes accused the U.S. of trying to force healthy Swedish youth to eat "plastic food." And later when a McDonald's first tried to open at the Piazza di Spagna in Rome, thousands protested against it. Today the McDonald's franchise is a growing concern overseas, but not without bumps along the way, including legal battles in France involving product quality and hygiene. The French in particular are bugged about this global "imperialism" that threatens their gastronomic integrity, but it doesn't keep the French kids from wolfing down the burgers and eating American-style pizza.

In the eighties the U.S. was at the forefront with the fads. There was "spa cuisine," which touted lighter cooking like that found at the spa or fat farm. Stouffer's offered Lean Cuisine dinners and entrees. Just pop it into the oven or microwave and you had a genuine processed gourmet dinner in no time at all. No fuss, no mess. And if you weren't thumbing through the pages of *Cooking Light* or *Food Arts* magazine, you could always catch the *Frugal Gourmet* on PBS with Jeff Smith showcasing his brand of "simple home cooking." Spaghetti was no longer spaghetti, now it was pasta—and anybody who aspired to be hip had to make their own at home with a pasta machine. And ice cream was no longer ice cream. Now it had to be granitas, gelati, or sorbet. Organic produce, whole grain breads and cereals, and free-range chicken were indicative of a growing interest in healthy eating. Consumption of red meat plummeted. Anything with LDL-type serum cholesterol (like egg yolks, butter) or nitrates (bacon, processed meats) were to be avoided. The baby boomers wanted to live forever.

A sense of normalcy came in the late eighties and early nineties when Americans rediscovered comfort food, or what was labeled in some circles as "Retro Food" (like meat loaf, fried chicken, and corned beef hash).

By the mid-nineties the American economy had improved and Americans were spending again. You now had a twenty-four-hour Food Network, just like the Weather Channel and the all-day news network. A foodie could immerse him or herself in the glories of cooking ad nauseam. And if you had any questions you could access good old Betty Crocker (a composite of seventy-five women) on the Internet, or *Gourmet's Club Network*, or *Epicurious* with recipes and advice from *Bon Appétit* and *Gourmet*. After all, most Americans had the gadgets for it. But now we weren't the only ones. The modern kitchen with all its equipment was known worldwide. In a French survey in 1989 only 19.9 percent of those questioned stated they owned a freezer or microwave oven. In 1990 it was up to one-third of French households. By

1995 the figure was over 50 percent.

Worldwide we had accepted convenience in cooking. One would be crazy not to. Like all things, there's a catch. Many had asked, and continue to ask, Does one have to sacrifice freshness for convenience? Or quality for mass production? Are precut frozen vegetables any less nutritious than fresh vegetables? Is a prewashed salad any less good than organic? Do we exchange taste for health?

As the century drew to a close we were back to the same time-worn arguments. Except that now modern science had more than a proportional say in what we cooked or ate. In 1996 the U.S. Food and Drug Administration ordered that most bread, flour, and pasta products be fortified with folic acid and a B vitamin in order to prevent two serious birth defects. The same year the F.D.A. approved a controversial fat substitute, Olestra, for limited commercial use in chips and snacks. The Olestra battle would continue with consumer advocates insisting that the fat substitute was a health risk.

This question of the beneficial union of science and food is ongoing. There are misgivings about genetically altered foods, what some consider "unnatural foods." There is the controversy concerning irradiated food, with some arguing that ionized radiation of food is harmful. Others disagree. For those who cook, whether at home, for recreation, or professionally, the new century is one of choices—whether we want irradiated food or not, processed food or organic, or to bypass the stove altogether (we can always order takeout). For those in the developed world the choices are many. For those in the underdeveloped world the choices are fewer. Most of us still have control over what goes into the pot, what we feed ourselves and others and how we dine. Whether we open the can, defrost the fish and vegetables, or do it from scratch, we still need to show our individuality, to create with the cooking.

PICKLED HERRING

The Settlement Cook Book first appeared in 1901. The book is unique in the annals of culinary history. The Settlement House was a vocational center in Milwaukee that sought to Americanize young Jewish immigrants. Mrs. Lizzie Kander taught domestic skills to young women at the Settlement and along with Mrs. Henry Schoenfeld and Mrs. Isaac D. Adler, lobbied local businessmen to buy advertisements for the publication of a cookbook featuring recipes and housekeeping tips. The book went from a fund-raising tool to one of the most successful cookbooks in American history, with more than forty editions. Despite such entrees as Frog Legs á la Newburg and such traditional American dishes as Brunswick Stew and Ham and Potato Casserole, it also included such traditional Jewish recipes as Gefilte Fish (Filled Fish), Matzos Fritters, and Pickled Herring, transcribed below in toto.

1 dozen milch herring
4 large onions, sliced
2 lemons, sliced
2 tablespoons black peppercorns
2 tablespoons mustard seed
12 bay leaves
1 tablespoon sugar
3 cups vinegar
1 cup water

Soak herring in cold water over night, drain and remove entrails, reserving the roe and the milt. If you desire, skin and bone them; cut off heads, run knife down center of back and skin towards the tail; scrape the meat off the bones, without cutting the bones, thus separating the herring in two parts.

Place herring in crock of layers, with sliced onion, lemon, a few pieces of bay leaf, a sprinkling of mustard seed and peppercorns.

Mix and mash the milt with the sugar, add a little vinegar to thin, strain through sieve, add the rest of the vinegar, or better still, in place of the vinegar 3 cups sour cream or milk, and pour over herring to cover.

Two medium sized sour apples, chopped fine, and 1 oz. of chopped almonds may be added; cover jar and keep in a cool, dry place. Will keep for a long while. Serve with boiled potatoes in their jackets.

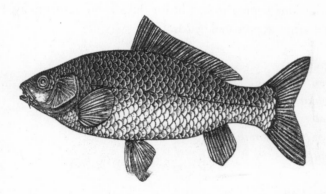

CREAM VICHYSSOISE GLACEE

Vichyssoise (pronounced "vihsh-ee-SWAHZ" or "vee-she-swahz") is a rich and creamy potato-leek soup that's served cold. And it's American, Ha-Ha. Its creator was Chef Louis Diat of the Ritz-Carlton Hotel in New York City, and he conjured it up in 1917. Still, we must give the French credit since the soup most likely evolved from the leek and potato soup very popular in France, *potage bonne temme*. In *Cooking à la Ritz*, Diat himself states that the name for the soup comes from Vichy, the French town near his childhood home. He calls it Cream Vichyssoise Glacée. Vichyssoise has entered the lexicon along with such nuggets as chicken tetrazzini and English muffin (another American novelty). Vichyssoise is popular because with a blender or food processor it's easy to make. My favorite recipe uses scallions not leeks, and I like to add cayenne pepper to it. But for the sake of authenticity, I enclose the original recipe as prepared by Mr. Diat.

4 leeks, white part
1 medium onion
2 ounces sweet butter
5 medium potatoes
1 quart water or chicken broth
1 tablespoon salt
2 cups milk
2 cups medium cream
1 cup heavy cream

Finely slice the white part of the leeks and the onion, and brown very lightly in the sweet butter, then add the potatoes, also sliced finely. Add water or broth and salt. Boil 35 to 40 minutes. Crush and rub through a fine strainer. Return to fire and add 2 cups of milk and 2 cups of medium cream. Season to taste and bring to a boil. Cool and then rub through a very fine strainer. When soup is cold, add the heavy cream. Chill thoroughly before serving. Finely chopped chives may be added before serving.

YIELD: 8 SERVINGS

FETTUCINE ALFREDO

Fettucine Alfredo is not an American invention, although it is one of the most popular dishes on the continent. It was created in Rome in 1920 by Italian cook and restaurateur Alfredo di Lellio. American-style Fettucine Alfredo is decked out, depending on preference, with cream and mushrooms, eggs, green peas, or garlic. The true Alfredo sauce is nothing more than butter, Parmesan cheese, and black pepper.

1 pound fettucine (fresh, if possible)
1 stick unsalted butter, softened at room temperature
1 cup freshly grated Parmigiano-Reggiano cheese
Freshly ground black pepper to taste

1. Cook the fettucine in a pot of boiling salted water. If using fresh fettucine this will take about 2 minutes. Otherwise cook until al dente.
2. Meanwhile, combine the butter and cheese in a heated serving bowl. Drain the pasta, add to the bowl, and toss everything together. Mix in the pepper and serve.

YIELD: 6 SERVINGS

CAESAR SALAD

On the Fourth of July weekend in 1924, in the town of Tijuana, Mexico, restaurateur Caesar Cardini discovered that all he had left in his storeroom was a crate of romaine lettuce, a slab of Romano cheese, bread, olive oil, and some eggs. Caesar's Place was popular with the movie stars and other luminaries from California who headed across the border into Tijuana to drink and party. It was the height of Prohibition and what better way to tie one on. Caesar, an enterprising fellow, took the ingredients he had and created a salad: lettuce, croutons browned in olive oil, grated cheese on top, and a dressing made with a one-minute egg and lemon juice, all mixed together in a bowl rubbed with garlic—Caesar Salad.

The catch is the egg. Some say the original salad called for a raw egg. Whether it's a one-minute egg or raw egg, these days it is not recommended due to pesky salmonella problems. You can skip the eggs altogether, but it will not be a true Caesar Salad. Or you can cheat by using one of the egg substitutes now on the market.

¾ cup olive (preferably extra virgin)
2 cups Italian bread cubes, crust removed
1 garlic clove, peeled and crushed
1 head romaine lettuce, washed, dried, and chilled
½ teaspoon salt
¼ teaspoon ground black pepper
4 ounces substitute egg product (equivalent to two large eggs), regular not
    frozen
Juice of 1 lemon
¼ cup freshly grated Romano or Parmesan cheese

1. Heat half the olive oil in a heavy skillet or saucepan until hot but not smoking. Add the bread cubes and sauté over medium heat until brown. Remove the bread cubes from the pan, drain on paper towels, and set aside.
2. Rub a large wooden bowl with the crushed garlic. Discard the garlic. Break the lettuce into bite-size pieces and put in a bowl. Sprinkle with salt, pepper, remaining oil, and toss well.

3. Pour the egg product over the salad, add the lemon juice, and sprinkle with cheese. Toss until well blended. Top with croutons and serve (some prefer the salad be served on chilled plates, some say on wooden plates).

Yield: 6 servings

SPAGHETTI AND MEATBALLS

In the 1920s the international cuisine was to affect American cooking in one respect: a new found interest in what was termed exotic cooking. Among these was Chinese cuisine, precisely Cantonese. Another was Italian cooking, an influence brought over by immigrants from southern Italy, mainly Sicilians, who opened up small family restaurants, some of them speakeasies where wine brewed in the basement could be served with your pasta. In the old country, Sicilian cooking relied mainly on vegetables, legumes, and starches. The new immigrants developed Italian-American hybrids in which meat sauces prevailed, everything came covered with parmesan and mozzarella cheese, veal was cooked with lemon or marsala, and everywhere huge platters of meatballs and spaghetti.

This is my mother's recipe. And in the Rivera family we make meatballs the size of baseballs.

1¼ pounds ground beef (my mother uses chuck)
1 tablespoon olive oil
1 medium onion, finely chopped
2 cloves garlic, peeled and finely minced
1 cup fresh bread crumbs
½ cup finely chopped parsley
1 egg, lightly beaten
Salt and ground black pepper to taste
2 to 4 tablespoons olive oil
1 1-pound, 12-ounce can tomatoes with their juice (preferably imported)
1 6-ounce can tomato paste
½ cup water
½ teaspoon dried crumbled basil
½ teaspoon oregano
½ teaspoon dried thyme
1 bay leaf
1 pound spaghetti
Grated Parmesan or Romano cheese

1. Put the meat in a mixing bowl.
2. Heat the oil in a large skillet. Add the onion and garlic and cook until the onion is wilted.
3. Add this to the meat along with the bread crumbs, parsley, egg, salt, and pepper.
4. Blend well with the hands and shape the mixture into meatballs, anywhere from 12 to 16 balls (or more), depending on size.
5. Using the same skillet as before, heat enough oil to reach a depth of about ⅛ inch. Add the meatballs and cook, turning as necessary, until brown all over.
6. Holding the lid over the skillet, drain the fat into a large saucepan or small kettle. Add the tomatoes, tomato paste, water, basil, oregano, thyme, and bay leaf. Adjust the seasonings, adding more salt and pepper if necessary. Bring to a boil, cover, and let simmer on low heat for about 5 minutes.
7. Carefully drop the meatballs into the cooking sauce and continue cooking for about 30 minutes.
8. Cook the spaghetti to desired doneness. Serve with meatballs and sauce and with cheese sprinkled on top.

YIELD: 4 SERVINGS

CLASSIC MEAT LOAF

In the United States, one of the popular thrifty menu foods of the thirties was meat loaf. It was a favorite during the lean war years, the hefty postwar years, and, after a brief period of decline, continues to be a favorite today. There are numerous ways to prepare the dish. I've come across highfalutin recipes where veal or veal combined with pork provides the meat filler. There is the Quaker Oats recipe that I saw printed on their boxes when I was a kid, and which uses rolled oats (quick-cooking or old fashioned). I've even come across plain meat loaf recipes without any tomato sauce.

This recipe is a classic from Irma Rombauer's *The Joy of Cooking*. Long before Julia Child, James Beard, Elizabeth David, and renowned others came on the scene there was Irma Rombauer, a St. Louis widow who amassed five hundred recipes from family and friends and paid to have them published in 1931. Her book went on to become what *Time* magazine referred to in Mrs. Rombauer's obituary as "the kitchen bible." I wouldn't venture to guess how many newly minted brides, from the thirties to the present, have received the book as a wedding present.

Position a rack in the center of the oven. Preheat the oven to 350° F. Lightly grease a 9 X 5-inch (8 cup) loaf pan. Combine in a bowl:

12 ounces ground beef chuck
1½ cup finely chopped onions
1 cup quick-cooking rolled oats or bread crumbs
⅔ cup ketchup
⅔ cup finely chopped fresh parsley
3 large eggs, lightly beaten
1 teaspoon ground thyme
1 teaspoon salt
½ teaspoon ground black pepper

Knead the mixture with your hands until everything is well blended. Fill the loaf pan with the meat mixture, mounding the top. Place the pan on a baking sheet and bake until the meat is firm to the touch and has shrunk from the sides of the pan or until an instant-read thermometer inserted in the center of the loaf reads 160 º F, 1 to 1¼ hours. Pour off the excess fat and let stand for 15 minutes.

YIELD: 8 SERVINGS

NOTE: Rombauer states that the dish can be served with Pan Gravy for Meat (for which she gives a recipe) and Mashed Potatoes (for which she gives a recipe).

Roquefort Cheese Balls and Mushroom Caps Filled with Roquefort

In 1939 actor-singer James Beard opened a catering business in New York City. A year later he published his first cookbook, *Hors d'Oeuvre and Canapés*. For decades to come James Beard was to have a major influence on developing food trends in the United States, all culminating in his massive landmark work, *American Cookery* published in 1972. You could say Beard was America's first cooking superstar. Long before it happened, he was there: in 1946 he hosted the first televised cooking show in the U.S., *I Love to Eat* on NBC-TV. In 1949 he became the restaurant critic for *Gourmet* magazine. By the fifties he had a cooking school in New York City. Well into the sixties and seventies he was a booster for the best America had to offer in terms of culinary excellence.

But I hark back to his first book, a little volume that showed Americans how enticing cocktail appetizers could be—as is the case with stuffed mushrooms. To most Americans in 1940 stuffed mushrooms must have seemed totally alien. Today it's hard to find some pretentious hole–in–the–wall joint that does not include this item (with whatever filling). Here is Beard's recipe verbatim along with his recipe for Roquefort Cheese Balls.

> Mix together four ounces each of Roquefort cheese and butter. Add to this one half teaspoon of dry mustard and blend well. Form into balls the size of a marble and roll them in a mixture of finely chopped parsley and chives. I suggest a mixture of two parts chives and one part parsley.

> Select twelve perfectly shaped, raw mushrooms and peel them very carefully in order to keep the smooth quality of the cap. Stuff them with the Roquefort mixture given above and sprinkle the cheese with chopped chives. The raw mustard flavor has a peculiar sympathy of flavor with the Roquefort.

Baked Frankfurters
with Stuffing

World War II was a time for stretching the rations and stretching the meals. The best book I've come across that describes all this is Joanne Lamb Hayes's *Grandma's Wartime Kitchen*. Despite its subject, it is a fun book with great vignettes about how Americans coped on the home front. One of Hayes's chapters is entitled "STRRRRRREEEEEEETCH IT." It tells how ingenious Americans became at "extending" a meal. This is one of the "Wartime Specials" featured in the book.

4 frankfurters
1 cup bread crumbs
2 tablespoons finely chopped onion
2 tablespoons butter, melted
1 tablespoon chopped fresh parsley

Split frankfurters lengthwise. Combine bread, onion, butter, and parsley. Divide into frankfurters. Bake at 375 degree oven for 30 minutes.

Yield: 4 servings

VICTORY PUDDING

So how did we manage desserts during wartime, especially when sugar was rationed? As *Grandma's Wartime Kitchen* shows in this Victory pudding, molasses replaced the sugar. According to Ms. Hayes, anything sweet was used as a substitute, including condensed milk and pudding mixes.

2 cups milk
⅔ cup cooked rolled wheat flakes or old fashioned rolled oats
⅓ cup light molasses
1 large egg, lightly beaten
1 teaspoon ginger
⅛ teaspoon salt
Plain or whipped cream, optional

Preheat oven to 350 degrees. Bring milk just to a boil in a heavy saucepan over low heat, stirring occasionally.

Meanwhile, lightly grease a 1-quart casserole or baking dish.

Combine cooked rolled wheat, molasses, egg, ginger, and salt in a heatproof bowl. Gradually heat hot milk into wheat mixture. Transfer to the casserole.

Bake until center is set, 35 to 40 minutes. Cool 20 to 30 minutes, then serve warm with cream if desired.

YIELD: 4 SERVINGS

HAMBURGER STEAK

The fifties are identified with backyard grilling. Mom may have been whipping up her casseroles and Del Monte fruit cocktails on the weekends, but it was dad who ruled the grill. Men who couldn't boil water became chef de cuisine (with apron, hat, and tongs) when it came to scorching a slab of meat on the grill. As noted in *The Complete Book of Outdoor Cookery* (1956): "Men love it, for it gives them a chance to prove that they are, indeed, cooks." This recipe from *Outdoor Cookery* gives an idea of what barbecuing 1950s style was all about.

For 4 persons you should have 2 pounds of ground beef chuck, top round, or top sirloin. Form the meat, being certain you can handle it lightly, into a large cake about 2 to 3 inches thick. Salt and pepper it well, and place it in a long-handled grill or a small gridiron over the coals. Broil it quickly, really just sear it well on each side, and get it crusty on the outside and soft and rare in the center. Remove to a hot platter, cut it in wedges, and serve. It is good with roasted corn and slices of raw onion which have been vinegared and salted and allowed to marinate for an hour or two.

YIELD: 4 SERVINGS

CALIFORNIA DIP

The U.S. in the 1950s was a nation of dips and spreads. Just as the extradry cocktail and canapés came into vogue, so did bowls of assorted mixtures for "dipping." Cocktail dips were not an invention of the fifties. They had been with us since at least the twenties. In the fifties they mushroomed in all their sour cream, cream cheese, and mayonnaise-based splendor. The hands-on favorite of the era was the California Dip, that familiar blend of dry onion soup mix and sour cream thought up by some anonymous cook sometime in the midfifties (some claim it was concocted in 1954; but the Lipton Company did not start printing the recipe on its onion soup boxes until 1958). The dip mania would continue through the sixties and beyond. Today, it is salsas that have captured the national fancy.

> *1 envelope dry onion soup mix*
> *2 cups sour cream*
> *Potato chips, crackers, or bite-sized raw vegetables*

1. Mix the soup mix and sour cream in a bowl and serve with the potato chips, crackers, or raw vegetables.

   Yield: about 2 cups

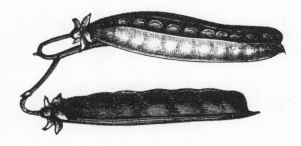

FILET OF TURBOT MENIERE

In the fifties foreign foods stoked the interest of Americans who, for the first time, were traveling abroad in great numbers. Any cooking that provided "exotic and delicious dishes" was in. Read into that: snob appeal. Myra Waldo in her *Complete Round-the-World Cookbook* (1956) assured novice cooks that they would "amaze and delight" their circle with recipes gathered by Pan American World Airways from the eighty-four countries they served.

Here's a simple, uncomplicated, and delicious *meuniere*-style dish.

> 6 boneless turbot fillets, about 1½ pounds (can also use flounder, cod, or
>   sole)
> 1 cup milk (or more as needed)
> ⅓ cup flour (or more as needed)
> Salt and ground black pepper to taste
> 1 teaspoon oregano
> ⅓ cup vegetable oil (or more as needed)
> ¼ cup butter
> 3 tablespoons finely chopped parsley
> 1 lemon cut into 4 wedges

1. Wash the fish under cold running water and pat dry with paper towels.
2. Pour the milk into a flat dish.
3. In another flat dish put the flour and season with salt, pepper, and oregano.
4. Dip the turbot fillets in milk and then dredge in the seasoned flour, shaking the fillets to remove the excess flour.
5. Add enough oil in a large skillet to cover the bottom to ¼-inch depth. Heat the oil, add the fillets, and cook over fairly high heat until they are golden brown on one side (about 1½ to 2 minutes). Carefully turn over and brown on the other side.
6. Remove the fish to a warm serving platter and keep warm.

7. Pour off the fat from the skillet and wipe with paper towels. Add the butter and cook over moderately high heat until nut brown. Do not burn. Immediately pour the butter over the fish fillets and serve, sprinkled with parsley and garnished with lemon wedges.

YIELD: 6 SERVINGS

NOTE: If you want to make this dish *amandine*, simply cook the fish as indicated and, when cooking the butter in the skillet, add ⅓ cup slivered blanched almonds. Cook until the butter is nut brown (do not burn). Finally, pour the butter and almonds over the fish, and you have *Fillet of Turbot Amandine*.

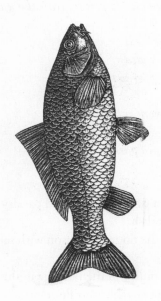

THE PHARAOH'S FEAST

CHEESE FONDUE

One fad I remember from the sixties was the Swiss fondue pot. I recall going to friends' houses and seeing this funny looking contraption in the middle of a table and saying to myself, what the hell is it? For a kid from Spanish Harlem this was the height of sophistication. Here was something with international cachet, yet simple and elegant, and it had its own dipping forks. This ingenious creation was invented by the Swiss as a way to make use of their hard cheese and stale bread. I remember "fondue parties" well into the seventies. Then it disappeared like the dodo bird. How many fondue pots are laying around in some basement or the back of a closet, I wonder?

The "classic" fondue was the cheese version. The cheese used could be anything—Swiss, Gruyère, Emmentaler, even processed American. And there were numerous variations for preparing the cheese. It could be grated or sliced, white wine or hot water was used for melting the cheese, and some recipes called for the addition of canned soup to thicken it. Then you dipped bread cubes or (for the more sophisticated) swirled the cubes in a figure-eight pattern in the melted cheese.

This is about the simplest cheese fondue recipe I know. If you don't have a fondue pot, a chafing dish can also be used.

1 clove garlic, sliced in half
1 cup grated cheese (Gruyère, Emmentaler, or a combination)
2 tablespoons flour
1 cup dry white wine
Salt and ground black pepper to taste
⅛ teaspoon ground nutmeg
Jigger of Kirsch cherry liqueur
Loaf of French bread cut into 1-inch cubes, and warmed in oven

1. Rub the interior of the fondue pot with the garlic cloves. Discard the garlic.
2. Combine the cheese with the flour and mix well.

3. Add the wine to the fondue pot and bring just to a boil. Add the cheese mixture and stir over medium heat until the cheese is melted.
4. Add the salt, pepper, nutmeg, and Kirsch. The cheese mixture should be creamy and smooth.
5. Dip the pieces of warm bread speared on fondue forks into the cheese.

YIELD: 2 SERVINGS

THE PHARAOH'S FEAST

PASTA PRIMAVERA

What may be considered America's greatest contribution to the pasta canon came about in the early seventies. Pasta Primavera has no lack of those claiming to be its progenitor. There are claims that it was first made at Le Cirque restaurant in New York when co-owner Sirio Maccioni, after having his wife serve friends a dish of pasta with freshly cooked vegetables, decided to add it to the restaurant repertoire. (But only as an "item for friends"— it is not on the restaurant menu.)

Another story has it that it was painter Ed Giobbi who dreamed up the dish in his home in Katonah, New York. Jean Vergnes, cofounder of Le Cirque liked this idea of combining fresh spring vegetables with pasta, and he decided to try it out at the restaurant. Initially, it was an appetizer; but the famous chef, Paul Bocuse, came in and ordered it as a main course. All agree that it was Maccioni who coined the term *primavera* (spring in Italian).

Whatever its origin, here it is.

> *1 cup fresh or frozen green peas*
> *1 head fresh broccoli florets*
> *½ cup asparagus tips*
> *2 small zucchini, unpeeled and cut into ¼-inch strips*
> *3 tablespoons butter*
> *1 cup sliced mushrooms*
> *6 tablespoons olive oil*
> *2 medium vine-ripened tomatoes, cut into 1-inch chunks*
> *1 clove garlic, finely minced*
> *½ cup heavy cream (or more as needed)*
> *1 pound spaghetti or fettucine (I prefer linguini), cooked al dente and drained*
> *½ cup minced fresh basil leaves*
> *¼ cup fresh minced parsley*
> *Salt and ground black pepper to taste*
> *½ cup freshly grated Parmesan cheese (or more as needed)*
> *⅓ cup pignoli (pine) nuts*

1. Place peas, broccoli florets, asparagus tips, and zucchini in a saucepan with about ½ cup water. Bring the water to a boil, cover, lower heat,

and steam the vegetables until crisp and tender. This will take 5 minutes, more or less, depending on whether the vegetables are fresh or frozen.

2. Drain the vegetables, place in a large mixing bowl, and store in the refrigerator until needed.

3. Heat the butter in a small skillet, add the mushrooms, and stir-fry over medium heat until tender. Remove the mushrooms from skillet and set aside.

4. Drain the skillet and wipe clean with paper towel. Heat 3 tablespoons of olive oil in the skillet, add the tomatoes and garlic and cook, stirring, until hot (about 3 to 4 minutes). Set aside.

5. In a large heavy kettle or Dutch oven, heat the remaining oil, add the vegetable mixture from the bowl, plus the mushrooms, and cook briefly until hot (2 to 3 minutes). Add the cream and heat until the cream is blended with the vegetables. Add the spaghetti and toss quickly. Add the basil, parsley, salt, pepper, and Parmesan and toss gently until the pasta and vegetables are coated with cream sauce. Stir in the tomatoes and their juice. Adjust seasonings, adding more salt, pepper, cream, or Parmesan, if desired. Sprinkle the pine nuts on top and serve on heated plates.

YIELD: 4 TO 6 SERVINGS

BRAN MUFFINS

In 1976 *Prevention* published a booklet featuring the *Prevention System of Eating and Good Health*. Among "the fabulous foods" included was bran, which "has proven itself the safest, most natural and most effective way to relieve constipation."

Well into the 1990s oat bran struck a chord with food reformers in the industrialized nations. There were claims that a steady diet of the stuff relieved such ailments as irritable colon and colitis.

The most obvious result of this was the mania for oat bran muffins. Everybody and his brother had their own recipe, like the one given. Inevitably it generated a backlash. Witness the old canard: "No matter how many bran muffins you eat, you're still gonna die."

2 cups oat bran
¼ cup brown sugar
2 teaspoons baking powder
½ teaspoon salt
1 cup skim milk
2 egg whites, slightly beaten
¼ cup honey
1 cup raisins

1. Preheat the oven to 425 degrees.
2. Spray 12 medium muffin cups with buttery cooking spray. Set aside.
3. In a bowl, combine the oat bran, sugar, baking powder, and salt. Mix well.
4. Stir in the milk, egg whites, honey, and raisins. Mix until the dry ingredients are moistened.
5. Fill muffin cups until ¾ full.
6. Bake 15 to 17 minutes or until golden brown.

YIELD: 12 MUFFINS

MUSSELS A LA TRIESTINA

By the late seventies the industrialization of food processing and distribution was a fait accompli in Europe and Japan. Supermarkets were everywhere and packaged brand-name foods were common throughout the industrialized world. Minute Rice and Pepsi could be found on the shelf in Osaka, Marseilles, and Rome. This did not diminish the importance of regional and national cuisines. Mass food distribution made it easier to get products, but the heart of the cuisine remained, as in this shellfish dish, which was popular in Trieste before and after the globalization of food.

The recipe is supplied by Marino Lettich, chef and owner of Marino's Restaurant at Eighty-fourth Street and York Avenue. He states that in Trieste the dish is normally served as an appetizer.

2 dozen mussels, rinsed, scrubbed, and debearded
½ cup dry white wine
2 tablespoons olive oil
2 cloves garlic, finely minced
½ cup chopped fresh parsley
½ cup fresh or dried bread crumbs

1. Place the mussels in a kettle or large saucepan. Add the wine and cover. Bring to a boil and steam until the shells open (5 to 10 minutes). For each mussel, discard the top shell but leave the mussel in the other (bottom shell). Set aside.
2. Using a fine sieve or strainer, strain the kettle liquid into a bowl, being careful to leave out the sediment. Set aside.
3. In a saucepan or skillet, heat the olive oil. Add the garlic, parsley, and mussel liquid. Cook over medium heat for 1 to 2 minutes. Add the bread crumbs and sauté until they are moistened (1 to 2 minutes). Remove the pan from the heat and let the mixture cool.
4. Spoon the mixture into each mussel shell so that it is on top and around each mussel. Serve cold or at room temperature.

YIELD: 6 SERVINGS

STEAK AU POIVRE VERT

To my mind, one food item that demonstrates the comingling of cultures prevalent in the latter part of the twentieth century is green peppercorns. An item mostly unknown in the sixties, by the eighties it was everywhere. The fresh green berries of common pepper (*Piper nigrum*) had been a staple in Madagascar for ages. But it wasn't until the 1960s when the process of canning and freezing made them available in Europe—first in France, then England—and finally in the United States, where it made the rounds in trendy restaurants and eventually found its way to the home kitchen.

The most popular green peppercorn dish, to my knowledge, is Steak Au Poivre Vert, which even firemen prepare between calls in local firehouses.

1 pound boneless beef round, top-round steak, 1-inch thick, trimmed of fat
Salt to taste
1 tablespoon green peppercorns
3 tablespoons olive oil

1. Sprinkle the steak with salt.
2. Using a mortar and pestle, crush the peppercorns; or place them in a plastic bag and roll with a rolling pin.
3. Sprinkle the steak with equal amounts of crushed peppercorns on both sides. Press the pepper into both sides of the steak with the heel of hand.
4. Heat the oil in a heavy skillet. Add the meat and brown quickly on both sides over high heat (about 10 minutes or longer depending on whether you prefer steak rare or well-done). Slice against the grain and serve at once.

YIELD: 4 SERVINGS

NOTE: For a variation, follow the 4 steps as instructed above, then remove the steak to a heated platter. Wipe the skillet clean with paper towels. Heat 2 tablespoons of butter in the skillet, add 2 tablespoons of chopped shallots and sauté until soft and wilted. Add ½ cup dry wine and cook, stirring, until the wine has almost totally reduced. Add ½ cup heavy cream and cook, stirring, over high heat for about a minute. Stir in 2 more tablespoons of butter. Pour the sauce over the steak and serve.

Sauteed Smoked Salmon and Caramelized Mango

Toward the last decade of the twentieth century it was only natural that the process that had begun with the discovery of the New World would accelerate with the blending of cuisines from different countries. Chinese migration to Cuba gave rise to the China-Latina restaurant concept so popular at one time on the East Coast. Modern day Jamaican cuisine is a prime example with its blend of Caribbean, African, and Indian flavors. My Uncle Phillip, of late memory, always said that the best Eurasian food he ever encountered was in London. And it is not uncommon in our part of the world to come across an establishment offering a menu blending Chinese and Japanese cooking, something unheard of years ago both in Japan and in the Chinese mainland.

This blending of cooking styles is nothing new. It has been with us since the beginning. The New World adapts Old World foods and vice-versa. In America this concept came to be known as fusion cooking, a term popularized in the nineties (although some claim that the term was being bandied about even in the eighties). In fusion cooking you were only limited by your imagination. You could combine diverse ingredients and techniques and still come up with something palatable.

To me, this concept is illustrated by the dishes I encounter at Mark's Restaurant at the Melia Hotel in Ponce, Puerto Rico. Mark French is a classically trained American chef whose ingenious pairings and combinations highlight this melding of cuisines.

This dish is a simple yet elegant smoked salmon paired with something very common to the Caribbean palate, mango. The second dish (see page 254) of fish with pigeon peas (gandules) is served accompanied by a salad of island ingredients.

Chunky salsa:
¼ cup diced tomatoes
¼ cup diced red onion
Juice of ½ lime
Juice of ½ orange

4 tablespoons olive oil
Salt and ground black pepper to taste

Parsley oil:
1 ounce parsley leaves
½ cup olive oil
Juice of ½ lime
Tabasco to taste
Salt and ground black pepper to taste

Salmon and mango:
4 teaspoons sugar
4 2-ounce portions of stacked smoked salmon
4 large lengthwise slices of ripe mango (a 2-pound mango will be ample)

1 small head Boston lettuce, cut into fine threads

1. In a bowl, combine and mix together the chunky salsa ingredients.
2. Puree well the parsley oil ingredients in a food processor.
3. In a semi-hot sauté pan sprinkle in a teaspoon of sugar. Add one portion of salmon and mango. Sauté one and a half minutes on each side until caramelized and dark in color. Remove from pan and keep warm.
4. Wash pan, dry with paper towels and repeat with other portions.
5. Arrange salmon and mango on individual plates. Garnish with chunky salsa over the top and sprinkle with lettuce. Drizzle parsley oil around the plates.

YIELD: 4 SERVINGS

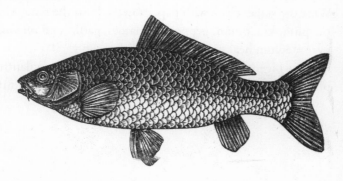

SAUTEED FRESH COD WITH PIGEON PEA STEW

2 5-ounce cod fillets
Salt and ground black pepper to taste
Flour
4 tablespoons olive oil
1 ounce diced pumpkin
1 ounce diced onion
1 ounce diced green peppers (pimentos), either red or green or combination
   thereof
1 ounce diced tomatoes
1 teaspoon chopped garlic
2 pieces aji dulce*
8 ounces green pigeon peas
2 cups vegetable stock
1 tablespoon tomato paste
1 tablespoon chopped cilantro
1 ounce grated green plantain
Pinch of cumin
Salt and black ground pepper to taste

1. Season the fillets with salt and pepper, and dust with flour.
2. Heat 2 tablespoons of olive oil in a heavy skillet or saucepan and sauté the fillets until golden on both sides. Remove from the skillet, set aside, and keep warm.
3. Wipe the skillet clean with paper towels. Heat the remaining oil, add the pumpkin, onion, peppers, tomatoes, garlic, and *aji dulce*. Sauté over medium heat until the vegetables are soft.
4. Add the pigeon peas, vegetable stock, tomato paste, cilantro, grated plantain, cumin, salt, and pepper. Stir well to mix. Lower the heat and

simmer, covered, until the stew is thick. Apportion on two heated soup bowls, and serve with the fish on top.

Yield: 2 servings

*Aji dulce *is sweet chili pepper* (Capsicum annuum) *and can be found in Asian and Caribbean markets. It is not a* hot *pepper.*

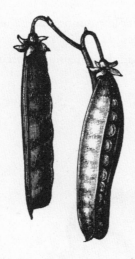

TROPICAL SALAD

½ bunch watercress
2 ounces fresh mango, peeled and julienned into strips
2 ounces red onion, peeled and julienned into strips
2 ounces cucumber, peeled and julienned into strips
1 scallion, diced
¼ cup fresh orange juice
4 tablespoons olive oil
Splash of white rum
Salt and ground black pepper to taste
1 teaspoon fresh chopped mint

1. Rinse the watercress under cold running water and pat dry with paper towels.
2. Place in a salad bowl and add the remaining ingredients, tossing all together.

YIELD: 2 SERVINGS

RICH CHOCOLATE CAKE

In my humble opinion, throughout the decades the one sweet that has dominated worldwide is chocolate. Ever since the Spanish brought it over from the New World, it has captivated us, first as a beverage, then in cakes, pastries, and sorbets. It's no accident that the Mayans two thousand years ago worshipped the cacao bean, the source of all chocolate, as an idol. Chocolate has been an ages old obsession. What would an anniversary be without chocolate? Or Saint Valentine's Day? How could one win the heart of their beloved if not assisted by a box of the goodies?

It's exceedingly logical that the last recipe be a rich dessert with an ingredient everyone can identify with.

The recipe is for a Rich Chocolate Cake. It's adapted from a well-worn cookery book I found on the street. That's right. I was strolling through my neighborhood and a discarded box of items on the sidewalk caught my eye. Inside was this recipe book and I could tell immediately it was from a previous era, a large color bound volume with six hundred color illustrations: *Cookery in Colour: A Picture Encyclopedia for Every Occasion*, edited by Marguerite Patten. The book gives no publication date but by the composition of the recipes I'd guess it's from the fifties. Some of the recipes include such ingredients as suet, red coloring, castor sugar, and measurements such as a "teacup."

The recipe calls for using "1 tablespoon golden syrup," and a few drops of "vanilla essence." I honestly do not know what the cook means by "golden syrup" so I've substituted honey. And I take "vanilla essence" to be vanilla extract—and it worked out. As per the recipe, the cake isn't frosted. It's just your basic chocolate cake. For frosting, the recipe states "Dust with icing sugar when cold." You can utilize whatever frosting you desire.

4 ounces butter or margarine
4 ounces sugar
1 tablespoon honey
½ teaspoon vanilla extract
5 ounces flour (with plain flour use 1 ½ teaspoon baking powder)
1 ½ ounces chocolate powder or 1 ounce Dutch-process cocoa powder
2 eggs
Milk to mix

1. Preheat the oven to 375 degrees.
2. In a large bowl, cream together the butter, sugar, honey, and vanilla until soft and light.
3. Sieve together the flour and chocolate powder into a separate bowl. Stir the eggs and chocolate mixture alternately into the butter mixture, and add just enough milk to make it a soft consistency. Be careful not to make this cake too soft. If you do, the weight of the honey will cause it to sink in the middle.
4. Grease and flour a 7-inch cake pan and pour in the batter. Bake for 1 ¼ hours.

YIELD: 4 TO 6 SERVINGS

NOTE: This recipe makes a relatively small cake, and it is not that pretty to look at. The top of the cake does not come out smooth. It has ridges and fissures, but this does not distract from the flavor. It's delicious. If you're bothered by the nonuniform top, then put frosting on it, or decorate any way you want.

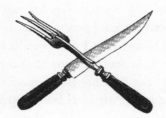

Cassius*: Will you sup with me to-night, Casca?*
Casca: *No, I am promised forth.*
Cassius: *Will you dine with me to-morrow?*
Casca: *Ay, if I be alive and your mind hold and your dinner worth the eating.*

Julius Caesar, Act 1, Scene 2

One order of Adam and Eve on a raft!
　　　An order for fried eggs on toast, as known in some of the old time diners

I t has been a long journey. But no matter how you cut it, whether it's two patricians plotting an assassination or Joe Schmo ordering eggs from the local diner, cooking comes into it. How can it not? From the earliest days we've been striving up from the pit—with the remains of last night's meal right alongside. First, it was eating the nuts and berries one could gather, then ingesting raw marrow from a bone. Then it was searing raw meat over an open fire, which led us through fits and starts and constant upheaval to today's deluxe menu, prepared in the home kitchen or ordered from else-where. Some people say that we've gone so far along this trail that cooking itself is now obsolete, defunct, or soon will be. There are pronouncements, just as there were before, about the kitchen of the future—which may entail no kitchen at all. The "global death of domestic cookery" as it has been chris-tened. No need to cook. We will select our food on the basis of time and energy and what is needed to gain sustenance. As we've seen in countless sci-fi epics, the food will come encapsulated in a pill that we will take in the morning or the evening, and that will be that, all the nutrition needed to get us through the day. Or else we'll be programmed to eat pseudofoods that will taste like beef or veal or sushi, and which will require no preparation what-soever and will contain no trace of animal, vegetable, or mineral.

I don't buy it.

The idea of the death of cooking has been with us since the advent of the first portable items like salted meat and fish came on the scene. True, for some, cooking has become an afterthought, something you do out of necessity and not much else. But for others, like yours truly, it will remain the essence of self-expression and conviviality. We cook because we must—we have to eat to sustain ourselves. But as our saga has shown, it is also a means toward the progression that got us out of the pit and into the kitchen. I refute the naysayers. Cooking will always be with us, if only for the fact that we are social animals and cooking and enjoying a meal is one of the most social stimulants we have.

I foresee in the future a continuation, indeed a further proliferation of the amalgam of cooking styles that we have today. The blending of food and food cultures will continue, especially in the West. But everywhere people will be more aware of what they cook and what they eat and the crosscurrents will be enhanced because yes, the cliché is true, we have become a global village. Mass communications, TV, and the Internet mean we can share recipes and recipe tips in every corner of the world. And even if we are subsumed by the ogre of mass processing, mass production, and fast food, there still will be those glorious nonconformists who will try and insist, by whatever method, to obtain the freshest ingredients and foodstuffs and hold on to that experience of cooking from scratch, just for the sheer pleasure of it. It is no accident that health food and natural food stores have proliferated at such a fast clip. Most people, if they have the means, are willing to pay more for a better and healthier diet.

In the beginning we ate simply to survive. The Neolithic revolution changed all that. We went from being hunter-gatherers to settled farmers, and then became stockbreeders, and then cultivators of grain. We learned to hoard and store food for the lean times and reap in times of plenty. We went from pit-boiling to cooking in pottery, and then in iron vessels and then steel, up to the modern composite cooking utensils of today. We learned along the way that cooking was not only functional but can be profitable and creative. We could celebrate special occasions, sign treaties, or commemorate a lunar cycle with a meal. And we explored, and we experimented, and discovered what was edible and what wasn't. I once was told by a learned person that it was a brave man or woman who first decided to eat an oyster out of the shell. Not an appetizing vision but it gets the point across.

We're still exploring and experimenting today. Every time you get into that kitchen, whether it's a mansion or a hut, one is continuing the journey, whether it's cooking something on a kerosene stove or the latest computerized range, on a charcoal grill or a hibachi. It doesn't matter, really, if one is preparing a seven-course extravaganza or a peanut butter and jelly sandwich. The time line goes back to that first fully cooked meal wherever it was or whoever did it, adding a bit of this and a bit of that, testing, trying for different flavor combinations, seeking the approval of those around us. It hasn't changed. It never will.

BIBLIOGRAPHY

Coon, Carleton S. *The Story of Man: From the First Human to Primitive Culture and Beyond.* New York: Alfred A. Knopf, 1954.

IN THE BEGINNING

Athenaeus. *The Deipnosophists.* Translated by Charles Burton Gulik. Vol. 1. Cambridge: Harvard University Press, 1927.

Bottero, Jean. "The Cuisine of Ancient Mesopotamia." *Biblical Archaeologist* 48, no. 1 (1985).

Bottero, Jean. "The Culinary Tablets at Yale." *Journal of the American Oriental Society* 107 (1987).

Diodorus Siculus. Historical Library. Book 4 and 5.

Kramer, Samuel Noah. *The Sumerians: Their History, Culture and Character.* Chicago: University of Chicago Press, 1963.

Limet, Henri. "The Cuisine of Ancient Sumer." *Biblical Archaeologist* 50, no. 3 (1987).

Saggs, H. W. F. *Everyday Life in Babylonia and Assyria.* New York, 1965.

Singer, Charles, E. J. Holmyard, A. R. Hall, and Trevor I. Williams. *A History of Technology.* Vol. 1. Oxford, 1958.

LAND OF THE PHARAOHS

Emery, Walter E. *Archaic Egypt.* Harmondsworth, Middlesex: Penguin Books Ltd., 1961.

Herodotus. *The Histories.* Translated by Aubrey de Selincourt. Harmondsworth, Middlesex: Penguin Books Ltd., 1954.

Posener, Georges, ed. *Dictionary of Egyptian Civilization.* New York: Tudor Publishing Company, 1959.

CLASSICAL GREECE

Alsop, Joseph. *From the Silent Earth.* New York: Harper & Row, 1970.

Archestratus of Gela, *The Hedupatheia.* S. Douglas Olsen and Alexander Sens. Oxford, 2000.

Dieting for an Emperor. Introduction and commentary by Mark Grant. Boston: Brill Academic Publishers, 1997.

Homer. *The Odyssey of Homer*. Translated by Allen Mandelbaum. New York: Banton Books, 1990.

Lichine, Alexis. *Encyclopedia of Wines and Spirits*. 4th ed. New York: Alfred A. Knopf, 1990.

Pliny the Elder. *Natural History*. Translated by H. Rackham. Cambridge: Harvard University Press, 1997.

THE INDUS VALLEY

An Account of the Vedas: With Numerous Extracts from the Rig-Veda. London and Madras: Christian Literature Society for India, 1897.

Prakesh, Om. *On Food and Drinks in Ancient India, from Earliest Times to c. 1200 A.D.* 1st ed. Delhi: Munshi Ram Manohar Lal, 1961.

Yule, Henry and A. C. Burnell. *Dictionary of Indian English*. Edited by G. B. T. Kurian. Madras: Indian University Press, 1966.

OF TOGAS AND CENTURIANS

Aries, Philippe and Georges Duby, eds. *A History of Private Life: From Pagan Rome to Byzantium*. Cambridge: Belknap Press, 1987.

Athenaeus. *The Deipnosophists*. Translated by Charles Burton Gulick. Cambridge: Harvard University Press, 1987.

Carcopino, Jerome. *Daily Life in Ancient Rome: The People and the City at the Height of the Empire*. Translated by E. O. Lorimer. New Haven: Yale University Press, 1955.

Chiquart's 'On Cookery'–A Fifteenth-century Savoyard Culinary Treatise. Edited and translated by Terence Scully. New York: Peter Lang Publishing, Inc., 1986.

Eban, Abba. *Heritage: Civilization and the Jews*. New York: Summit Books, 1984.

The Epigrams of Martial. Translated by James Michie. New York: Vintage Books, 1973.

Juvenal. *The Sixteen Satires*. Translated by Peter Green. Harmondsworth, Middlesex: Penguin Books Ltd., 1967.

Martial in English. Edited by J. P. Sullivan and A. J. Boyle. New York: Penguin Books, 1996.

The Roman Cookery of Apicius. Translated by John Edwards. London: Hartley & Marks Publishers, 1985.

The Satyricon of Petronius. Translated by William Arrowsmith. Ann Arbor: University of Michigan Press, 1959.

Scullard, H. H. *Roman Britain: Outpost of the Empire*. London: Thames and Hudson Ltd., 1979.

Suetonius. *The Twelve Caesars.* Translated by Robert Graves. Harmondsworth, Middlesex: Penguin Books Ltd., 1989.

MEDIEVAL EUROPE

della Casa, Giovanni. *Galateo.* Translated by Konrad Eisenbichler and Kenneth R. Bartlett. Toronto: University of Toronto Press, 1986.

Duby, Georges. *Rural Economy and Country Life in the Medieval West.* Translated by Cynthia Postan. Columbia: University of South Carolina Press, 1968.

The Forme of Curry: A Roll of Ancient English Cookery, Compiled about 1390, by the Master-cooks of King Richard II, Presented afterwards to Queen Elizabeth by Edward Lord Stafford. London: J. Nichols, printer to the Society of Antiquaries, 1780.

The Goode Huswifes Handmaide for the Kitchin: A Period Recipe Book. Edited by Stuart Peachey. Bristol: Stuart Press, 1992.

The Goodman of Paris: A Treatise on Moral and Domestic Economy by a Citizen of Paris (c. 1393). Translated by Eileen Power. London: George Routledge & Sons, 1928.

Tirel, Guillaume. *The Viandier of Taillevent: An Edition of All Extant Manuscripts.* Edited by Terence Scully. Ottawa: University of Ottowa Press, 1988.

Painter, Sidney. *Medieval Society.* Ithaca: Cornell University Press, 1963.

THE ARAB WORLD

Arberry, A. J. "A Baghdad Cookery Book." *Islamic Culture: The Hyderabad Quarterly Review* 13 (1939).

Bernal, J. D. *Science in History.* London: C. A. Watts & Co., 1954.

Chejne, A. G. "The Boon Companion in Early Abbasid Times." *Journal of the American Oriental Society* 85 (1965).

de la Mata, Juan. *Arte De Reposteria.* Madrid: Antonio Marin, 1747.

Ibn Ishaq. *Life of Muhammad.* Translated by Edward Rehatsek. London: Library of the Royal Asiatic Society, fol. 1057.

Ibn al-Mabrad. "Kitab al-Tibakhah: A Fifteenth Century Cookbook." Translated by Charles Perry. *Petits Propos Culinaires* 21, London: Prospect Books Ltd., 1985.

Miranda, Ambrosio Huici. *Traduccion Espanola De Un Manuscrito Anonimo Del Siglo XIII Sobre La Cocina Hispana-Magribi.* Madrid: Patrocinado por el Excmo Ayuntamiento De Valencia, 1966.

Randolph, Mary. *The Virginia Housewife: Or, Methodical Cook.* Baltimore: Plaskitt & Cugle, 1831.

Analects of Confucius. Translated by Arther Waley. London: Unwin Hyman, 1988.

Birch, Cyril and Donald Keene. *Anthology of Chinese Literature.* New York: Penguin Books, 1967.

Carletti, Francesco. *My Voyage around the World.* Translated by Herbert Weinstock. New York: Pantheon Books, 1964.

Gernet, Jacques. *La Vie Quotidienne En Chine A La Veille De L'Invasion Mongole, 1250-1276.* Librairie Hachette, 1959.

Needham, Joseph. *Science and Civilization in China.* Vol. 4, Part 2. Cambridge: Cambridge University Press, 1965.

The Sacred Books of China: The Texts of Confucianism. Translated by James Legge. Part III, *The Li-Ki, Book of Rites,* I-X, from *Sacred Books of the East.* Translated By F. Max Muller, Volume XXVII. Oxford: Oxford University Press, 1976.

Schafer, Edward H. *The Golden Peaches of Samarkand: A Study of T'ang Exotics.* Berkeley and Los Angeles: University of California Press, 1963.

The Travels of Marco Polo. Translated by R. E. Latham. Harmondsworth: Penguin Books, 1958.

Yule, Henry, ed. and trans. *Cathay and the Way Thither: Being a Collection of Medieval Notices of China.* 4 vols. London: The Hakluyt Society, 1913-1916.

THE NEW WORLD MEETS THE OLD

Beckford, Peter. *Familiar Letters from Italy to a Friend in England.* Salisbury: J. Easton, 1805.

Bostrom, Ingemar. *Anonimo Meridionale.* Libro A. Stockholm: Almqvist & Wiksell International, 1985.

Cruz, Juan. *La Cocina Mediterranea en el Inicio del Renacimiento.* Huesca: La Val de Onsera, 1997.

da Como, Martino. *Libro De Arte Coquinaria.* Milan: Guido Tommasi Editore, 2001.

la Varenne, Pierre Francois de. *Le Cuisinier Francois, Ensiegnant la Manierre de Bien Apprester & Assaisonner Touts Sorte de Viands.* Paris: Chez Pierre David, 1654.

Mallet, Michael E. *The Florentine Galleys in the Fifteenth Century (with the Diary of Luca Di Masso Degli Albizzi, Captain of the Galleys 1419-1430).* Oxford: Oxford University Press, 1967.

Markham, Gervase. *The English Hus-wife: Containing the inward and outward virtues which ought to be in a complete woman; as her skill in physic, cookery, banqueting-stuff, distillation, perfumes, wool, hemp, flax, dairies, brewing, baking, and all other thing belonging to a household.* Edited by Michael R. Best. Kingston and Montreal: McGill-Queens University Press, 1986.

Tommasseo, Par M. N. *Relations des Ambassadeurs Venitiens sur les Affairs de France au XVI Siecle.* Vol. 2. Paris, 1838.

Rumpolts, Marx. *Ein New Kochbuch.* Frankfort Am Mann, 1581.

THE AMERICAS

Beauvilliers, A. B. *The Art of French Cookery.* London: Longman, Rees, Orme, Brown, and Green, 1827.

Columbus, Ferdinand. *The Life of the Admiral Christopher Columbus by His Son Ferdinand.* Translated by Benjamin Keen. London: Butler & Tanner, 1959.

de Sahagun, Fr. Bernardino. *Historia General de las Cosas de Nueva Espana.* Vol. 2. Editorial Pedro Robrero, 1938.

Diaz, Bernard. *The Conquest of New Spain.* Translated by J. M. Cohen. London: Butler and Tanner, 1963.

Markham, Gervase. *The English Hus-wife.* Edited by Michael R. Best. Kingston and Montreal: McGill-Queen's University Press, 1986.

Oliver, Roland and J. D. Fage. *A Short History of Africa.* New York: Penguin Books, 1962.

Salaman, Redcliffe E. *The History and Social Influence of the Potato.* Cambridge: Cambridge University Press, 1949.

Ucko, Peter J., and G. W. Dimbleby. *The Domestication and Exploitation of Plants and Animals.* London: Gerald Duckworth & Co., 1969.

Wyndham, H. A. *The Atlantic and Slavery.* London: Oxford University Press, 1938.

Yule, Henry and A. C. Burnell. *A Glossary of Colloquial and Anglo-Indian Words and Phrases.* Compiled by Hobson-Jobson and edited by William Crooke. Curzon Press, 1995.

THE COOKING WORLD EXPANDS

Carletti, Francesco. *My Voyage Around the World.* Translated by Herbert Weinstock. New York: Pantheon Books, 1964.

Gerstacker, Fredrick. *Gerstacker's Travels.* London: T. Nelson and Sons, 1854.

Lichine, Alexis. *New Encyclopedia of Wines and Spirits.* New York: Alfred A. Knopf, 1974.

Schulz, J. W. *My Life as an Indian: The Story of a Red Woman and White Man in the Lodges of the Blackfeet.* New York: Doubleday, Page & Company, 1907.

Simmons, Amelia. *American Cookery, or the art of Dressing VIANDS, FISH, POULTRY & VEGETABLES and the best Modes of making PASTES, PUFFS, PIES, TARTS, PUDDINGS, CUSTARDS & PRESERVES and all Kinds of CAKES from the IMPERIAL PLUMB TO PLAIN CAKE adopted to This Country & All Grades of Life.* Grand Rapids: William B. Eerdmans Publishing Co., 1965.

THE INDUSTRIAL ERA

Acton, Eliza. *Modern Cookery, in All Its Branches: Reduced to a System of Easy Practice, for the Use of Private Families.* Longman, Bowen, Green and Longmans, 1850.

Beecher, Catherine Esther. *Miss Beecher's Domestic Receipt-book: Designed as a Supplement to her Treatise on Domestic Economy.* New York: Harper & Brothers, 1846.

Beeton, Isabella. *The Book of Household Management.* 1861.

Burnett, John. *Plenty and Want: A Social History of Diet in England from 1815 to the Present Day.* London: Thomas Nelson and Sons, 1966.

Carême, M. A. *The Royal Parisian Pastrycook and Confectioner: from the Original of M. A. Carême.* Edited by John Porter. London: F. J. Mason, 1834.

Farmer, Fannie Merritt. *The Original Boston Cooking-School Cook Book.* 1896. Southport: Hugh Lauter Levin, 1996.

Fulford, Roger. *George the Fourth.* London: The Camelot Press, 1935.

Mann, Mrs. Horace. *Christianity in the Kitchen: A Physiological Cook Book.* Boston: Ticknor and Fields, 1867.

Soyer, Alexis. *Shilling Cookery for the People: Embracing an Entirely New System of Plain Cookery and Domestic Economy.* London: Geo. Routledge & Co., 1855.

MODERN TIMES

Beard, James. *Hors D'Oeuvre and Canapes.* New York: M. Barrows and Co., 1940.

Brown, Helen Evans and James A. Beard. *The Complete Book of Outdoor Cookery.* Garden City: Doubleday, 1955.

Centre de Recherche et d'Etudes sur les Conditions de Vie. Points de vente, no: 393-1990.

Crocker, Betty. *Your Share: How to Prepare Appetizing, Healthful Meals with Food Available Today*. Minneapolis: General Mills, 1943.

Diat, Louis. *Cooking á la Ritz*. New York: J. B. Lippincott Company, 1941.

Hayes, Joanne Lamb. *Grandma's Wartime Kitchen: World War II and the Way We Cooked*. New York: St. Martin's Press, 2000.

Levenstein, Harvey. *Paradox of Plenty: A Social History of Eating in Modern America*. New York: Oxford University Press, 1993.

Lovegren, Sylvia. *Fashionable Foods: Seven Decades of Food Fads*. New York: Macmillan, 1995.

Rodale, Robert. *The Prevention System for Better Health*. Emmaus: Rodale Press, 1976.

Rombauer, Irma S., Marion Rombauer Becker and Ethan Becker. *Joy of Cooking*. 1931. New York: Simon & Schuster, 1997.

The Settlement Cookbook. Compiled by Mrs. Simon Kander, Mrs. Henry Schoenfeld, and Mrs. Isaac D. Adler. Milwaukee: J. H. Yewdale & Sons Co., 1915.

Sonnenfeld, Albert. *Food: A Culinary History from Antiquity to the Present*. New York: Penguin Books, 2000.

Stewart, Katie. *The Joy of Eating*. Maryland: Stemmer House, 1977.

Survey by CREDOC, Asparations et modes de viedes Francais.

INDEX

Abraham, 6
Achilles, 29, 49, 42
Acton, Eliza, 201
Africa, 160-161
aji dulce, 255
Akkadian tablets, 12
akvavit, 138
al-Baghdadi, 91, 93, 96, 100
Alcman, 34
Alexander the Great, 48
al-Mabrad, Ibn, 98
al-Mu'tasim, caliph, 90
al-Mutazz, Ibn, 89
American Airlines, 215
American Cookery
   author: James Beard, 238
   author: Amelia Simmons, 187
American Home, 215
Americas, 156–163
Amiczo, Chiquart, 87
Andalusia, 94
Anderson, J. Walter, 219
anonymous Andalusian cookbook, 99, 101
Anonymous Southerner (Anonimo Meridionale), 139
Antony, Mark, 73
A & P (Great Atlantic and Pacific tea Company), 212
Apicius, 40, 63, 68, 70, 71, 75
Arab World, 89–92
Archestratus, 31–33, 39
Argentina, 180, 183
The Art of French Cookery, 168
Aryans, 48–50
asafoetida, 33
asopao, 4
Atharva-veda, 49

Athenaeus, 8, 32, 34, 35, 39, 44, 45
Athens, 31
Audot, Louis Eustache, 198
avocado, 154
A & W Root Beer Company, 219
Ayurvedic doctrine, 51
Aztecs, 137, 156–159

Babylonians, 8, 12
Baghdad, 89
bamya, 26
The Banquet by Philoxenus, 44, 46
barbacoa, see barbecue
barbecue, 160,241
barley, 29–30
bean curd, 105
   deep-fried (Peking-style), 132
   spicy (Chinese), 121
beans and legumes:
   fava beans (*ful medames*), 24
   mess of pottage, 10
   new peas for a fish day, 83
   new peas for a meat day, 82
   pigeon peas, 57
   see also lentils
Beard, James, 217, 222, 236, 238
Beauvilliers, Antoine, 168, 169
Beecher, Catharine, 205
beef:
   beef a la mode, 203
   classic meat loaf, 236
   hamburger steak, 241
   lion's head (Chinese), 128
   matambre, 183
   meat stew, 14
   steak au poivre vert, 251
   vinegar garlic beef, 148
beer, 6–9

Beeton, Isabella, 203
Beijing (Peking) cuisine, 130–132
Bell, Glenn, 219
*Better Homes and Gardens Guide to
  Entertaining*, 221
Betty Crocker, 216, 226
bird's nest soup, 106
Bisquick, 215
Black Death, 4, 80
Blackfeet Indians, 177
blank mang (*blamanger*), 80
Bocuse, Paul, 220, 247
Bomb Shelter Chocolate-Cherry Delight
  Cake, 221
Bon Appétit, 225, 226
Book of Household Management, 203
Borgia, Alexander VI, 134, 160
bourbon, 180, 192, *see also whisky*
Brahmin(s), 49
bran muffins, 249
brandewin (brandy), 138
Brazil, 160
bread:
  barley bread, 35
  beer bread(s), 8
  cappadocian, 66
  flat bread, 19
  Roman bread, 66
Bronze Age, 30
Buddha, 49
buran, 96
Burger King, 219

Caesar salad, 232
California dip, 242
Campbell's soup, 213
cannibalism, 158–159
canning, 195, 214
Cantonese-style cooking, 110–115, 234
capon armado, 145
Cardini, Caesar, 232
Carême, Marie Antoine, 198, 199, 200
Carib Indians, 160
Carletti, Francesco, 109
caroenum, 65

Carson, Rachel, 223
cassava bread, 156
The Casserole Cookbook, 217
cassoulet, 4
caspa, 94
Chao hun, 103
chapatis, 50
charqui, 181
cheese:
  cheese fondue, 245
  Chevre, 39
  Feta, 35, 42, 46
  Pecorino Romano, 39
  Roquefort cheese balls, 238
chicken, 48
  limonia, 139
  melokiyah, 20
  poulet à la marengo, 209
  poussin, 12
  steamed, Cantonese style, 110
  zirbaya, 99
Child, Julia, 222, 236
chili peppers, 117, 157
China, 103–109
"Chinese-American" cooking, 110, 224
chocolate, 137, 257
chop suey (origin of), 110
chopsticks, 108–109
Christianity in the Kitchen, 206
chuñu, 159
Churchill, Winston, 215
Circe's kykeon, 42
Civil War, 195
classic meat loaf, 236
Claudius, Roman emperor, 73
Cleopatra, 73
coal stove, 196
coca (leaf), 181
Coca-Cola, 212
cocoa (cacao) bean, 137, 257
Code of Hammurabi, 8
coffee, 161
cognac, 138
coleslaw, 178
Columbus, Christopher, 94, 134

comalli, 157
comfort food, 214, 226
comissatio, 63
Confucius, 104
Cooking à la Ritz, 230
Coon, Carleton, 2
Conquistadors, 137, 158
Cordoba, 94
corn, *see maize*
Corning (Pyrex baking dishes), 213
Corning game hens, 12–13
corn pone, 170
Corson, Juliet, 209
Cortez, Hernando, 137, 156
cream vichyssoise glacée, 230
C-rations, 216
Crete, 30
criollo aristocracy, 180
crock pot cookery, 223
Crusades, 3, 78
curry, 50
Cyclamate, 215

dahi, 50
dal, 57
Davis, Adelle, 223
defrutum, 65
dehydrated food, 216
deipnon, 33
de la Verenne, Pierre Francois, 143, 144
de Medici, Catherine, 3, 135, 143
de Medeci, Marie, 136
De Mille, Cecil B., 18
de Nola, Ruperto, 145, 147
de Pordenone, Oderic, 106
De Re Coquinaria, 40, 63
The Deipnosophists (*The Sophists at Dinner*), 32
del Castillo, Bernal Diaz, 156
della Casa, Giovanni, 79
desserts:
  hais, 100
  Indian pudding, 187
  Philoxenus' cheesecake, 46
  rice cake, glazed and ornamented, 199

rice pudding, 151
rich chocolate cake, 257
sweetened dates, 27
tiropatinam, 75
victory pudding, 240
zabaglione, 142
Diat, Louis, 230
Diet for Invalids and Children, 209
di Lellio, Alfredo, 231
Diocletian, Roman emperor, 77
Dionysus, 7
dishwashers, 213
Dixie cup, 213
dog (as food), 104, 157–158, 198
The Doubleday Cookbook, 225
duck:
  boiled and roasted, 22
  smoked (Chinese), 124
Du Fait de Cuisine, 87
Dutch East India Company, 138, 161
Dutch East Indies, 196
Dutch stoves, 176
duxelles, 143

Eating European Abroad and at Home, 221
Eban, Abba, 61
eggplant, 96
  stuffed, 207
Egypt, 18–27
Ein New Kochbuck, 148
Eisenhower, Dwight D., 217
El Dia de Acción de Gracia, 171
electric stove, 196–197
Empedocles, 91
England, 138
The English Hus-wife, 149, 151, 172
English stove, 176
Epic of Gilgamesh, 7
Epicurius, 226
Esau, 6, 9
Escoffier, Auguste, 220
Ethiopia, 161
Eucharist, 73
Family Living on $500 a Year, 209

faraga (Chinese pepper), 117
The Fannie Farmer Cookbook, 207
Farmer, Fannie Merritt, 207
fast food, 219
The Fast Gourmet Cookbook, 221
ferula asafoetida, 33
fettucini alfredo, 231
Fifteen Cent Dinners for Workingmen's Families, 209
figs, 27
filet of turbot meuniere, 243
fish:
  a la Mithaikos, 39
  baked whole fish, 44
  filet of turbot meuniere, 243
  grilled pike in wine sauce, 84
  poached sturgeon, 141
  sautéed fresh cod, 254
  sautéed smoked salmon, 252
  sweet and sour (Chinese), 126
First World War, 212, 213
five flavors concept, 103
Fleischmann's Yeast Company, 213
Food and Wine, 225
Food Network, 226
food processor, 225
Forme of Cury, 81, 84, 86
"four humors" principal, 91
fraises Romanoff (Strawberries Romanoff), 200
Francatelli, Charles Elme, 198, 209
Franco-Italian cuisine, 135–136
frankfurter(s), 213
  baked frankfurters with stuffing, 239
Franklin stove, 176
Frederick the Great, 169
freezing, 196
The French Chef, 222
French cuisine, classical, 197–199
Frigidaire electric refrigerator, 213
fritters, 81
frozen food, 215
Frugal Gourmet (TV show), 226

fruit:
  Aztec fruit cup, 167
  jujubes, 53
  mangoes, 53
  pears cooked without coals or water, 87
  pomegranates, 53
frumenty, 79
ful medames, 24
fusion cooking, 252

Galen, 66, 91
garum (*liquamen*), 64
gas ranges, 213
gas stove, 196
gastra, 34
gaucho, 180–181
gazpacho:
  con ajo blanco, 94
  Malaga-style, 95
General Electric Company, 212, 218, 222
General Foods, 213
General Mills, 215
General Tso's chicken, 122
George V, monarch, 197
Germany, 137
ghee, 49
Giobbi, Ed, 247
gin, 138
Glaucus of Locris, 31
Good Housekeeping, 223
The Goode Huswives Handmaide, 84
Gourmet's Club Network, 226
Gourmet, 226, 238
Gourmet Meals for Easy Entertaining, 221
grain pastes, 29, 62
Grandma's Wartime Kitchen, 239, 240
granola, 223
Great Depression, 214–215
Greece, 29–46
"grog," 163
guacamole, 164

hais, 100
halva, 55
hamburger steak, 241
Han dynasty, 104–105
haq, 8
Harappa, 48
hardtack, 162
harisa, 90
Hayes, Joanne Lamb, 239
Hazelton, Nika, 221
The Hedupatheia, 32
Hellenistic era, 34
Herakleides of Syracuse, 31, 35
herb, 37, 81
Herodotus, 19
Hinduism, 49
hing, 33
home economist, 214
Homer, 30, 42
hominy, 162, 170
Homo erectus, 1
Homo sapiens, 1, 2
honey, 35
Hors d'Oeuvre and Canapés, 238
House and Garden, 218
Hunan-style cooking, 122–127

iced tea, 213
I-Ching, 106
Id-al-Fitr, feast of, 3
The I Hate to Cook Book, 218
Iliad, 29, 42
I Love to Eat (TV show), 238
Incas, 159
India (Indus Valley), 48–52
Indian pudding, 187
Indian slapjack, 190
Industrial Revolution, 194–198
instant coffee, 216
ipocras, 147
Irish potato famine, 194
iron stoves, five-plate, 176
Isabelle of Castille, 134
isfanakh mutajan, 93

Italy, 135–136

Jacob, 6
jambalaya, 185
Jazz Age, 213
Jell-O, 212, 213
Jesus Christ, 3, 73
Jians, 49
johnnycake, 178, 187, 189
The Joy of Cooking, 236
Juvenal, 63

kadhi leaves, 50
Kander, Lizzie, 228
Karanis, 62
kari, 50
karil, 50
kasha, 138
Kellogg's Corn Flakes, 213
Kentucky Fried Chicken (food chain),
  219
kerosene stove, 196
kesar doodh, 59
ketchup, 126
Khrushchev, Nikita, 217
King Srenika's bash, 53–59
kofta, 25
Kool-Aid, 214
Koran, 90
Kraft Television Theater, 217
Kroc, Roy, 219
Kublai Khan, 73

Lamb:
  buran, 96
  Hunan lamb, 122
  kofta, 25
  lamb and turnip stew, 11
  Mongolian hot pot, 130
  roast leg of lamb, 40
  tharid, 98
Lao-tzu, 109
Last Supper, 3
Le Cuisinier Francois, 143

Le Cuisinier Impérial, 168
Le Ménagier de Paris, 81–83, 85
Le Viandier de Taillevent, 85
lentils, 6, 10, 57
Libre del Coch, 145
Libro de Arte Coquinaria, 141
libum, 46
Li-Ki, 104
limeys, 163
limonia, 139
Lincoln, Abraham, 171
Lindqvist, Frans Wilhelm, 196
Lipton Company, 242
lobster Cantonese a la Larry Quan, 115
lobster thermidor, 218
Long Island *Star Journal,* 218
Lun Yu (The Analects), 104

macaroni(s), 136
Maccioni, Mario, 247
MacPhee, John, 221
maize, 156, 157
Mann, Mrs. Horace, 206
margarine, 196
Markham, Gervase, 149
Mastering the Art of French Cooking, 222
Martial, 62
matambre, 183
McDonald's, 219, 226
meat, *see beef; ham; lamb; pork*
meatballs (kofta), 25
Medieval Europe, 77–80
Medina, 90
melokiyah, 20
Mesopotamia, 6–7, 12, 14
mess of pottage, 10
microwave, 222
Middle Ages, *see Medieval Europe*
mint julep, 192
Minute Rice, 216, 250
Miss Beecher's Domestic Receipt Book, 205
Mithaikos, 31
Mnesitheus cabbage, 37
The Modern Cook, 198
Modern Cookery for Private Families, 201

Modern Times, 212–217
Mohammad, 89–90
Mohenjo-Daro, 48
Mongolian hot pot, 130
Montezuma, 137, 156–157
Moors, 94
mortrews, 80
Mott, Jordan, 196
Mouriés, Hippolyte Mège, 196
Mozarab, 94
mulligatawny soup, 201
mulsum, 63, 68
mussels a la triestina, 250
Mustakfi, Caliph, 89

nadims, 90
nam pla, 65
napoleon (pastry), 4
National Review, 221
Neanderthals, 1, 2
Neolithic revolution, 2, 8, 250
Nero, 62, 73
Nestor at Knossos, 30
New Deal, 215
New England colonies, 161–162,
  175–177
Newsweek, 221
Nicholas V, pope, 160
1904 St. Louis World's Fair, 213
1939 New York World's Fair, 212
Ninkasi, 6
noodles, 107
  Szechuan style, 117
North America, 161–162, 175–180
North American Indians, 162, 177
northwest passage, 161
nouc mam, 65
nouvelle cuisine (*La cuisine minceur*),
  223

Odysseus, 29, 40, 42
Odyssey, 29, 42
okra, 26
Olestra, 227
olive oil, 30

onion(s), 14
Oribasius, 37
Outdoor Cookery, 241
oxymel, 37

pancakes, 149
Pardon My Foix Gras, 218
partridge, 16
Passover Seder, 73
passum, 65
pasta, 136, 227, 234
    pasta primavera, 247
Patten, Marguerite, 257
Pearl Harbor, 215
Peking man, 1
pemmican, 177
pepper (*Piper nigrum*), 251
Peru, 159
Petronius, Gaius, 61–62
Philoxenus' cheesecake, 46
Philoxenus of Leucas, 44, 46
pickled herring, 228
Pilgrims, 162, 171–172
ping, 107
Pizarro, Francisco, 159
pizza, 219
Pizza Hut, 219
Pizzeria Uno, 219
*A Plain Cookery Book for the Working
    Class*, 198, 209
Pliny the elder, 29
"pocket soup," 178
Point, Fernand, 220
Poland, 137
Polo, Marco, 73, 106, 107, 136
Pompeii, 62–63, 66
Poppy Cannon's Can-Opener Cook Book,
    218
pork:
    baked frankfurters with stuffing, 239
    roasted loin, 86
Portugal, 134, 160–161
potato(es), 159–160, 194
    German potato salad, 169
    pomme de terre a la lyonnaise, 168

potato pie, 205
Pramnian wine, 31, 42
prandium, 66
Prevention, 249
Prohibition, 213, 214
prozymi, 35
puls (*pulmentum*), 62
Puranas, 49
Pyrex Prize Recipes, 218

quail, 16
Quaker Oats, 236

rabbit:
    rabbit Athenaeus, 45
    roasted rabbit, 71
Raitas, 58
rationing, 215
ratl, 100
"red cooking" technique, 128
refrigerator, 215
Renaissance, 77, 92, 136, 139
"Retro Food," 226
Retsina wine, 30
Revere Ware, 215
Revolutionary War, 177, 180
Ricardo, Ric, 219
rice, 4, 195
    arroz con pollo, 4
    fragrant boiled rice, 56
    rice cake, glazed and ornamented, 199
    rice pudding, 151
    rijst, 4
    risotto, 4
Rig-veda, 48
rishta, 107
Ritz crackers, 215
Rombauer, Irma, 236
Rome, 61–65
Romulus Augustulus, 77
Roquefort cheese balls and mushroom
    caps filled with Roquefort, 238
Rossi, Martino, 141
Rumpolts, Marx, 148
Ruta graveolens, 37, 65

rue, 37, 65
rum, 163, 179–180
rum punch, 191
Russia, 137–138

saffron, 59
Saint Patrick's Day, 3
salads:
  Caesar salad, 232
  green salad, 23
  tropical salad, 256
salsa, 242,
  chunky salsa, 252
salt, 213
samidu, 12, 16
Saturday Evening Post, 221
The Satyricon, 61
sauces:
  Cameline sauce, 85
  Roman sauce for boiled meat, 70
  sauce poivrade, 144
  tempura dipping sauce, 154
sautéed fresh cod with pigeon pea stew,
  254
sautéed smoke salmon (and caramelized
  mango), 252
scurvy, 162
sekanjabin, 101
The Settlement Cookbook, 228
Sewell, Ike, 219
Shanghai cuisine, 128
sheera, 55
Shen Nong, 107
Shih ching (*The Book of Songs*), 104
Shilling Cookery for the People, 209
Sicilian cooking, 234
Siculus, Diodorus, 8
silphium, 32, 65
Simmons, Amelia, 187
slave trade, 156, 160–161, 179–180
Smith, Jeff, 226
"soul food," 179
soups:
  cream vichyssoise glacée, 230

mulligatawny soup, 201
toor dal, 57
South America, 181–182
soybean, 105
Soyer, Alexis, 209
"spa cuisine," 226
spaghetti (origin of), 136
  spaghetti and meatballs, 234
Spain, 134–135, 136–137, 156–160
SPAM, 217
squab, 16
squid (Szechuan style), 119
Srenika, Indian king, 51–52
Standard Brands, 213
Starbuck's, 223
steak au poivre vert, 251
stews:
  asopao, 4
  cassoulet, 4
  lamb and turnip stew, 11
  meat stew, 14
  mess of pottage, 10
  pigeon pea stew, 254
  pigeon stew, 16
  tarru-bird stew, 12
  see also soups
stir-frying, 104–105
stoves, cast-iron, 175–176
succotash, 162, 170
sugar, 19, 160
sugarcane, 53, 160
suhutinnu, 14
Sullivan, Thomas, 213
Sumer (Sumerians), 6, 11
Swiss fondue, 245
Szechuan-style cooking, 117–121

Taco Bell (Taco Tia), 219
tamales, 157, 165
Tang, 221
tarru-bird stew, 12
tea, 107–108
tea bag, 213
Teflon, 30, 215

tempura, 152–154
Thanksgiving Day feast, 171–172
Tharid, 98
Thompson, Benjamin (aka Count
  Rumford), 196
Tirel, Guillaume, 85
tiropatinam, 75
tlacatlaolli, 158
tofu, 223
tomato(es), 94, 157
  tomato omelette, 209
tortillas, 157
tournedos rossini, IX
trencher, 79
tropical salad, 256
Tupperware, 217
turkey fowl, 158, 172
turnip(s), 11
  raised turnips, 15
Twinkies, 215

udom, 4
Ulysses, *see Odysseus*
uqiya, 100
Ur, 6, 11
U.S. Food and Drug Administration,
  223, 227

Vasco da Gama, 134
Vayu Purana, 49
vegetables:
  artichokes, oil and minced eggs, 69
  bamya (okra), 26
  basic stir-fry (Chinese), 111
  isfanakh mutajan (spinach), 93
  Mnesitheus cabbage, 37
  raised turnips, 15
  tamales de vegetales, 165
  third course (King Srenika's bash), 54
  vegetable tempura, 152
vegetarianism, 49, 224
Velveeta, 218
venison, roasted, 171–173
Vergnes, Jean, 247

Viard, Antoine, 168
vichyssoise (cream vichyssoise glacée),
  230
Vishnu Dharma Sutra, 49
vitamization, 213
Vitellius, Roman emperor, 63
vizcacha, 159

Wait, Paul B., 212
Waldo, Myra, 243
Washington, George, 179
What Cooks in Suburbia, 221
whisky, 138, 180, 192
White Castle, 219
wine, 30–31, 73
wok, 105, 111
Woman's Day, 215
wo-min, 4
World War II, 215–217

Yale Babylonian Collection, 12–16
yerba mata, 183
Yi Yin, 103
yin and *yang* (principal of), 103
yogurt, 58, 98

zabaglione, 142
zirbaya, 99